WALK ON WATER

"I wasn't in the hospital ward any more, but on a beach looking out to sea. The sea was a beautiful blue, the sort of color you see in holiday brochures but never in real life. The horizon seemed very close, and on it there was the most lovely light, a warm, glowing white light that filled the sky. I had a strong feeling that I could walk across the water to the light: not wade through it, but walk on top of it. I could see other people standing in the light, and they appeared to be standing on top of the water, too. I could see them beckoning to me, and I wanted to go and join them."

—from the recollection of Sue Adams and her near-death experience in 1989

DEATH'S DOOR

True Stories of Near-Death Experiences

from
*The News of the World's
Sunday Magazine*

Jean Ritchie

A Dell Book

Published by
Dell Publishing
a division of
Bantam Doubleday Dell Publishing Group, Inc.
1540 Broadway
New York, New York 10036

The trademark Dell® is registered in the U.S. Patent and
Trademark Office.

ISBN: 0-440-22172-2

Printed in the United States of America

Published simultaneously in Canada

March 1996

10 9 8 7 6 5 4 3 2 1

RAD

This book is dedicated to the many people who so willingly shared the stories of their near-death experiences with the author.

The author would particularly like to thank Drew MacKenzie for his contribution to the American research. Thanks are also due to Tony Harris, Pete Picton, Lili Gooch, Martin Malin, and to Mark Lomas for his cover design.

Contents

Introduction

I should be glad of another death.

T. S. ELIOT

This book tells the story of what it is like to be near death or, in some cases, to actually die and be brought back to life. It is one story and it is lots of different stories: more than 300 people volunteered to talk about their experiences. Only a fraction of them have been included here, but the reason for that is purely space. All their stories are fascinating, all their stories are individual. Yet all their stories are in several compelling ways almost exactly the same.

If so many people experience the same unusual sequence of events when they are close to dying, it must mean something significant. If the journey they embark on in those few critical seconds when their lives hang in the balance follows the same route as so many others take, it cannot be a dream or a hallucination.

But does that mean it is "real"? For the people who have the experience, there is never any doubt: it actually happened. There are certain phrases that you hear time and time again when you talk to them, and among the most common are "I know it was real," "I know it happened," "I know I did not dream it," "It's the most real thing that has ever happened to me."

That's not proof, of course. The stories told in this book cannot be dissected and examined in a laboratory, they cannot be analyzed scientifically. They cannot, if you like, be proved. Yet that does not make them invalid. If so many people have experienced them, and are experiencing them every day, and if similar stories can be traced back to the

1

beginning of civilization, and if they happen in all different cultures and races, the sheer volume of evidence is overwhelming.

There will always be skeptics who argue against near-death experiences (NDEs), either by refusing to believe those who tell the stories or by coming up with complicated scientific hypotheses to explain them away. This book does not ignore the possibility that eventually science *may* come up with an explanation for what happens in those fading seconds of life (see Chapter Eighteen). But, at the same time, it would be unfair to give credence to a few convoluted theories in preference to the witness evidence of so many who have had NDEs.

You only need to talk to anyone who has had one to know that, to them, it was a very powerful, very moving, unforgettable event. They almost all find it changes their lives. Very few of them are now afraid to die: in fact, many of them talk longingly of the day when death finally comes to them, although they know that the decision about when that day should be is not one they can make. As one woman said, "I look forward to it like I look forward to a fantastic holiday."

It is the testimony of these people, the ones with firsthand knowledge of the NDE, that constitutes the backbone of this book.

And it is to them that this book is dedicated.

If you want to know what it is like to die, and where we may all be going after death, read on. You will find it reassuring.

The surnames of some individuals who have had NDEs have been deleted to protect their privacy.

Chapter 1

WHAT IS AN NDE?

In one of the most famous pieces of writing in the English language, Hamlet's "To be or not to be" speech, Shakespeare describes death as "the undiscover'd country from whose bourn no traveler returns." But is it really undiscovered? Does no traveler ever visit the land of death and return to the land of the living?

From the beginning of time there have been stories of people dying and coming back to life, usually with their lives transformed in some way for the better. Nowadays, with doctors and hospitals equipped to resuscitate people when they have gone beyond what, in Shakespeare's day, would have been the point of no return, there are a great many more stories (see Chapter Three).

Medical science has progressed to the point where clinical death has had to be redefined. The old-fashioned idea that when the heart stops beating you're dead has had to be reappraised: many heart attack victims have been successfully resuscitated. As long as their brains have not been deprived of the oxygen pumped in by the blood for too long, they can be brought "back to life" without any permanent damage. Some—and there are examples in this book—have even had their hearts stopped for so long that there *ought* to have been brain damage, but miraculously they make full recoveries.

Astonishingly, people who have come close to death or have even technically died frequently report a sequence of events that is remarkably similar. Between a third and a half of all those who, through accident or ill health, hover

3

on death's doorstep tell of an experience which they can remember vividly, which affects them profoundly, and which, with some variations, is consistently the same.

At first it was only those who worked with the dying who were aware of this phenomenon. But since the 1970s, the subject has been talked about and experts have studied it. The events that are reported have been dubbed the near-death experience (NDE), and attempts to dismiss them as hallucinations or dreams have failed. Other attempts have been made to explain them away scientifically, as part of the natural processes of a dying brain (see Chapter Eighteen), but these theories are only informed speculation: they offer no proof and have some fundamental flaws.

So, first of all, what is a near-death experience?

The first person to collect near-death stories, and the man who coined the name for them, was Dr. Raymond Moody, whose book, *Life After Life,* was published in America in 1975, and broke the ground for many further studies of the phenomenon. His interest in the subject was sparked when, as a student, he heard about the experience of a psychiatrist who had "died" from double pneumonia, only recovering after his doctors had pronounced him dead to his family. The psychiatrist experienced and wrote about his NDE. It was not the first time a psychiatrist had chronicled the details of an NDE: Swiss-born Elisabeth Kübler-Ross, who worked with survivors of Nazi concentration camps, had become convinced that something unexpected happens close to death, and had written about it in her book *On Death and Dying,* a more general work about dying than Moody's, but containing the first real exploration of the NDE by a doctor. Dr. Kübler-Ross was so affected by what she witnessed that it convinced her that there is life after death.

Moody took up the challenge of researching this relatively unknown territory. He came up with a classic description of an NDE.

It is a made-up compilation—it did not actually happen in all this detail to any one person—but it contains all the features that have now been recognized as part of the NDE, although the order of the early stages is usually slightly different from this. Very few people ever have an experience this full: most only go through two or three of the stages, possibly because some are actually nearer to death than others, who come back to life sooner. Whatever the reason, the first few stages of the NDE are far more common than the later stages.

But Dr. Moody's imaginary case is a detailed and thorough exploration of a complete NDE, and so here it is:

"A man is dying and, as he reaches the point of greatest physical distress, he hears himself pronounced dead by his doctor. He begins to hear an uncomfortable noise, a loud ringing or buzzing, and at the same time feels himself moving very rapidly through a long dark tunnel. After this, he suddenly finds himself outside his own physical body but still in the same immediate physical environment, and he sees his own body from a distance, as though he was a spectator. He watches the resuscitation attempt from this vantage point and is in a state of emotional upheaval.

"After a while he collects himself and becomes more accustomed to his condition. He notices that he still has a 'body,' but one of a very different nature and with very different powers from the physical body he has left behind. Soon other things begin to happen. Others come to meet him and to help him. He glimpses the spirits of relatives and friends who have already died and a loving, warm spirit of a kind he has never encountered before—a 'being of light'—appears before him. This being asks him questions, nonverbally, to make him evaluate his life and helps him along by showing him a panoramic instantaneous playback of the major events of his life. At some point he finds himself approaching some sort of barrier or border, apparently representing the limit between earthly life and the next life. Yet he finds that he must go back to earth, that the time for his death has not yet come. At this point he resists, for by now he is taken up with his experience of the afterlife and does not want to return. He is overwhelmed by intense feelings of joy, love, and peace. Despite his attitude though, he somehow reunites with his physical body and lives.

"Later he tries to tell others but he has trouble doing so. In the first place he can find no human words adequate to describe these unearthly episodes. He also finds that others scoff, so he stops telling other people. Still, the experience affects his life profoundly, especially his view about death and its relationship to life."

British psychologist Margot Grey, who herself experienced an NDE, gives a shorter, but just as relevant, summary of the NDE: "Many people who nearly die, whether in an accident, during surgery, or in other traumatic circumstances, subsequently report a remarkable experience while physically unconscious. This event brings with it a profound and permanent alteration of their understanding of the nature of reality. There are many elements, recounted independently by thousands of people, common to all these accounts. These frequently involve an encounter with a compassionate being of light, a meeting with deceased loved ones, and feelings of inexpressible beauty, peace, and transcendence, leading to a loss of fear of death, greatly increased sense of life's purpose, and a more loving and open attitude."

Dr. Moody's book gave details of a number of NDEs that had been personally recounted to him. He stressed that he had not collected them scientifically, but the marked similarities he had noted in them compelled him to assemble them together.

Although his, and Margot Grey's, summaries of the NDE are good, it is probably useful to go through the different steps in more detail. This version of the NDE is based on the evidence of the many people who contributed their stories to this book, but it also corresponds with most of those reported by Dr. Moody back in the 1970s and by many different researchers since.

The experience starts with a realization of being dead, although not all NDEers are conscious of definite thoughts: many aspects of the experience they just "know," without being aware of where the knowledge comes from. It is, they say, more a feeling than a thought. It is just there: it is the reality of that moment. The vast majority do not feel at all distressed to find themselves dead.

Then they feel themselves floating out of their bodies. There are, as with all elements of the experience, some variations on how this happens, but the majority simply feel themselves float upwards, away from themselves.

There is peace, calm, happiness. All earthly worries and problems slip away. All pain—and remember, many NDEers are in acute pain because of the medical condition that has brought them to the brink of death—slips away and they feel whole and well. People with permanent disabilities find they have gone. Even the blind can see as well as other NDEers.

Some, a small minority, feel they have an actual second body, of the same shape and size as the one they leave. Most don't: they are unaware of how they look. Yet they are all convinced that it is the real "them" that has left the earthly body. It's a notion they find hard to express. One person said, "The body down below was just a shell, it was as much to do with me as an old coat that I had been familiar with wearing. The real me, the essence of me, the important part of me, my soul, my spirit, my personality—whatever you like to call it—was up on the ceiling.''

Next the subject finds they can look down from their vantage point up above (usually directly above, but often to one side, particularly in a corner), hovering just below the ceiling. They can see themselves. At this stage they may see things they could not possibly know if they were lying on the bed unconscious. They see their own bodies, they see medical staff working on them, when they have been in an accident they see firemen and ambulance personnel struggling to free them. They may, afterwards, be able to repeat entire conversations that happened while they were unconscious. Occasionally they can move around into other rooms. One classic case, reported in 1963 before NDE research was fully under way, came from a woman who was in a hospital, seriously ill with peritonitis. The ward was L-shaped and as she lay in her bed she could not see around the corner.

"One morning I felt myself floating upwards and found I was looking down on the rest of the patients. I could see myself propped up against the pillows, very white and ill. I saw my sister and nurse rush to my bed with oxygen. Then everything went blank. The next I remember was opening my eyes to see the sister bending over me. I told her what had happened and at first she thought I was rambling. Then I said, "There is a big woman sitting up in bed with her head wrapped in bandages and she is knitting something with blue yarn. She has a very red face." This certainly shook her, as apparently the lady concerned had had a mastoid operation and looked just as I had described. She was not allowed out of bed and, of course, I hadn't been up at all. After I'd given her several other details, such as the time by the clock on the wall (which had stopped working) I convinced her that something strange had happened to me, at least.''

The next stage is the tunnel. This is the best known aspect of an NDE, but, like all the other stages, not everyone experiences it. Some describe darkness, without seeing it as a tunnel. Some describe situations that, symbolically, are the same as tunnels: roads through steep mountain passes, long corridors, etc. The NDEers may feel they are walking along the tunnel, but most usually feel they float, often at high speed.

Then they see the light. The light is at the end of the tunnel, and everyone who has seen it finds it very hard to describe. Over and over again they use phrases like ''bright and yet soft,'' ''gentle yet strong'' and, all the time, ''more beautiful than anything I have ever seen.'' For some of them the light contains colors, the colors found in the rainbow spectrum. Again, these are described as incredibly beautiful.

At the end of the tunnel they pass out into the light. There may be a barrier at the end, which they sometimes pass and sometimes don't, or they may come to a barrier (a door or a gate) when they have moved from the tunnel. What lies beyond the tunnel, in the light, varies a great deal from person to person, but has one essential fact in common: it is beautiful. Beautiful becomes a very overworked word in any conversation with an NDEer: so much of what they see is beyond description in ordinary terms, they say, and the nearest they can get is to keep stressing its beauty.

Some of them only see ''beautiful'' countryside when they get out of the tunnel, others meet people. Some have already met friends and relatives in the tunnel who have previously died (a few are actually taken into the tunnel by one of their dead loved ones), but the real meetings, with conversations, generally take place beyond it. How much communication there is varies enormously: some have normal, everyday sort of talks, others simply "know" that they are being told things without a word being spoken.

Occasionally, not very often, the subject has a "life review." This means that they see brief clips of episodes and incidents in their lives: probably the origin of the saying "his life flashed before him." Sometimes this review happens in the presence of a person or spirit who appears to be judging them.

Some subjects meet people they don't know. They often describe them as angels or spirits. For some, there is one supreme being waiting, the "being of light," so named because often there is no physical form, just a glow of light from which emanates a feeling of power and goodness. Some have conversations—again, often nonverbally—with this divine being, others simply see and feel the presence.

At some point (and it can be at any point along this sequence of events) the subject is "sent" back to his or her body. One of the people they meet may send them back, or they may hear a voice telling them to go back. The expression that is frequently used is that it is "not your time yet." Some are specifically told to return because there are things left unfinished.

Some feel that they made themselves return, by concentrating their minds on what they were leaving behind. This was particularly true in the case of parents with young children. One woman said, "If it happened today I'd be so happy to go, I wouldn't fight it. But at the time I knew my children needed me."

Most are not aware of the return journey. They simply find they are suddenly back in their bodies. Some are conscious of actually reentering their physical shell.

Almost all NDEers are changed by their experience: they become less materialistic, more caring, more spiritual, and they are almost unanimously no longer afraid of death. A very small minority, about 3 percent, have unpleasant NDEs (see Chapter Sixteen).

Dr. Moody's work was regarded at first as controversial by the medical profession, some of whom accused him of simply collecting together hallucinations. The NDE stories, they said, could not be proved. It's true—it is impossible to produce scientifically acceptable proof, because NDEs are not things you can put in a laboratory and examine under a microscope. But it is certainly possible to eliminate hallucinations: psychiatrists who have studied patients with psychotic illnesses that trigger hallucinations know that no two patients have the same hallucination, nor do they remember them in the way that NDEers do. Hallucinations are chaotic, unpredictable and are usually associated with feelings of depression and despair, or unnatural elation, whereas the characteristic emotions of the NDE are calm, joy, serenity, peace.

One of the staggering things about NDEs is the way people remember them. The majority of stories told in this book were first written down by the NDEers two years before the book was researched. Asking them, after such a long gap, to repeat the details of their NDE produced in every case an identical report, although they did not have their original written account in front of them. Not close, but exactly the same.

If you asked people to repeat stories about any other event in their lives with a two-year gap between the first and second tellings, you would find a whole lot of discrepancies creeping in. Human memory is notoriously fickle. Even important events fade, details become distorted, and those that we do remember correctly are patchy. Try asking two people, for example husband and wife, to give an account of the same event, perhaps their wedding. You'll find one remembers bits the other has forgotten, although both were there, and vice versa. As for dreams, very few of us remember them for more than a few minutes after waking, and those dreams which are colorful enough to impinge on our memories for a few days (nightmares, more commonly than pleasant dreams) very rarely last a lifetime. Yet NDEs do.

Certain phrases were used over and over again by the 300 people whose stories were collected for this book: one of the most common was "I can remember it as though it were yesterday." Many of those who volunteered their stories added that they did not have particularly good memories. "I can't remember what happened last week, let alone ten years ago. Yet this is still as fresh and vivid as if it had just happened," was a typical comment.

Dr. Moody's work aroused the interest of other researchers, notably psychologist Kenneth Ring from the University of Connecticut. He set out with an open mind to investigate Moody's theory that many dying people experienced something similar. He did not know whether his research would find anything to support Moody's ideas or not. He interviewed not only those who had had NDEs, but those who had nearly died and had nothing so exciting to report. He confirmed Moody's findings and, by conducting his research in a more thorough, scientifically rigorous way, he made NDE research academically respectable, at least in the United States.

Ring outlined five core elements of the NDE, and these are probably a better guide to it than Moody's hypothetical case: feelings of peace, separating from the body, entering the darkness (a tunnel in Moody's description), seeing the light, and entering the light.

Most NDEers experience these key stages in the same order, and in declining numbers, so that according to Ring's research as many as 60 percent of all people who brush with death experience feelings of peace, 37 percent separate from their own bodies, 23 percent go into darkness, 16 percent see the light, and 10 percent go into the light. "It seems to be the same journey with different individuals encountering different segments of what appears to be a single common path," said Ring.

As his work with NDEers progressed, he came up with a more detailed version of his core elements: a sense of being dead, feelings of peace, separation from the body, going into darkness, meeting a "presence" or hearing a voice, taking stock of one's life, seeing beautiful colors, entering into the light, and meeting visible spirits.

Another pioneer researcher was Michael Sabom, a cardiologist, or heart specialist. He was very skeptical about Raymond Moody's book, and felt that he could demolish it by speaking to heart patients who had survived brushes with death. The first two he asked confirmed his idea that it was all hocus-pocus, but to his astonishment the third patient he spoke to described a classic NDE. As he went on questioning, he found more and more examples, and like the other researchers he became fascinated by the common threads running through them all.

After Dr. Moody's book opened the subject for discussion at all levels, people who had previously felt uncomfortable talking about their experience came out into the open. There are still, particularly outside the United States, residual feelings of disquiet among NDEers that they will be treated as, in the words of some of those interviewed for this book, cranks and nuts. The reason we have what appears to be an epidemic of NDEs nowadays is not only because of the advances in medicine: the freedom to talk openly about these strange and supernatural-seeming events has allowed people who previously only confided in their closest friends and families to speak up. When they did talk, it was to those they believed would be sympathetic: a survey of clergymen has shown that 70 percent have had reports of NDEs from parishioners.

As, like a snowball, the numbers coming forward to tell
their stories grew and grew, so did the funding for research.
And as serious study of the subject increased, extra core
elements were identified. For example, many NDEers feel
very alert and observant during their experience, more so
than ever before in their lives: colors look sharper, noises
are clearer, senses are heightened.

In 1981, in the United States, the Association for Near
Death Studies was set up by Dr. Kenneth Ring, and this
has since become the International Association for Near
Death Studies. It is a forum for the exchange of research
findings and it offers access to research material. It has also
worked well as an umbrella organization for support groups
for people who have had NDEs (there are several across
the United States), and these provide a resource of cases
for experts to study. There is a British branch of the
IANDS.

Among the questions explored by researchers is the obvious one: how many people have NDEs? Ring's work suggests that as many as 60 percent who have been close to
death have some sort of experience, with 37 percent having
a recognizable NDE. Other experts have come up with figures varying from 22 percent to 48 percent. It is a very
difficult subject to work on: how close to death do you have
to be for an NDE? Michael Sabom, working with Sarah
Kreutziger, conducted one of the most reliable studies, and
came up with a figure of 43 percent of those close to death.

In the general population, it is even harder to put a figure
on what proportion of people have had an NDE. One poll
in the United States put it as high as 15 percent: people
were asked if they had had ''an unusual experience'' when
they were ''on the verge of death.'' Without being more
specific about the type of unusual experience, it was obvious that many people would answer yes: just being seriously ill or in a life-threatening accident is, in itself, an

"unusual experience." And "on the verge of death" was not specifically defined: if the figure of nearly half of all those who are near death having an experience is correct, this statistic of 15 percent would mean that at least 30 percent of the population have been so ill or in such a serious accident that they have been near death: a very unlikely figure. Most of us only meet death once in a lifetime.

Why do some people have NDEs and some people don't? The researchers have been busy on this question, too, and they have discovered that NDEs are spread across the board: they happen equally to men and women; they are not influenced by how religious the subject is, or his or her age, education, class, wealth, or any other variable. In other words, it's a lottery as to whether, when you are near death, you have one or not. It does not matter, either, whether you have ever heard of NDEs or not: talking about them more, the writing of books, and the showing of television programs about them, has not produced a higher percentage of them. One difference does exist between the sexes: women are more likely to talk about them, to write about them, to share them. Perhaps men are more afraid than women of being mocked as nuts or cranks. Women accommodate the spiritual more easily than men do, they are also more used to talking about their feelings and emotions—and having an NDE is a very emotional business. More women than men have taken part in the research for this book, but their experiences are neither deeper nor involve more stages of the NDE. In fact, the men who have contributed have usually gone farther through the core elements: it is possible that, the stronger the experience, the more they feel compelled to share it.

One study showed that NDEers are more likely to have had troubled backgrounds when they were children than non-NDEers: a higher proportion came from families where parents were divorced or separated. But it is also possible, as has been pointed out, that people who had stressful child-hoods are simply more likely to have had life-threatening illnesses or accidents.

Another study shows, perhaps not surprisingly, that the longer a person is clinically dead, the more likely he or she is to have an NDE. And, contrary to the general argument that NDEs are only hallucinations, experts have found that they are actually less likely to occur when the subject is influenced by drugs such as anesthetics, other medication, or hallucinogenic chemicals like marijuana, LSD, or alcohol.

There are some general facts that have emerged from all the statistical analysis of NDEs:

- people who have accidents are more likely to feel great joy and be very reluctant to return to their earthly bodies;

- those whose hearts stop are more likely to meet friends and family who have already died;

- those under anesthetic have a greater awareness of the bright light;

- those who have accidents are more likely to have a sense of time slowing down, or becoming totally unimportant;

- those who suffer cardiac arrest are more likely to have gone along a tunnel;

- younger people report more mystical elements in their NDEs;

- NDEs that happen at night usually involve more colors, brighter colors, and more vivid awareness of light and shade, and so do NDEs that happen when the subject nearly drowns;

- for many people, just believing they are near death is

enough to trigger an NDE. A British study showed that, of fifty-eight patients who had NDEs and who genuinely believed they were near death, doctors assessed only half as actually being on the brink of death and only saved by medical intervention. The others, though seriously ill, would probably have recovered anyway, even without the help of modern medicine. But because they believed they were dying, they were just as likely to have an NDE. One of the stories in this book is of a woman who had a horrific accident with a chain saw: she thought it had cut her jugular vein and that she would bleed to death. She had an NDE. Although her injuries were appalling and she needed a great many stitches, she had not, in fact, cut the jugular nor was she in immediate danger of death.

Some of the most interesting research into NDEs has been done with children and they, it appears, do need to be on the brink of physical death to have an NDE—probably because their experience of life and their very limited, or non-existent, medical knowledge mean that they have no concept of how ill they are.

The research with children is very important. Chapter Eighteen includes some of the arguments against the existence of the NDE as anything more than a brain function, and it is, of course, always possible that future research into the workings of the brain will come up with cast-iron proof that the NDE is not a spiritual experience, or a taste of the afterlife. But there are some very strong reasons for suspecting that science will never be able to argue away the NDE.

One of these is that children have them. Adults may be conditioned, by their religion, by their culture, even by having read or seen television programs about other people's NDEs, to expect one and perhaps even generate one from their heightened emotions at the time of a physical crisis. But children are clean slates—the younger they are, the cleaner they are. They haven't been told that it is odd to find yourself on the ceiling looking down. Going down a tunnel towards a light is, to them, an adventure, but then so is their first train journey, their first airplane flight. They have no preconceived ideas of what is "normal" and what is not.

Another American doctor, Dr. Melvin Morse, limited his first NDE study to children only, a field in which he had a great deal of expertise as a professor of pediatrics. His book, *Closer to the Light*, studied children who had been resuscitated and returned to life telling miraculous stories about the experience, and was based on interviews with twenty-six children who had survived cardiac arrest.

His fascination with the subject began when he was professionally involved in caring for a little girl called Katie, who nearly drowned in a swimming pool. She was recorded as not having a pulse for nineteen minutes, way beyond the time at which doctors could hope to revive her in anything more than a brain-damaged vegetable state (when no blood is pumped to the brain it is starved of oxygen, and after a very short time brain damage sets in). Dr. Morse worked hard at resuscitating Katie, but he had very little hope that she would survive. Her family never shared his pessimism, and spent hours at her bedside praying, talking to the unconscious child, and holding her hands. Three days after she was admitted to the hospital she regained consciousness and, defying all medical prognosis, made a full recovery with no brain damage.

Trying to find out more about what had caused the accident at the pool when she hit her head, Dr. Morse casually asked her what she could remember. To his astonishment she said, "Do you mean when I saw the heavenly father?" She proceeded to give him a detailed version of an NDE, including looking down watching him and the other medical staff working on her body, traveling along a tunnel, meeting an "angel," being taken to look down at her own family at home, and finally returning to her body. "You'll see, Dr. Morse. Heaven is fun."

Katie's story so fired Melvin Morse that he began to study the research that had already been done on NDEs, and began to collect his own material. He found that children often described the experience as "a weird dream." But, as with adults, the memory of the NDE did not fade as dreams do, and childhood NDEs last a lifetime with the people who experience them, as the testimonies of those interviewed for this book confirm (see Chapter Twelve).

"I discovered many things, but the most important thing I learned was to listen. By listening to the wisdom of these children we can begin to learn about the greatest mystery, the one that has puzzled humankind since the beginning: What happens to us when we die?" he said.

Dr. Morse is one of the few researchers who are prepared to accept that the NDE is actually a foretaste of what it is like to die, and therefore is proof of an afterlife. Even those who totally accept that NDEs happen are reluctant to commit themselves as to what they mean.

But there is no doubt in the minds of the NDEers. Their lives—as well as their attitudes to death—are transformed by their experiences.

Chapter 2

THE LIGHT BRINGS CHANGE

"If my wife was listening I would have to tell you that the most important thing that ever happened to me was meeting and marrying her. But the truth is, my NDE is the most important event in my life. It changed *me* more than any other single thing. It shaped *me*. It changed my personality—and even though my wife has been trying for years to do that, she's never succeeded! Having an NDE is the most profound thing anyone could go through, apart from death itself."

The words of one of the men interviewed for this book sum up the feelings of the majority of NDEers. Going beyond life changes life. The feeling of being given a second chance makes people value life more than they did before: it encourages them to sort out their priorities. They usually become more spiritual, waste less time in the pursuit of the material, value their human relationships more highly. With very few exceptions, they are convinced of the existence of an afterlife, and they are no longer afraid of death.

Quite a few change their careers, moving (often for less salary) into caring professions such as nursing. Others take up volunteer work. Some, employed in rat-race professions, simply prefer being out of work to a job that involves competing with others and flourishing at the expense of others. Many want to spend more time with the people they love.

"There's an old saying, 'You don't lie on your deathbed

thinking "I wish I'd spent more time in the office," but you may well lie there thinking I wish I'd spent more time with my kids.' Well, I've been there, and I can tell you, that old expression is true. After my NDE I didn't want to work long hours. No amount of overtime payment in the world could make up for time spent away from my family," said one NDEer.

For many, there are similarities to a religious conversion—even down to seeing the light. They don't necessarily turn to organized religion, in fact some turn away from it. But they have a deeper personal religious conviction. Many say they *believed* in life after death before their NDE, but now they *know* it is true.

Some seem to have been given more energy to get on with their lives by the NDE, other are more laid back and perhaps less energetic. The need to plan the future and control life seems to evaporate, and many NDEers report that they are more able to enjoy the minute rather than thinking ahead and worrying about the future. Some fears and phobias disappear—NDEers may lose their fear of flying or phobia about spiders, for example. It is as though they recognize the futility of these fears and no longer need to allow them to get in the way of their lives.

A large number report that they are more open, more m approachable, less suspicious of other people.

"I tended to think others were always trying to bring me down. I was always questioning their motives. Now I take people at face value: okay, one or two have let me down, but they are the exceptions," said one man.

One of the women in this book reported a much greater tolerance about small things: "I used to get mad if I was in the slowest line in the supermarket—I was always looking to see which line was moving the fastest. I used to get cross if salespeople were rude or offhand.

Traffic jams made me fume. Now I accept that these are ridiculous things to be concerned about. I just don't worry about them.

"I don't care about material possessions so much. If the kids break something I'm not pleased, but I don't go off the deep end. My family have all noticed the improvement in me."

The researchers who work closely with NDEers are all aware of the long-lasting effects: "Almost always they are extremely grateful that [the NDE] happened. Many say that it's their single greatest experience," said Dr. Kenneth Ring, one of the leading near-death researchers. In this book, *The Omega Project*, which looks at the aftereffects of NDEs, he found the people he studied became kinder, more compassionate, more concerned for others, more religious, and more spiritual after their brush with death.

A study of three groups of people—those who have never come close to death, those who have come close but not had an NDE, and those who have had an NDE—shows that the NDE does have a profound effect on its subjects. Both groups who had come close to death valued life more than those who had not. But the study, conducted by Dr. Bruce Greyson at the University of Connecticut, showed that those who had NDEs became more adventurous and started to take more risks, whereas those who had been close to death without the NDE became more cautious, more protective of themselves.

"The near-deathers are ready to go anytime," said Dr. Greyson. "They tend not to be afraid of death. Paradoxically, the others tend to be afraid of life."

Surprisingly, considering their experience of an afterlife is so seductive, people who have had NDEs after attempting suicide are less likely to try again.

"They sense a new meaning and purpose in life," says Dr. Greyson. "Their problems don't go away, but they see them more as challenges and opportunities for growth than as something they must run from."

There is also no evidence that a taste of a wonderful afterlife makes NDEers want to hasten their own end: they consistently report a sense of knowing that death will happen when it is "their time" and that that decision is not theirs to make. They may talk of looking forward to death, but none of them contemplate suicide in order to achieve it.

Some NDEers report that they become more sensitive, and have more psychic awareness and experiences, afterwards. Others find that the rush of information that they are sometimes given during the NDE—they talk of knowing so many things or being taught so many things, without necessarily meaning going through a conventional teaching and learning process—continues after they return to life, and they find their minds flooded with information. They don't know where it comes from, but some talk of another dimension.

A detailed analysis of the changes in attitude among NDEers was carried out by Russell Noyes, a professor of psychiatry at the University of Iowa, and he broke the changes down into five different categories: reduced fear of death, a sense of invulnerability, a feeling of special importance or destiny, a belief in having received a favor from God or fate, and a strengthened belief in an afterlife.

The most common change was the reduced fear of death: although Noyes found this in only 41 percent of his survey, it seems to be an almost universal reaction to an NDE. Dr. Melvin Morse found in his research that the deeper into the NDE the person went, the less fear of death they had afterwards.

A feeling of invulnerability is much rarer, but it has also been noted by Dr. Michael Sabom, a heart specialist, among

patients who have survived cardiac arrests. Like Dr. Greyson he noted that those who didn't have NDEs tended to
wrap themselves in cotton to avoid another heart attack:
changing their diets, their lifestyles, worrying about their
health. Those who had NDEs tended to be far less concerned, and sometimes took up exciting and dangerous hob-
bies.

Noyes talked to one young woman who had her NDE
after narrowly escaping death in a skydiving accident. She
went back to skydiving afterwards, saying "I somehow feel
invulnerable now." Climbers who experienced falls came
away from the NDEs feeling more confident and even, in
one case, "a relative degree of invincibility."

One in five of those in the survey felt they had been
chosen to survive death in order to fulfill some mission:
perhaps it was only to bring up their families, but it may
have been as life changing as a complete switch of career.
Some felt they were on a mission to spread the word about
NDEs.

One in six felt they had been favored by God or fate,
and for some that meant that they believed in God—or an
all-powerful force governing the universe—for the first
time in their lives. Others had stronger religious beliefs as
a result.

The physical effects of the NDE are only just beginning
to be studied, but there's already some evidence of NDEers
having lower blood pressure afterwards, which can be a
great benefit, particularly to those who come near to death
through heart conditions or strokes. Some NDEers develop
changes to their sense of smell, as though it has become
more sensitive. Sometimes they cannot stand certain smells
that they tolerated happily before.

There are also some examples of NDEers having a pe-
culiar effect on electrical equipment, causing computers,
microwaves, and tape recorders to go on the blink around

them—the result, some doctors believe, of changes in their electromagnetic fields. Dr. Melvin Morse discovered an undertaker who had had an NDE who was unable to wear a watch: they all stopped working on him. His NDE had occurred as a child, and Morse believes he was attracted into a profession connected with dying because of it.

There are a few negative aspects of having an NDE, and not just among the small minority who have unpleasant ones. Even though the experience itself is very beautiful, it can cause problems for the person returning to life. An immediate, and very temporary, reaction is anger at having been brought back, and this may be followed by guilt for not wanting to come back (mothers of small children who did not think about them during their NDE feel the most acute guilt). Disappointment at being back, especially for those facing lots of problems in their lives, is another negative reaction, and occasionally is coupled with real depression. And there is often a deep sense of frustration at not being able to explain the experience: even though it is easier to come out and admit having an NDE today, many people are still wary of being labeled odd. Time and time again, those who have told their stories in this book stressed how they have never previously been interested in the supernatural, how hardheaded and down-to-earth they are. But the frustration is also at their inability to describe what happened: they can always recite the details of the NDE, but feel they cannot do justice to describing the beauty of it, or the feelings of ineffability.

It is above and beyond all human experience, and therefore it is very hard to share with those who have never been there.

Some NDEs are so powerfully disruptive to the subject's life that they result in broken marriages. "Very often people come back with a very different concept of what love is," says Dr. Greyson. "They often feel that they love everybody. And that's real hard for spouses to accept sometimes."

The changed set of values can be difficult for families to accept, especially if the NDEer wants to give up a well-paid job. A fundamental change in spirituality can also be difficult for those who have not shared the experience, and sometimes a divide opens up between married couples.

Far more commonly, though, NDEers find the whole experience refreshing, stimulating, exciting, unforgettable and, to use the most overworked word in this book, beautiful.

Chapter 3

DOWN THE CENTURIES AND ACROSS THE WORLD

People have been going down the tunnel and into the light since man first walked the earth. Near-death experiences are not new. There may be more people having them today than ever before, but they have been recorded since civilization began, and they have not changed greatly over the centuries.

In fact, although we may have more near-death experiences to record and analyze today thanks to medical science, that same science has reduced the number of actual death experiences that ordinary people witness. It's not that we've discovered immortality and stopped people dying, it's just that we have institutionalized death. It's no longer an everyday part of society: the family gathered around the deathbed, neighbors and friends coming in for a last goodbye. We've sanitized it into hospitals and nursing homes, and we've eased its arrival with massive doses of painkilling drugs. There is nothing wrong with killing pain in the dying with drugs, but it may well reduce the actual death experience as much as it reduces the near-death experience in those who are brought back from the brink of death: the more heavily anesthetized the patient, the less likely he or she is to have an NDE, which explains why a proportionately higher number happen to those who have accidents rather than illnesses.

How do we know that the actual death experience is the same as a near-death experience, only without the subject being summoned back to life? The families and friends who gathered around the bedside knew about it, and stories of what happens at the point of death were passed down in folklore for generations. Those who were there heard the "ramblings" of the dying, some of whom were able to describe the vision that was before them cogently and lucidly. Others, while not being able to articulate what was happening to them, clearly lost their pain and suffering and, by the moment of death, were very happy and peaceful. Stories of deathbed visions were commonplace, and totally accepted. There was no suspicion of nuttiness or crankiness attached to them, partly, perhaps, because a God-fearing age would have readily accepted the idea that death brought a passage into a brighter, better land. The materialism and skepticism of the latter half of the twentieth century have combined with modern medical techniques to remove most of us from any spiritual experience through the death of others. We have retained the grief, but eliminated the life-enhancing aspects of what J. M. Barrie described as "an awfully big adventure."

So how do we know what previous generations and even civilizations experienced at the point of death? There is plenty of written evidence. In Tibetan Buddhist writings there are literally hundreds of near-death stories, recounted by people who have come back to life at the point of being buried or cremated, and telling usually of meeting dead friends and relatives. Sometimes they brought back messages for the living from their deceased loved ones. Tibetan culture accommodated these people, and accorded them the chance to preach about their experience as prophets on a mission to convert the living to higher standards of moral behavior. There was implicit in their teachings the message that the better the life on earth, the better the afterlife.

The ancient Greeks similarly accepted NDEs as evidence of what awaited them all after death. Plato recorded a full NDE in his *Republic*. It is the story of a Greek warrior who was assumed to have died in battle, and whose body was left on a funeral pyre awaiting cremation. But before the torch could be set to the bonfire he regained consciousness and climbed down. He then described his NDE: he had traveled with others to a place of judgment. There were gateways on either side, some leading to beautiful places and some to places of punishment. Some of the others were stopped and judged and sent through one of the entryways, but the warrior was told to return to earth and tell others about his experience. Instantaneously, without knowing how it happened, he was back in his body on the funeral pyre.

One of the most common elements of the NDE, the tunnel, is an image which has been depicted in art from the Middle Ages onwards, and NDEs were recorded in medieval times. Although there are many similarities, there are also some differences between these medieval NDEs and those we hear about today. In 1987 Carol Zaleski wrote a book comparing medieval and modern NDEs, and found that in the older stories there were many more accounts of unpleasant experiences at the brink of death, with demons and devils and the like grappling for the soul of the subject. But there were core features that tie in closely with the stories recounted nowadays: the sense of floating out of the body and hovering above it, being able to watch what was going on below; tunnels or valleys or pathways to travel down; a mystical experience of heightened awareness and understanding; and a strong feeling of being compelled to return. Far more fundamental to the medieval experience than the modern one was the sense of being judged, of confronting the past and reviewing the deeds and words of a lifetime. Whether modern religious teaching, with far less emphasis on Judgment Day, has influenced the type of NDE that is prevalent is arguable. Religion does not appear to have as much influence over NDEs as might perhaps be expected: there is no higher incidence of NDEs among those who believe in God and an afterlife than among those who have no religious convictions.

One of the first Western collections of NDEs was made in 1892 by Swiss geologist and climber Albert Heim, who was inspired by his own experience after a fall in the Alps to collect stories from other mountaineers, finding thirty who had survived potentially fatal falls. Here is an excerpt from his own account: ". . . no grief was felt, neither was there any paralyzing fright. There was no anxiety, no trace of despair or pain, but rather calm seriousness, profound acceptance and a dominant mental quickness. The relationship of events and their probable outcomes were viewed with objective clarity, no confusion entered at all. Time became greatly expanded."

At the end of the nineteenth and beginning of the twentieth century, when serious physical research was first getting under way, deathbed visions were also collected and recorded. Early researchers, though, were less interested in NDEs than they were in other phenomena, because they felt that visions and experiences that occur at a time of crisis may have been induced by the stress or pain of the moment. It is still an argument being debated today (see Chapter Eighteen).

Three of the founding members of the Society for Psychical Research, a serious and respected organization dedicated to furthering real investigation into the paranormal, published in 1886 a seminal book called *Phantasms of the Living*, which contained 700 reported cases of ghosts or apparitions.

One of the deathbed reports in the collection dated from the time of the American Civil War. A sergeant major from a regiment of volunteer infantrymen was taken to a hospital with mortal wounds. The surgeon who looked after him reported the case, saying that the soldier could only speak in whispers and eventually appeared to be dead. The patient's father was there.

"When we thought him dead the old man put forth his hand and closed the mouth of the corpse and I, thinking he might faint in the keenness of his grief, said 'Don't do that! Perhaps he will breathe again,' and immediately led him to a chair in the back part of the room, and returned, intending to bind up the fallen jaw and close the eyes myself. As I reached the bedside the supposed dead man looked suddenly up in my face and said, 'Doctor, what day of the month is it?' I told him the day of the month and he answered, 'That is the day I died.' His father had sprung to the bedside and turning his eyes on him he said, 'Father, our boys have taken Fort Henry and Charlie [his brother] isn't hurt. I've seen mother and the children and they are well.' He then gave quite comprehensive directions regarding his funeral."

The surgeon reported that the soldier again asked what the date was, and again said, "That's the day I died." Very shortly afterwards he was dead. The news about the taking of the fort, and the fact that his brother Charlie was unhurt, subsequently proved to be true.

It may not have all the features of a deathbed experience along the lines of a classic NDE, and it is obviously impossible to add to it or clarify any of it, but it is possible that the second sight of the dying man—being able to predict the outcome of the assault on the fort and his brother's survival—was nothing to do with traveling outside his body. But he actually says, "I've *seen* mother and the children," which suggests that he was in some way able to travel to their location and observe them.

Other early accounts of NDEs were published in the papers of the Society for Psychical Research, and some were reprinted in a collection made by G.N.M. Tyrrell in 1943.

One was the story of a doctor from Kansas who, early this century, was ill with typhoid and had a very low temperature and pulse. He felt he was dying, and said his farewells to his family and friends. He straightened his legs and folded his arms over his chest, as if anticipating the work of the funeral director. His own doctor, who was present, recorded that for hours he had no pulse or perceptible heartbeat. He was thought to be dead, and the church bell was tolled. The doctor occasionally thought he saw the "corpse" give a little gasp, so he stuck a needle into the flesh. There was no response. Eventually the "dead" man suddenly opened his eyes and started breathing normally. He was later able to give an account of what happened to him while he was unconscious.

He described how he had felt a need to get out of his body, and had done this by rocking to and fro until he broke his physical connection with the tissues of his body. He felt himself retreat inside the body, until he had moved up into his own head, and was then able to leave it through the line of the junction of bones in the skull.

"I recollect distinctly how I appeared to myself something like a jellyfish as regards color and form. As I emerged I saw two ladies sitting at my head. I measured the distance between the head of my bed and the knees of the lady opposite the head, and concluded that there was room for me to stand, but felt considerable embarrassment as I reflected that I was about to emerge naked in front of her. . . . As I emerged from the head I floated up and down and laterally, like a soap bubble attached to the bowl of a pipe, until at last I broke loose from the body and fell lightly to the floor, where I slowly rose and expanded into the full stature of a man. I seemed to be translucent, of a bluish cast, and perfectly naked."

He then described leaving the room and walking down the street, commenting that "I never saw it more distinctly than I saw it then. I took note of the redness of the soil and of the washes the rain had made." He tried, and failed, to let other people know that he was there. He noticed that he was attached to his body by a fine cord, like a spider's thread, which joined him at the shoulder. He then seemed to be propelled, as if by a pair of hands, and found himself on a roadway above a scene of mountains and forest which was typical of the Kansas countryside. He eventually came to some rocks blocking the road and tried to climb over them, but at that moment a black cloud descended on him and he was back in his body.

Again, not all the components of the classic NDE, but enough to be worthy of note: the sense of leaving his own body, being able to look at his own body, traveling away from it, being unable to communicate with other people. The road may have symbolized the tunnel down which so many NDEers pass, and the rocks that blocked it are symbolic of the barriers that so many others find ultimately sealing off their route. The feeling of being propelled as if by hands is also common to many NDEs.

The idea of being attached to the body by a cord is rarely found in modern NDEs, but the idea of an "astral body" linked to the human flesh by a cord was prevalent at the time: it was propounded by the Theosophical movement, whose teachings were an amalgam of Eastern doctrines. (Although the movement's founder, Madame Helena Blavatsky, was exposed as a fraud, the movement survived the disgrace and still exists today.) The theory was that severing the cord which bound the astral body to the earthly one would result in death; while the cord was intact, it was possible to return to life.

Another case from the early reports of the Society for Psychical Research is that of a Huguenot minister, whose hobby was mountaineering in the Alps and the Pyrenees. He and his party ignored the advice of their guides and tackled a particularly difficult climb. He was exhausted and could go no farther, and decided to sit and wait for the others on their way down. As he waited he felt a cold inertia creep over him, and he realized he was dying (probably of exposure).

"My head was perfectly clear but my body was as powerless and as motionless as a rock," he later wrote. He felt an acute pain and seemed to die. Then he thought: "Well, at last I am what they call a dead man and here I am, a ball of air in the air, a captive balloon still attached to earth by a kind of elastic string and going up and always up. How strange! I see better than ever and I am dead—only a small space in the space without a body."

He then looked down and was able to watch the movements of his climbing party, watching the guide taking them by a route they should not have followed, and even seeing the guide drinking a bottle of Madeira and stealing a chicken leg from another member of the party. When the group returned, they found the minister unconscious but were able to revive him. When he told the guide what he had seen, the man ran off.

Again, there is a suggestion in the story of being attached to the body by a cord. But there is also evidence that the NDEers could look down and see things he would not otherwise have known.

Another story recounted in Tyrrell's book comes from an account of the Boer War, written by a British officer who was taken to Bloemfontein Hospital suffering from typhoid fever.

"In my delirium night and day made little difference to me. . . . Mind and body seemed to be dual, and in some ways separate. I was conscious of the body as an inert, tumbled mass by the door; it belonged to me but it was not 'I.' I was conscious that my mental self used regularly to leave the body, always carrying something soft and black,

I did not know what, in my left hand, and wander away from it under gray, sunless, moonless, starless skies, ever onwards to a distant gleam on the horizon, solitary but not unhappy, and seeing other dark shades gliding silently by until something produced a consciousness that the chilly mass, which I then recalled was my body, was being stirred as it lay by the door. I was then drawn rapidly back into it, joining it with disgust . . .''

He was under the impression that he went back into his body whenever it was being attended—washed, fed, talked to—by the nursing staff, and as soon as he was left alone again he parted from it and resumed his wanderings. On the final occasion that he reentered his body he found it warmer, more comfortable, and he was not so disgusted by it.

Again, on his wanderings, he was able to see events he would not otherwise have known about, including the death in another part of the hospital of an army surgeon he knew. He also recalled, as so many modern NDEers do, the exact words used by the doctors who stood over him discussing his case.

One of the first attempts as a systematic study of what happens at the point of death was that of Sir William Barrett, a professor of physics who researched the paranormal and was a founding member of the Society of Psychical Research. In 1924 his wife, a doctor specializing in obstetrics, told him about a woman patient whose deathbed visions changed her from a state of high agitation, pain, and fear into one of serenity and radiance in the minutes before she died. Barrett collected and published many similar stories reported by those who were present when someone else died, stories which are consistent with the NDEs of those who survive a brush with death. A beautiful light, sweet music, lovely surroundings, being greeted by dead friends and relatives, seeing angels or similar beings of light were all reported. In one case, a young woman who died after childbirth talked of seeing her sister—yet she had not been told, because of the state of her health, that her sister had died just a matter of weeks before.

Carl Jung, the Swiss psychiatrist who founded analytical psychology, had an NDE in 1944 after suffering a heart attack. As he lay in bed, a nurse saw him surrounded by a bright halo of light: she claimed to have seen the same light many times, always around patients who were dying. Jung did not die, and later recorded his memories of what happened to him while he was unconscious.

He floated above himself, and then found himself high over the earth, and could make out the Himalayas and the Mediterranean. He felt that he was leaving the earth. Then he saw a block of stone which had been hollowed out into a temple. To the right of the entrance a black Hindu was sitting in the lotus position. Jung felt that he was expected to go into the temple, and as he drew closer he was aware of all his earthly and material desires slipping away from him, and he was aware that he could fully understand the meaning of life. A doctor appeared whom he recognized as his own doctor, although in the guise of the Roman god of healing, and told him that he had to return to his body. Jung did so, but very reluctantly. He felt anger towards the doctor, who was attending him when he regained consciousness. But he also felt that the way in which he had seen the doctor during the NDE was a sign that the doctor would not live long: he had seen him, Jung believed, in his primal form. Sure enough, shortly afterwards the doctor died.

Jung's experience may have transformed him, or may have helped a transformation which was already well under way as, in his old age, he moved more and more towards the study of the spiritual and the supernatural.

One of the acid tests of the truth or otherwise of the near-death experience is whether it is consistent across cultural as well as historical boundaries. We have seen from Tibetan and Greek examples that it appears to be, and there are numerous other examples of NDEs from the folklore of different countries across the world. North American Indians believe in them, and have traditional stories involving traveling outside the body after death. Descriptions of NDEs have been found in the beliefs of Bolivian and Argentinian Indians, too, in Buddhist and Islamic texts, and in stories from China, Siberia, and Finland.

In an attempt to come to grips with the cross-cultural nature of the experience more scientifically a huge survey of the observations made by doctors and nurses at their patients' deathbeds was carried out in the late fifties and early sixties by a pair of parapsychologists, one American and one Norwegian, Karlis Osis and Elendur Haraldsson. They wanted to discover if deathbed visions were real, and evidence of what comes after death, or whether they were caused by the dying brain beginning to malfunction.

They believed that if the second theory was right, the visions would vary according to the religious beliefs and lifestyles of the patients; levels of medication would also be crucial. To achieve a sufficient contrast in the religions, the expectations, and even the types of treatment of the patients, they questioned medical staff in America and India. More than 1,000 Americans and some 700 Indians took part in the survey, and from them nearly 900 cases of deathbed experiences were obtained. There were some differences between the two groups, but more startling were the similarities. The core experience was the same. The people seen in the afterlife were more likely to be dead relatives or friends for the Americans, and more likely to be religious figures for the Indians. As many as 60 percent of Americans visualized their own mothers, whereas female figures were very rare for the Indians. The Americans were also more likely to feel a strong urge to go with the experience, while the Indians were more likely to fight it and struggle to return to their bodies.

Not surprisingly, where religious figures were seen, they came from the religious background of the person having the vision: Christians saw Jesus or the Virgin Mary, Indians saw one of the Hindu deities (and in Navajo Native American folklore, a great chief is seen in a beautiful field).

However a later study, not of deathbed visions but of NDEs, carried out by Satwant Pasricha and Ian Stevenson, found some more fundamental differences between the two continents. In their study the Indians did not float above and look down on their own bodies, but were simply escorted away by messengers who took them to a man or woman with a book, who told them a mistake had been made and they were not wanted; they were then taken back to their earthly lives. The mistake was often spelled out: it was someone with a similar name who was needed, or someone with the same name but a different job, or from a different village. In contrast, the Americans were not usually given a reason for their return, although in some cases they felt it was because of their love for members of their family. Sometimes they were told that their time had not yet come.

Pasricha and Stevenson point out that the Indian experience may have roots in Hindu beliefs: the king of the dead sends out messengers, and the newly dead are brought before a man with a book containing a record of their life. But they are at pains to stress that their survey was small, and that the differences between the American and Indian NDEs may not be as significant as appears at first sight.

"We should remember that if we survive death and live in an after-death realm, we should expect variations in that world just as we find them in different parts of the familiar world of the living. . . . There may be different receptionists and different modes of reception in the 'next world' after death. They may differ for persons of different cultures.''

A more recent study of Indian NDEs was carried out by Dr. Susan Blackmore, who believes there is a biological explanation for NDEs rooted in the way that the brain behaves near death. If her theory is ever to be proved it is essential that all NDEs should have common factors: it may be possible to explain differing means of getting to the afterlife in cultural terms if the experience is accepted as spiritual, but if it is an actual physical process then it must be the same whether the brain belongs to an Indian or an American. Dr. Blackmore was concerned that there did not appear to be any reference to the tunnel experience in recorded Indian cases. She put an advertisement in the Indian newspaper the *Times of Bombay*, asking for people who had come close to death to relate their experiences to her. She was careful to give no clue as to what she was looking for. Of nineteen replies, twelve involved some kind of strange near-death happening, and eight of those twelve contained some elements of the recognized NDE.

''One heard sweet music, three reported a tunnel or dark space, four saw bright light, four experienced joy or peace and three claimed effects on their lives or beliefs—in other words, although this was only a small study, the features were similar to those reported in the West,'' she said in her book *Dying to Live*.

Although Dr. Blackmore can extrapolate from this evidence that the dying brain works the same whatever the race, creed, or cultural background (see Chapter Eighteen), the same evidence can also be quoted to verify the ''realness'' of the near-death experience.

If everyone has an experience that has certain core features (albeit with different additions and variations) then it can be argued that it really happened.

That is certainly what the NDEers whose stories are told in this book believe.

Chapter 4

CELEBRITIES WHO HAVE SEEN THE LIGHT

Elizabeth Taylor had one. Jane Seymour had one. Even Bart Simpson's dog had one. It stands to reason that if up to a half of all people who face death through accident or illness have an NDE, there will be quite a few celebrities among the ranks of the NDEers. Surprisingly, over the years not many have ever come forward and talked about their experience—or perhaps it is not surprising, considering that until relatively recently anyone who announced that they had traveled down a tunnel and had an encounter with a light filled with love and warmth would have been thought of as slightly cracked. Celebrities, ever protective of their public images, have been happier sharing the time-tables of their love lives with the public than baring their souls about the intimate and spiritual experience of an NDE.

One of the first British celebrities to talk openly about what happened to him was Hughie Green, the veteran host of *Opportunity Knocks*. He probably has no idea how re-assuring it was to hundreds of people when he did tell the story of his NDE, even though he never got any farther into the experience than looking down on himself from outside his body. Many of those who have helped the research for this book by sharing their stories have commented that it was reading his that gave them the courage to speak up about their own. As far as Hughie Green is concerned, he has no explanation for what happened to him. But after more than thirty years he knows that it did happen, and can still recall it clearly. It never occurred to him not to mention it: he's intrigued by it.

In the sixties *Opportunity Knocks* was an enormously successful television program which gave ordinary people a chance to parade their talents in front of millions. Every year more than 9,000 volunteered for auditions, which were held in every major city in Britain. Hughie Green himself could not attend all of the auditions, but tried to be at half of them. He had to operate on a tight schedule, and quite regularly traveled to audition venues late at night in order to be there for an early start the next day.

One evening in 1964 he left his home in Marylebone, London, with his assistant Doris Barry, to drive to Bristol. Doris, the sister of world-famous ballerina Dame Alicia Markova, was in charge of auditioning classical acts for the show, although her own background as a Windmill Theatre dancer meant that she also had a foot in the popular entertainment camp, making her a huge asset to Hughie Green (it was Doris Barry who discovered the poet Pam Ayres). Doris was in the passenger seat of the Jaguar and Hughie, who was forty-four at the time, was behind the wheel as they sped down the Great West Road, through Maidenhead, towards Reading.

At Sonning they came to a sharp left-hand turn, almost at a 90-degree angle, over a railway bridge. It was a well-known accident black spot and Hughie, who had driven the route many times before, approached it cautiously at low speed. Coming towards him over the bridge was a 30-ton truck. Tragically, as Hughie negotiated the bend, the steering on his car stiffened and refused to budge. Within a split second the Jaguar went into the rear offside wheels of the truck. The passenger door was thrown open and Doris was catapulted out; Hughie was trapped in the wreckage of his totaled car.

"I was unconscious, and I remember nothing from the first few minutes after the crash. The alarm must have been raised quickly, and the fire brigade rushed to the scene. At this stage I can clearly remember being above the car, looking down on my own unconscious body, with two firemen working hard to release me. I could see that I was badly injured. I remember looking at myself quite dispassionately and thinking, 'You're in a bad way,' but I knew it was me.

"I felt peaceful and there was no pain. But there was also a feeling of anxiety, as though I might be in trouble for damaging the car. It wasn't that I was worried about causing the accident: I can only think that it was a throwback to my wartime service as a pilot in the Canadian air force. If you damaged a plane through bad luck or carelessness you wet your knickers with fear, because you were in big trouble. I felt just like that about the car."

Hughie's NDE lasted only seconds, and then he was back in his body, conscious and in great pain. He heard one fireman say to the other: "We've got to get the bugger out before it bursts into flames." He was conscious as the firemen freed him, and he was loaded into an ambulance.

"I had the presence of mind to ask the ambulancemen to give me a blood test: I was stone cold sober and I did not want there to be any question afterwards about whether or not I had been drinking."

Hughie was rushed to a hospital in Reading, where he spent ten days. He was given an emergency tracheotomy operation to allow him to breathe. He had broken every rib in his body in the crash, but the worst thing that happened was that an abscess developed between his liver and his lung. He was transferred to the King Edward VII Hospital close to his home in London, and spent ten weeks there. Doctors had to wait for the abscess to be big enough to be opened, which they then did by removing one of his ribs.

"If the same thing had happened today I could have been

treated easily and without any aftereffects by laser, which
shows how much medical science is progressing all the
time.''

Doris Barry also suffered a catalog of injuries, but fortunately recovered completely after a few weeks in the hospital.

Hughie has no explanation for his NDE. He believes in
God, but has little time for organized religion. During the
war, when other aircrew and pilots were seeing their padres
and their priests before flying, he took the line that he did
not need an intermediary between him and God.

''If I want to talk to Him and He wants to talk to me,
we should just get on with it. He might not have anything
very nice to say to me, but He can say it to me direct. What
happened at the scene of the crash has not affected how I
think about God or death. I think I came to terms with the
prospect of death during the war. When you are twenty-
three years old and sitting at the controls of a B-24 bomber
on a runway at three A.M., with snow falling, and your crew
think you're the greatest pilot since Pontius but you know
you are only a fallible human being, you do a bit of adjusting. Most of us got through by generating the idea
within ourselves that death was something that happened
to other people—even though the statistics showed that we
were in the running for it. But I saw some people who had
a definite feeling that something was going to happen to
them, and it did.

''The day will come when the whistle will blow and that
will be the end of the line for me. I don't know what comes
after death, but I think something will happen. It's hard to
believe that we all simply turn to dust. But who knows?

''There are some things we cannot explain, and perhaps
we don't want to. I was ferrying planes from Montreal to
Karachi at one point during the war, and I used to always
take the opportunity to go into the city of Karachi to buy

gold, which I smuggled back and sold for a handsome profit. There were always lots of beggars in the streets, but one day one of them came up to a chap who was with me and said he could tell us his name and where he came from. He said the chap came "from beside big waterfall" and that his name was Comerford. He was absolutely right: the name was correct and the chap's home town was next to Niagara Falls. I don't know how he did that.

"It's the same with my experience after the crash. I don't know why it happened or how it happened. But it did. When I think about it, it is as clear today as it was when I woke up in the hospital in Reading: it all flooded back into my mind straightaway. I believe at the moment it happened my life was hanging in the balance, and it could have gone either way. But why that put me above myself, looking down, I have no idea."

For actress Jane Seymour, the queen of the television mini-series, her brush with death came when she was thirty-six years old and filming in Spain. She was playing the part of Maria Callas in a series called *The Luckiest Man in the World*, about the life of Greek shipping tycoon Aristotle Onassis. The extravagant and expensive production was being filmed on location in the searing heat of the beautiful city of Madrid. Costs had already rocketed over budget, so when Jane started sniffing and sneezing she determined not to take a couple of days off sick, as she knew any delay would cause major problems. Feeling under the weather and wanting nothing more than to have a restful day in bed, she struggled to get up before daybreak each morning and put in a twelve-hour day in front of the cameras.

She thought that, given a day or two, she would be on the right side of her cold. But the symptoms persisted, got worse, and soon it was apparent that her cold was in fact a severe bout of flu. Eventually, too weak to continue filming, Jane was ordered to bed by the film's producers and an English-speaking Spanish doctor was called to her plush hotel suite.

He arrived with a male nurse and examined the actress, diagnosing a bronchial infection for which he wanted to give her an injection of penicillin. He asked if she was allergic to the antibiotic, but Jane, who has taken penicillin on many occasions, told him she was not. "By that time I felt so weak that I welcomed anything that might make me better. The doctor made up the shot, and then he left the room, leaving the male nurse to administer it."

The injection was given. "My mouth went dry, my throat closed. I saw tiny white lights everywhere. I felt as if I was dying. I did not know enough about what was going on to object, I just let the professionals do it. But the effect was instantaneous. I started to black out. I was losing consciousness, gasping for breath and desperately trying to tell the nurse what was happening to me. I cried out that something was wrong, but the nurse could not understand my English. Then the room seemed to start flying. My legs were flying. My arms were flying. I had no control of my body at all, and I had no blood pressure.

"I thought my heart would explode. It was pumping away too fast, I could feel it going boom, boom, boom, like it was going to burst any moment. God, it was like a nightmare. It was the most frightening thing I've ever experienced. I kept jamming my fingernails into the palms of my hands because I thought that as long as I could feel pain I would remain conscious.

"The nurse did not seem to understand what I said, then I remembered some Latin from my schooldays so I went "muerto, muerto, muerto," thinking it must mean dying. The nurse went white and ran from the room to get the doctor."

The physician rushed back into the room and immedi-

ately recognized the signs of arterial shock. By now Jane
was having convulsions, shaking so violently that she had
to be held down by one of the hotel staff, who had come
to her room after hearing the commotion.

While shouting at the nurse to order an ambulance to
take Jane to the hospital, the doctor administered large
doses of adrenaline and cortisone. But it was almost too
late. Jane had already slipped out of consciousness and was
just minutes away from death. And it was in those moments
that she had her NDE.

"I literally left my body. I had this feeling that I could
see myself on the bed, with people grouped around me. I
remember them all trying to resuscitate me. I was above
them, in the corner of the room looking down. I saw people
putting needles in me, trying to hold me down, doing
things. I remember my whole life flashing before my eyes,
but I wasn't thinking about winning Emmys or anything
like that. The only thing I cared about was that I wanted
to live because I did not want anyone else looking after my
children. I was floating up there thinking, 'No, I don't want
to die. I'm not ready to leave my kids.' And that was when
I said to God, 'If you're there, God, if you really exist and
I survive, I will never take your name in vain again.' Although I believe that I 'died' for about thirty seconds, I can
remember pleading with the doctor to bring me back. I was
determined I wasn't going to die."

Jane, who had two children, Katie, born in 1980, and
Sean, who is four years younger, suddenly found herself
back in her body.

"Almost as soon as the doctor stuck the needle in, I
could feel myself coming back."

The actress still shudders at the memory of that day in
1985. And yet, like so many NDEers, she insists that ultimately it was a valuable experience. She nearly died, and

she is horrified to think how close her children came to losing their mother, but having survived she can see a lot of positive results from her brush with death. She believes it helped her put her life into perspective, and it also confirmed her belief in God.

"All I can say is that my attitude towards everything has changed. All these movies and TV series I do: it's lovely, but it's not terribly important anymore. Life is very short and very precious. A freak thing can happen at any moment, and then you're gone. You can't count on tomorrow. That's why I now tell my children that I love them every single day. I hug and kiss them several times a day without fail because I don't know if I'll be there tomorrow or not. Only God knows.

"My career was once the be-all and end-all of my life. Now what matters most are the children. Coming so close to death gave me a new set of priorities. I always loved my kids, but after this horrible thing happened to me I began to love them even more, if that was possible. And I decided not to disrupt their lives by having them sitting around hotel rooms waiting for me to finish a long day's working."

At the time of her NDE Jane, who first came to fame as a Bond girl in the 007 movie *Live and Let Die*, was married to businessman David Flynn, her second husband and the father of her children. But after ten years of an often stormy on-off relationship, the couple split up in 1991. Since then Jane has married actor-director James Keach, the brother of *Mike Hammer* TV-star Stacy Keach. By an incredible coincidence, her new husband has also had an NDE which convinced him that there is life after death.

"I was underwater with my scuba-diving instructor and I indicated that I was going up," he said. "I reached the top but I could not see my instructor, so I went back down looking for him. The next thing I knew I was completely tangled up in seaweed, and I couldn't breathe because my air had run out. I felt I was leaving my body, literally. Suddenly a strange voice said to me 'Scream.' ''

With no oxygen, James was seconds away from death. Even though he was underwater and it would not seem to be very sensible advice, he obeyed the command of the strange voice, opened his mouth and screamed. Seconds later he was rescued by another diver who cut him loose and helped him to the surface.

Jane says that their similar traumas, and the NDEs they had as a result, have brought the couple closer together, and closer to God. ''We want to grow together, spiritually. That is our main quest now,'' she said.

They are not the only two Hollywood stars to have talked about their NDEs. Elizabeth Taylor ''died'' briefly four times while suffering from a mystery virus, possibly meningitis, during the filming of the epic *Cleopatra* in 1963.

''I had a strange disembodied feeling,'' she said. ''I could see myself in bed, with all the doctors around me. I was certain that I had died. I felt very calm. There was enormous peace, and a feeling of floating easily on warm and calm water.''

Although it was a happy experience, she felt a strong desire to live. ''When I concentrated hard on that thought I seemed to merge back into my earthly body on the bed.''

Burt Reynolds, who went into a coma when trying to withdraw from sleeping pills, says he had ''the whole out-of-body experience.''

Actress Rebecca DeMornay, who starred in the film *The Hand That Rocks the Cradle*, discovered as an adult that she'd experienced an NDE when she was just seven years old. The star remembers that she was rushed by her parents to a hospital in Mexico City after a doctor had diagnosed her as suffering from a peptic ulcer.

"One night the doctors told my mother that there was only a fifty-fifty chance that I'd make it. I remember that I was tied to three IVs [intravenous drips] but I recall getting out of bed and looking out of the window: it was snowing. There was an old-fashioned lamppost and barefoot children were dancing around it, singing. I went back to bed and the next morning the crisis was over. In 1983 I started thinking about it: 'Does it ever snow in Mexico City? Do they have these strange kind of lampposts there?' I went back to Mexico and I didn't see those lampposts anywhere. Nor does it ever snow there."

Rebecca no longer fears death. "Corny as it may sound, the experience made me see the tenuousness of life at a very early age. And that has made me stronger. I truly think my illness was a blessing."

American actor Robert Pastorelli had an NDE which literally changed how he was living, in a very dramatic way. Robert, who starred in the TV series *Murphy Brown* with actress Candice Bergen, admits he was an unruly teenager whose life was on a crash course. When he was nineteen he was driving his sister's car, a Pontiac Le Mans, at breakneck speed near his home in New Jersey when another car crossed a red light and ran into him.

"It smashed right into the driver's door. It hit me so hard it actually knocked the shoes off my feet. My car rolled over about four times on this big highway and the next thing I knew I was in intensive care with a collapsed lung. Every one of my ribs was shattered. I had lacerations to my head and face, and my kidneys, spleen and gall bladder were all ruptured. I was a mess.

"I was in excruciating pain. Then, in the next second, there was no pain. Suddenly I realized I was out of my body. I was floating above myself, looking down at my unconscious body lying in the hospital emergency room with my eyes closed. I could see tubes down my nose and throat. I knew I was dying and I thought, 'Well, this must be death.' I even saw a priest giving me the last rites. But it was the most peaceful feeling in the world. Then I saw my father starting to faint out of grief. Two nurses grabbed him and sat him down in a chair across the room.

"When I looked down and saw my father's pain it had an effect on me. I firmly believe that at that moment I made a decision to live, not die. The next thing I knew I was waking up back in my body. Later, in the recovery room, when I was fully conscious, I told my father what had happened, his fainting and all. He was astounded.

"I already believed that we all have a soul. But after this happening to me, it became the difference between believing in the soul and truly knowing that it exists. And all of a sudden I had a different outlook on life because I knew it was never ending. So I wasn't afraid of death and I felt totally free to live my life the way I wanted.

"I'd always wanted to be an actor, but it was something that I had been afraid to try until then. The month after I got out of the hospital I was in acting school in New York. Now every day I try to live my life to the fullest because I'm just happy to be healthy and alive. I had an NDE and it will affect me for the rest of my life."

Hollywood star Donald Sutherland was taken ill with acute meningitis during the filming of *Kelly's Heroes* in 1979. "Suddenly the pain, fever and acute distress seemed to evaporate. I was floating above my body, surrounded by soft blue light. I began to glide down a long tunnel, away from the bed . . . but suddenly I found myself back in my body. The doctors told me later that I had actually died for a time."

Another show business star who has had an NDE is Erik Estrada, famous for his role as a motorcycle cop in the TV series *Chips*. During the filming of an episode of the show he had a serious motorcycle accident, and was rushed to the hospital.

"Suddenly I was in a long corridor with bright lights, beautiful music, and a feeling of great peace. But something seemed to be blocking my progress. A voice told me, 'You've got to go back. You've a lot still to do. You've achieved success and stardom but you haven't achieved personal happiness and peace of mind.' "

After hearing the voice he returned to his body. There were tubes coming from his nose, neck, and lungs, and the medical staff had been very worried about his condition, but he made a full recovery.

British comedian Ronnie Dukes died in 1981, after suffering his fourth heart attack. The well-loved roly-poly comedian had already had three earlier brushes with death, and it was after one of these heart attacks that he described a classic NDE, in which he found himself moving up a tunnel towards a bright light.

"It looked and felt very inviting. I was tempted to go onwards towards the even brighter lights I could see in the distance." But something made him turn back, and he was later told by his doctors that he had been clinically dead for a few seconds.

It made him, he said, feel happier about the eventual prospect of death. It also gave his family some comfort after his death, because he had shared with them his belief that there was an afterlife. "I used to be afraid of death," he said, "but now I know there is something that takes away all the pain."

British actress Ann Todd, who died in 1993 at the ripe old age of eighty-four, experienced the feeling of disappointment and anger familiar to many NDEers when, after a close encounter with death, she found herself returned to

her earthly body. Ann, whose most famous film role was
starring with James Mason in the 1945 classic *The Seventh
Veil*, had had a serious operation and was recovering in a
convalescent home.

"There did not seem to be any air in the room and I
could not breathe properly. Then the fruit and flowers by
the bed and the bed itself were encircled by light and I felt
so very happy. I've always believed that I have a guardian
angel—ever since I was four years old. Now I felt him take
my hand and we seemed to shoot upwards as though we
were in a lift, towards a bright light. There were flowers,
trees, wonderful music. It was everything beautiful that we
have on earth, only better.

"I saw Tanty, my mother's eldest sister, holding out her
arms. She was laughing at my surprise. Then I was being
tugged back into the darkness and I heard one of the doctors
say, 'Thank God, we have got her back.' I was furious.
How dare he say that when I had so nearly gone over into
the spirit world."

Another classic description of an NDE was given by the
Marquis of Tavistock, heir to the Duke of Bedford's estate.
In February 1988, when he was forty-nine, Robin Tavistock, who runs the 13,000-acre Woburn Abbey estate with
its famous safari park, suffered a massive stroke. After a
major brain operation surgeons gave him only a 1 percent
chance of survival. It was during those first six critical
hours immediately after the stroke that he believes he went
out of his body.

"I was floating up out of my body. I did not know how
I got there. I was going somewhere where I was much
happier. It was totally peaceful. Indeed, it was wonderful
to see what it was like up there.

"I could see what happens in the next world. I saw loved
ones who had long since died, especially my mother who
died when I was five years old. I don't remember how it

ended, because somebody up there said, 'We don't think we want you yet.' It wasn't a voice, more a feeling. But I do know now that I am not frightened of death.''

After a difficult struggle—in which he had to relearn to talk—he is now recovered from the stroke that left him temporarily paralyzed, speechless, and incontinent. He now has very little memory of the months immediately after his operation. But he commented soon afterwards that he felt his life had been permanently changed by his NDE: he was, he said, more philosophical, less tense, and more able to enjoy life—sentiments shared by the majority of NDEers.

One exception is no doubt Bart Simpson, the grotesque American cartoon kid. It's difficult to imagine anything making Bart relaxed, philosophical, and more spiritual. Predictably, when he had his NDE, it was a nasty one. Bart had been riding his skateboard with reckless abandon and had been hit by a car driven by his dad's boss. He floated out of his body: but ended up in hell. It was there that the devil discovered he wasn't due to arrive for another hundred years, and Bart was unceremoniously dispatched back to his two-dimensional body.

He's not the only member of the dreadful Simpson family to have had an NDE. When the family pet, that strange mutt named, inappropriately, Santa's Little Helper, was taken seriously ill, the rest of the Simpsons were too busy wondering whether Homer had won the lottery to notice the languishing dog. Eventually the mutt's life is saved by an operation—but not before he's had a brief glimpse of doggy heaven.

Chapter Five

SO THIS IS WHAT IT'S LIKE

All near-death experiences are slightly different, and they all come about in individual ways. Not many of them go right through all the stages. So that's why this one is particularly interesting, and deserves a chapter to itself. It's the perfect example of a full NDE.

Gillian Cross had an accident in the school gym when she was fourteen which, more than twenty years later, took her to the brink of death and gave her an NDE which has stayed vivid in her mind ever since. It was in 1960 that Gillian's class was having the gym lesson that changed her life: as she climbed up a rope another girl, halfway up her own rope, started to swing wildly and careered into Gillian, hitting her in the face with her kneecap. Gillian dropped to the floor, her nose a bloody, pulpy mass.

At the hospital that evening a doctor had to insert two long needles, one up each nostril, to pull her broken nose back to the center of her face. He told Gillian's mother that he could not set the nose properly at that stage, and that Gillian would have to come back when the bruising and swelling had subsided to have her broken nose set and straightened.

But the whole experience had been so horrible that Gillian determined to make do with the twisted, slightly off-center nose that she was left with. Luckily, she was a good-looking girl, with high cheekbones, attractive eyes, and a full mouth. Nobody noticed her nose, which was small. It was only as she grew older, into her thirties, that Gillian herself began to worry about it.

"I had a bit of a problem with it whenever I had a cold, but I also began to notice it more. Somebody told me that as you get older your nose gets bigger, and I could see myself with a face completely dominated by my nose. Also, as you start to lose your looks, you become more worried about imperfections. So I decided to get it done privately."

When the surgeon saw it he told Gillian that he would do it on the National Health Service plan, and, having put up with it all those years, she was prepared to wait. Eventually the date of the operation, at Whiston Hospital, near Liverpool, came close and Gillian, who admits she is a coward about hospitals and operations, was not looking forward to it. She'd been operated on for a gynecological problem before, and it had all gone well, so she constantly psyched herself up by reminding herself that she would simply go to sleep and wake up back on the ward, the operation over.

A couple of weeks before she went into the hospital Gillian and her husband Leon, who live in Moreton, Merseyside, had a visit one evening from a couple of proselytizing Mormons, members of the Church of Jesus Christ of Latter-day Saints. They were two clean-cut young men who explained their religion to Gillian and Leon, and Gillian was impressed. She commented to Leon that it sounded like a very attractive religion to belong to: she herself has always been convinced of the existence of God, but has not been particularly committed to organized religion, believing that there are many different roads to God. The young men came back again, and Gillian was beginning to feel herself drawn to their church.

"Then I asked them some questions, because I knew that their religion was supposed to believe in one man having many wives. They told me that Moses had lots of wives. But I knew that wasn't true: I've read the Bible about Moses, and I've always been attracted to him. I've always been interested in the basic beliefs of Christianity, things like the Ten Commandments, which are simple laws to live your life by. So I argued with them, and in the end I sent them away. I was quite angry with them.''

Afterwards Gillian wondered if she had been a bit abrupt and rude with the two young men, but she did not have time to agonize about it as she was preoccupied with her impending stay in the hospital, which came just two days after this encounter. She was so worried that she prayed long and hard, especially asking God to send Jesus to be with her during the operation.

After being given the anesthetic, the first thing that Gillian remembers is traveling down a long dark tunnel. She was being pushed on a hospital trolley, although she could not see who was pushing her. She was traveling fast, and there were small points of light on the ceiling of the tunnel which whizzed past as she traveled along it.

"I remember wondering why they hadn't given me the same anesthetic as last time, as I felt I was not asleep but really was being moved down this tunnel. I'm not a good traveler, I get carsick, and I began to feel queasy. I remember thinking that if I ever had to have an operation in the future I would take something to settle my stomach beforehand. I had my eyes closed after a while, to try to shut out the sense of motion.

"Then I opened them and I was not moving, and I was on a high bed. The sensation felt just like waking up. I could see the surgeon and the nurses, and I assumed the operation was over and they were going to say, 'Are you all right, Mrs. Cross?' at any moment. Then I realized I was still in the operating theater. The surgeon had curly hair, and bits were sticking out under his operating cap, which surprised me. I could hear everything he said quite clearly: he appeared to be talking to another doctor who was on the other side of me, who I could not see. I was expecting them to notice that my eyes were open at any minute, and explain to me what was happening. I really did think that perhaps they were using a kind of anesthetic that meant I would be awake, and they would say, 'Don't worry, we know you can see and hear us but you won't feel anything.' But nobody seemed to notice my eyes open, and I could not speak or move. Then he picked up a large instrument and he seemed to go straight into my face with it. I could not feel anything, but because I could see it I had this horrible sensation of it going into me, and of his hand being right inside my face.

"I started to pray, hard. I said to God that I knew the age of miracles was supposed to be over, but I asked him to perform one more, for me, and to put me to sleep. I remember thinking that I did not want to die without seeing my husband and my mum again."

Immediately Gillian found herself standing in front of an archway, so dark inside that she could see nothing, but with a beautiful light coming from all around it. She had felt no sensation of leaving her body, but she realized that she had slipped away from it. She looked down and saw that she was still wearing her white operating gown, but that her feet were bare. Although she was standing on the ground, her body felt weightless.

"I had a very strong feeling that beyond the archway was God. I could feel a power coming from it, and I knew that I could not go into it, or even see into it, because it was something too powerful for human eyes. I felt no pain, and I felt very calm, and a little bit in awe of the power I could feel coming from the arch.

"But I also felt silly, looking down at my bare feet. I felt grateful, because I had asked him to get me off that operating table and he had done that, he had answered my prayers. But I felt bewildered about where I was and why. I did not know what to do, but I felt I should acknowledge Him, so I bowed towards the arch. It sounds silly, but I can remember thinking: should I curtsey or bow?

"Then there was a strong sensation telling me that I had to walk away. I could sense that there was something to my left, so I started to walk in that direction. Again, although I was taking walking steps, I seemed to be completely weightless.

"As I walked to my left I came upon a circle of men, all wearing long white gowns. They were standing on a raised circular concrete dais, and they were facing inwards talking to one another. I wondered if Jesus was one of them, because I had especially asked for him to help me through the operation, but I knew without anyone telling me that he was not one of them.

"As I walked towards them one of the men, who seemed to be the leader, turned to speak to me. He was the only one whose face I saw, but the others all seemed younger, with shoulder length dark hair.

"He was very old, with white hair just over his ears in length and curling over his forehead. His skin was golden brown; not the sort of brown you get with a suntan, it seemed to glow. He, like the others, was wearing a long white robe and sandals, and on his head was a band of very finely woven material in spun gold. It looked almost like a halo, and it seemed to mingle with the pure white of his hair.

"He had a kind but very strict face, a strong face. I remember wondering if he was Moses, but his eyes were blue and I can remember thinking that Moses would surely have had brown eyes.

"I started to talk to him. I told him I was having an operation and he replied that he knew. I asked him questions, but he seemed to avoid giving direct answers. I remember asking him if Joseph Smith, the founder of the Mormon religion, had really existed. The thought just popped into my head, probably because I was still a bit concerned about whether I had been rude to those two young men. The old man said yes, Joseph Smith had existed. I asked if he was there, because I wanted to apologize for being rude to his followers, but the old man said Joseph Smith was not there. At least, he didn't say it outright, but that was the impression I got. It was as if he was not allowed to tell me, although he did not actually say that. I sensed it.

"I asked him if this was life after death, and he said it was for some people. Then he said to me, 'You believe in Moses, don't you?' I replied that I did, and he told me that if I continued to love him and keep the laws that he gave to us I would never have anything to fear when I died. I interpreted that as meaning that there was an alternative to this lovely life after death: there is a hell for those who don't obey those laws. I wanted to ask him if he was Moses, but I felt it would be impolite. When he said the word 'fear' I felt a sensation of real terror run through me, just for a second. The rest of the time that I was talking to him I felt safe and secure, and I think he said that word just to demonstrate to me the power that he represented.

"I asked him if, when I got back—because somehow I always knew I was going back—I should tell people that there was life after death. He replied that people only believe what they want to believe and that when my experience was over, even I would doubt whether it had truly happened, because although I had a strong faith it was not strong enough to eliminate all doubt.

"As I talked to him I seemed to 'know' lots of things. I felt I could see into the future, but it wasn't by making an effort, it was by simply 'knowing' what was going to happen. I said to him, 'I have to go into the hospital again, don't I?' He said yes, and said I would go in before the summer. There would be something wrong with me but I would not have an operation until later. He said I would naturally be worried, but I had to remember that everything would be all right 'within a time and a half.' I did not know what that meant.

"It sounds ridiculous when something so important was happening to me, but a lot of what he said went in one ear and out of the other. I was so amazed to be there, to be speaking to him, and yet at the same time it seemed perfectly natural. I could only see what was straight ahead of me: it was like looking through a telescope without the magnification. I could see immediately in front but I had no side vision, and I cannot say what kind of surroundings the concrete dais was in, because that was all I could see. I remember noting that the ground under my feet was hard, yet I could walk on it with ease because I was weightless.

"I had a very strong feeling by now that I had to go back, and I said this to him. He just nodded. I felt in awe of him, slightly frightened, but at the same time I knew he was a very good person. While I was talking with him I felt so much wiser and more free than I am normally, I felt I understood everything. But I had to turn and walk away, something was making me go."

There was nothing but darkness all around as Gillian walked away, again with no feeling of weight in her body. After only a moment or two her attention was caught by a light in the distance, to the right of her. She walked towards it for what seemed like a long time, until eventually she walked into the light. She could see a high table with a young woman lying on it, her face to one side with her mouth wide open.

"I thought she was on a ship because there seemed to

be little portholes letting in light all around the walls. Again it was as if I was looking at it down a telescope: I could see the circle of light with the girl in it, but all around was darkness. There were people on the edge of the darkness, fussing around the girl, and I wondered what was going on. As I recognized the room as an operating theater, I still did not take in who she was. I was thinking, 'Why has she got her mouth open?' It dawned on me slowly that it was me on the table. I went up to myself to have a look: I remember that the table was high, because I put my fingers on the rail that was holding her on to it and my hand was at chest height.

"I could see two men in white, and they were laughing and talking together, but I could not hear what they were saying. To get to the table I seemed to walk right through one of them, without him noticing. I knew I had to go back into my own body, but I don't know how I did that or what it felt like, because the next thing I remember is waking up on a trolley in the lift, being taken somewhere by two nurses. I remember vividly thinking: I must make a noise so that this time they know that I'm awake. I started moaning, and they realized I was coming round. I was in great pain, and very cold, which I noticed especially as I had been so warm and comfortable before."

Gillian told her mother and her husband about her experience. Her mother believed her, but her husband thought she had simply been dreaming while under anesthetic. When she fully regained consciousness she was no longer wearing her operating gown, but chatting to one of the nurses she learned that they had been short of the socks that patients normally wear in the operating theater, and that she had been taken in with bare feet.

As the months wore on towards the summer, Gillian began to think about the prediction that she would be going into the hospital again twice. "I decided to give up smoking, because if I was going to be ill I didn't want to make matters worse. Leon came with me for acupuncture to help us give up cigarettes. The following day I had gripping pains across my stomach and they got worse over the next few days. At first the doctor thought I had pulled a muscle, but eventually I was so ill I was sent into hospital, where they diagnosed an abscess on my appendix.''

Gillian was told that she would not be able to have her appendix removed until the abscess had shrunk. After three or four weeks of treatment she was sent home, and six months later she was readmitted to have her appendix removed.

"I think Leon realized then, when the prediction came true, that perhaps I had not been dreaming. Even the "time and a half" prediction came true, because it was eighteen months, or a year and a half from my meeting the old man to me being discharged after the appendix operation. It slotted in perfectly.

"The old man was also right that there have been times when I myself have doubted it all, and asked myself whether I couldn't have imagined it all while under the anesthetic. But there was something about the experience that was very real."

Although Gillian had felt calm and not at all frightened during her NDE, when she went into hospital for the appendix operation she prayed that she would not have a repeat of the experience.

"I did not mind it, but I would not choose to go through it again. I felt very peaceful and relaxed during it, but I also found it disconcerting to be able to know things in the future. It has reassured me that there is a life after death, and the prospect of being judged has helped me be more patient and tolerant with other people. But I felt strongly that I did not want to go there again, yet. When my time comes I will go happily, but I don't like the idea of having another preview."

The appendix operation went smoothly. As with the first operation she had, Gillian found herself going quietly to sleep under the anesthetic and waking up back on the ward when it was all over. It was during her recuperation on the ward, though, that she had another unusual experience: not connected with her NDE, but the sort of psychically sensitive event that has happened throughout her life.

As a young child of about nine or ten she "saw" a man in white robes walk across a stream on whose bank she was sitting, stringing daisies into a chain. She had been playing with two cousins, but they had left her to go searching for chestnuts. She sat there alone, concentrating on her project, when she looked up, aware that the birds had stopped singing, the leaves had stopped rustling, and the water, less than three feet away from her, had stopped making its rushing, gurgling noises. As she looked up she saw the man, whom she assumed must have been to a costume party the night before, because of the robes he was wearing. He did not approach her or speak to her, but crossed the shallow water without touching it, and disappeared among the bushes on the opposite bank. A few seconds later all the noises of the countryside resumed.

Gillian was never sure whether she had really seen him or had hallucinated the vision. Another paranormal experience came when she was newly married, and was staying in her aunt's house while the aunt was in California visiting her family. Gillian felt drafts on the staircase, as if someone was pushing past her, and regularly felt that her husband Leon was walking into the kitchen behind her and walking out again. When challenged, Leon would insist he had been nowhere near the kitchen. Finally, one morning when she was in bed after Leon had gone to work, Gillian awoke to find a woman standing at the foot of the bed. It took a few moments before she realized that the woman was wearing an old-fashioned dress with fur around the cuffs and a dropped V-shaped waistline.

"At first I assumed she was someone who had called round to see me, and that Leon would pop his head round the door and introduce her any moment. She did not speak, although she smiled when I smiled at her. I felt cross with Leon for letting her in and not telling me. But then she walked away, out of an upstairs window! And I realized then that Leon had left for work twenty minutes earlier. Yet she had appeared as solid flesh to me. My aunt later told us that other people had detected odd things about that house, and that my cousin, when he was a toddler, had always talked about 'the lady' who came in and went out again.

"I never found anything out about the history of the house, except that the family who had lived there years ago, before my aunt, had been of auburn coloring: the lady I saw had striking auburn hair."

So Gillian has, over the years, learnt to accept that she is fairly sensitive to the supernatural. Yet even she was reluctant to believe what happened as she lay in bed recovering from her appendix operation.

"I was used to the staff coming round every few hours, even in the night, to take my temperature and my pulse. So when I heard a rustling around my bed I pulled myself up into a sitting position with the pillows. I could make out the shape of a man, who I thought was a doctor, and a very small nurse, less than five feet tall. There had been a tiny nurse on duty during the day, and I remember thinking it was odd that she should also be on duty at night. The 'doctor' started to pass his hands over my feet—not touching them, just a few inches above them—and move upwards along my whole body. When he reached my chest I looked down and noticed that his hands were very large, with a scar on them, just like my father-in-law's hands. My father-in-law had been dead for a couple of years at this time. I was fascinated that the doctor should have such similar hands, but when I looked up into his face he had vanished, and so had the nurse. I wondered if they had gone through the window at the back of my bed, but the next morning I could see it was closed.

"The next day one of the other patients, a nursing sister herself, remarked that she was no longer frightened of her treatment because she had received a visit from her dead mother during the night, and her mother had reassured her. Then another patient, who was in the bed opposite me, said she had been visited by two of her departed aunties in the night, and a patient on my side of the ward had seen her late father. I was reluctant to say what had happened to me, but I asked the patient whose father had been whether he was a big man with large hands—she replied that he was small and frail. When I told them all what had happened to me they all thought it really had been my father-in-law, and that in passing his hands over me he was performing some kind of healing.

"We all agreed that it had to be more than just a coincidence that we were all visited by relatives who were no longer alive on the same night."

Gillian, who is no longer able to work because of tendonitis and rheumatoid arthritis, does not believe that her NDE has increased her sensitivity, but it has confirmed what she already believed: that there is a life after death, and that our behavior during this life preordains the nature of the next. She admits that there have been times when she has been tempted to be rude or abrupt with people who have annoyed her, only to check herself by remembering her conversation with the man with the long white robes.

She is resolutely not flaky. Every experience she has she has always attempted to explain in matter-of-fact, down-to-earth ways, wondering, for example, why the small nurse was doing a night shift as well as a day shift, feeling that it was impolite to ask the man she spoke to in her NDE if he was Moses, expecting her husband to introduce the lady at her bedside with a practical explanation for her presence.

"Everything that has happened has seemed completely real, normal and natural at the time. I have never been frightened while it has been happening, although I have felt a bit scared afterwards."

Chapter Six

THE MOST NATURAL THING
IN THE WORLD . . .

Childbirth may be the most natural process in the world, but it has also always been one of the most risky. Before medical science intervened, thousands of women died every year in the "natural process" of pregnancy and birth. The reduction in the death rate for both mothers and babies is one of the most staggering advances in the whole field of medicine. Even fifty years ago, twenty-six times as many women died giving birth as do today.

With the drop in the death toll has come a lot more interventionist treatment: in other words, the minute there's the slightest sign that things are going wrong, the doctors are ready to start work. They don't wait to let nature take its potentially fatal course. Consequently, many more babies are born on the operating table, after cesarean operations, than previously. And many more pregnant women are taken into the hospital for observation when there is an abnormal rise in their blood pressure, or any other symptom of problems to come.

As a result, childbirth produces a large crop of near-death experiences. For many normal, healthy women, having babies is the only time they ever go into a hospital; for others who, not that many years ago, would not have survived, childbirth takes them physically very close to death. As with any illness or accident, only some of these women report NDEs. But it is a sizable number: two out of every five women who have given details of their NDEs for this book experienced them during pregnancy, childbirth, or associated gynecological problems.

67

• • •

It should have been such a happy week for Gloria Taylor.
Her second baby was born quickly and easily, without any
labor pains. Gloria had gone to the hospital for a regular
checkup, and as she was leaving had suddenly realized that
she was about to give birth. Half an hour later she was in
a bed on the maternity ward holding beautiful little Kirsty
in her arms. Although Kirsty was five weeks early, she
weighed over six pounds and was perfectly healthy: a great
relief for Gloria, whose first child Andy had also been pre-
mature, and at only four pounds birth weight had given his
mom and dad plenty to worry about in the first few weeks
of his life.

So Kirsty's birth seemed so smooth and happy. Twenty-
four hours after she was born, Gloria proudly took her
back to the family home in the village of Curry Rivel, near
Langport in Somerset. Friends and family were delighted
with the new arrival, and Gloria's husband Brian was
thrilled to have his wife and baby daughter to care for. He
arranged to take some time off work, but when he couldn't
be at home with Gloria, her friend Hazel was happy to
help out.

The only problem that Brian and Hazel had for the first
day or two was getting Gloria to rest. She felt absolutely
exhausted, but she would not stay in bed, despite both the
midwife and the doctor ordering her to have some rest. By
the third day she was losing clots of blood that were larger
than normal, enough to concern the midwife. Again, Gloria
was told to stay in bed and try to rest.

Again, she defied the order.

"There was a voice telling me to get up out of bed and
walk about. It was saying, 'Keep walking, keep walking.'
Somehow, it made me keep on walking until I couldn't
walk anymore. Yet if I dropped off to sleep I would feel a

tapping on my shoulder and the voice would say, 'Gloria, don't go to sleep, wake up. Don't lie down, walk.'

"It was a female voice and it seemed to be in the bedroom. I looked inside the wardrobe and the drawers, because it was so real I was sure there was either a person or a recording of the person's voice somewhere in the room with me. I asked why I had to walk, but there was no answer except for 'You've got to.' I was so tired and ill I'd think, 'For God's sake, shut up woman,' but the only thing that stopped it was to get up and walk. I began to think I was going bonkers.

"I tried to shut it out: I'd climb back into bed and close my eyes, but the tap would come on my shoulder again."

By the third and fourth day, Gloria was becoming delirious. She was too ill to look after Kirsty—in fact, she had forgotten that she had even had a baby. She still heard the voice and struggled to obey the command to walk. By the end of the fourth day she heard a second voice, a man's voice, more authoritative and commanding than the first one. "You've got to keep her awake," the voice said, not addressing Gloria directly.

When Brian and Hazel reported to the midwife that they could not persuade Gloria to rest, Gloria explained to the nurse that she had been told to walk. The midwife called the doctor, who again told her to stay in bed.

"By the end of the fourth day I was so exhausted and ill I just wanted to die. I told the voice to leave me alone and let me die. Brian and Hazel have told me since that they brought Kirsty in to me and that I held her, but I have no memory of it. I was too ill to be bothered, I could not cope with myself let alone a baby. Luckily, I'd decided to bottle feed her from the beginning, so Hazel and Brian were able to do that. One explanation for my raised temperature and my delirious state was that I had milk fever."

The household activities on the fifth day after Kirsty's birth have completely gone from Gloria's memory. She was by this time so ill that she had given up walking, and by the evening of that day she passed a very large clot which the midwife later told Brian was part of the afterbirth, the membrane that had contained the baby in her womb, and which should have been cleared before she was discharged from the hospital. It had been turning septic within her, and poisoning her system. She had only managed to pass it because it had broken up—and it had broken up because she had been walking about so much.

But Gloria was too ill to understand how the voice she had been hearing had saved her life. She was no longer part of the world around her. Her husband, her son, her new baby daughter: they did not exist for her anymore. Instead of the familiar surroundings of her bedroom, she could see a bright light, glowing with pale pastel colors.

"It looked like a tunnel, filled with a pale lilac light with a stripe of white with a pale yellow streak in it across the top. Then it was pale pink, and pastel green, each time with the silvery white stripe with the yellow streak. The tunnel was revolving very slowly, and out from the mist at the top came a girl dressed all in white. She was wearing a plain, round-necked gown that came down to midcalf. It had short sleeves. I knew that her feet were bare, though I could not see them because there was a mist through which she seemed to be walking. She had blond hair bobbed just above her shoulders, she was aged between twenty and thirty, and she was very, very beautiful.

"She stretched her arms out towards me and said 'Come now, Gloria, come now.' She held her hands out towards me and I held mine out to her, but I could not move towards her. I really wanted to, but it was as though my feet were glued to the ground. I could not move, although I wanted to go so badly. It was the deepest longing I have ever experienced. She simply said, 'You're not ready yet, I'll see you again.' She turned and started to go back through the tunnel, but she stopped part of the way back and turned again, stretching out her arms and saying, 'Come now.' Again, I tried to go to her, but I couldn't move. She said, 'Quick, or it will be too late,' then she waved and said good-bye, and seemed to flow into the glow of colors in the tunnel.

"I could hear voices coming through the tunnel, but not clearly enough to tell what they were saying, and at the end of the tunnel, beyond the colors, was a mist. The colors were at the top of the tunnel, and revolving slowly inside it.

"I knew the girl had come for me, but I was not thinking about death. It just seemed the most natural thing in the world to go with her, and I was very distressed to find I couldn't. I didn't think about my home, my husband, Andy or Kirsty at that moment, I just wanted to go."

Gloria came around suddenly, to find her doctor patting her cheeks and calling her name. "There were a lot of people in the bedroom: Brian, Hazel, the midwife, and the doctor. The doctor was cradling me in his arms and telling me to stay awake, not to close my eyes. After a few minutes I became more conscious, and he told me I was a very lucky lady because I had nearly died."

From that point onwards, Gloria started to get better. It took her a few days to recover any strength, but she never lost consciousness again and she heard no more voices.

"I told the doctor afterwards about the voice that told me to keep walking, but he said I must have dreamt it. I know that it was not a dream, nor was the girl who came out of the tunnel for me: this happened in 1981, and if I had dreamt it I would have forgotten it by now. But I can still see it, so clearly.

"I will never know if it was the same girl telling me not to sleep, but whoever it was saved my life."

In some ways, Gloria feels cheated. She has no memory of Kirsty's first week: "I want to remember Brian holding me and pleading with me to get better; I want to remember Andy, who was seven at the time, with his arms around me, so upset that his mother was ill; I want to remember Kirsty's first feeds.

"But the only memories I have are odd flashes. I can remember the midwife ripping up sheets to bind me because of the milk fever, I can remember odd snatches of conversation. But nothing is clear, except my meeting with the girl."

Unlike other NDEers, Gloria did not recognize the young woman who came to meet her. She is certain that they had never met before—but she's equally confident that they will meet again.

"Brian still thinks I dreamt it, and he and Andy don't like me to talk about it, because they think I am talking about death. I don't want to leave my family, but the one thing I learnt was that time has no meaning there, at the other end of the tunnel, and that we will all be together for ever."

Gloria, who celebrates her fiftieth birthday in 1995, has a serious heart condition. "I've been told that I may live another fifteen years, or I may live only a matter of a couple of years. Nobody knows: I could have a heart attack at any time. But I'm not afraid of dying. I'm not religious—you only find me in church for weddings and funerals—but I've become much more spiritual. I now believe in life after death, whereas before I would probably have said I didn't know."

Unlike Gloria, Jennifer Mallett recognized the person who came to greet her when she came face to face with death:

it was her grandmother, who had died four months before. The old lady was wearing her familiar wraparound pinafore and her slippers with little balls on the front. She had been over eighty when she died, but when Jennifer met her, her face was wrinkle free and serene.

"She didn't look like a young woman: she was my grandmother, as I knew her and had seen her only a few months before. But her face was much smoother, and she looked free from all worries. She said, 'Come with me, Jennifer, it's just like being on earth.' "

Jennifer's NDE happened in 1971, when she was twenty-eight years old. She was having her third baby, and was worried because, at the time, money was tight and she did not know how she and her husband Brian could afford to feed another mouth. She had planned to give birth at home, but after several hours of labor her midwife decided that she was not going to be able to have a normal birth because the umbilical cord was prolapsed, caught around the arm of her breech-position baby. An ambulance was called to rush Jennifer to the hospital.

An emergency cesarean operation was performed and her third son, Vincent, was born hale and hearty. But Jennifer was unconscious for several hours, and hospital staff asked her husband Brian, a butcher, to help bring her around by calling her name.

"I was very frightened as I was rushed into the operating theater, as I had never had an operation before in my life," said Jennifer, who lives in Norwich and who was treated at the Norfolk and Norwich Hospital.

"But all I remember after that was such a wonderful feeling. I was looking down a tunnel, which was dark round the edges, but at the end of it was a bright light and such green grass. I've never seen a green like it, it was so intense and beautiful. My grandmother was standing in the middle of the tunnel, and she spoke to me as clearly as if she was alive. I really wanted to go to her. I was delighted just to be there, looking at her and feeling so content and peaceful.

"Then I heard my husband's voice saying, 'Jenny, Jenny.' I don't know what happened next, because I was suddenly back with him, in the hospital. He was holding my hand and saying my name. I was pleased to be back, but sad to have left that lovely place. When I was there, looking at it down the tunnel, I did not think about my family: I just wanted to go there. Now I'm glad that I didn't, because of Brian and the boys. But I know that there is nothing to fear about dying, and even as I remember it I think, 'Wow, I wouldn't mind some of that.'

"I sat with my mother when she was dying of pneumonia in 1993. She suffered from Alzheimer's disease, which made her rather confused, but in the hours before her death her mind seemed to clear. At one stage, just a few hours before she died, she said to me, 'Look at that, over there.' I could not see what she was looking at, but she seemed so happy and peaceful that I feel sure she was enjoying a glimpse of the place I saw, and that she was going to. I wished at the time that I could see it, too."

Jennifer's experience has taken away all fear of death, and changed some of her attitudes towards her life. She was brought up as a member of the Salvation Army, and even though she left the army at fifteen she continued to have Christian beliefs. "But I don't know that I truly believed until this happened to me. Before, I felt that there was a God and a heaven: now I know it."

When her sons were old enough for her to start working, she had "a serious think about what I was doing with my life." She felt a strong need to help others, and now works as a physiotherapy helper in a psychiatric hospital for the elderly. She has also worked as a nursing auxiliary, and in her professional capacity has found herself sitting with elderly patients who were dying.

"I don't tell people about what happened to me, and I never preach about my faith in God. But I somehow believe that the old people I have looked after feel comfortable with me beside them. The fact that I can accept that what is happening to them is something to look forward to seems to communicate itself to them. I hope it's a comfort. It helps me accept the work I do."

Jennifer's husband, Brian, always believed what she told him about her experience, and her sons have grown up hearing her talk about it: "On one level they think it's just one of mum's stories, something they've always heard me talking about. But on another level perhaps they will one day get a lot of comfort from it.

"Some people I have mentioned my experience to have laughed. They've said it was a dream, or a hallucination caused by the anesthetic. But you do not remember a dream so vividly and clearly after more than twenty years. I can call the picture of it to my mind as if it happened yesterday, and when I see it again I get the same feeling of peace."

Joyce Evans shared Jennifer's experience of being welcomed at the end of the tunnel by a close relative. Joyce came very close to death when her son David was born in 1972, when an emergency hysterectomy had to be carried out at the same time as the cesarean operation to deliver David. Joyce, from Stone in Staffordshire, was told by her doctor afterwards that she was the first patient he had known to survive all the problems she faced, and that it was a miracle that both she and her baby son lived.

But while the medical team were working hard to save her, Joyce was unaware of the panic: she was traveling very fast along a tunnel towards a bright light, where she could see her father waiting for her.

"I knew very clearly that I was dying. There was beautiful music playing, the air was filled with it. The light at the end of the tunnel was very bright, yet not dazzling: it was a very bright glow. I can remember thinking, 'It's the end of the line for you,' yet I felt absolutely no fear. I moved very quickly through the tunnel, and there was a gate at the top of it which I went through, but only just through—I did not go beyond it. I was within inches of my father, who was smiling at me. He had died fourteen years earlier, when I was sixteen, and he looked exactly as I remembered him from my childhood. I felt so pleased to see him and be with him, and there was an overwhelming feeling of peace and tranquillity. Then he put his hand up and said, 'It's not your time, go back, go back. You have a baby who needs you.' ''

The next thing Joyce remembers is coming around after her operation. She was still very ill: she was blind for three days, a condition caused by a loss of blood. She had not been aware she was pregnant with David, who has a sister Louise who is eighteen months older than he is, because throughout the pregnancy she continued to have periods, caused by massive fibroids in her womb. She also had a placenta praevia, which means that the afterbirth which nourishes the baby developed in the lower part of the womb instead of the upper part, and without the cesarean operation could have blocked the birth of the baby. She was told by her doctor afterwards that the combination of complications she suffered would happen only once in a million births.

"It was marvelous to wake up and find myself alive, because I did not want to leave my husband Michael or Louise or my new baby. I felt I had been given a second chance. But at the same time I also know that I have seen what death is like, and there is nothing to be afraid of. I saw how well and happy my father looked, and that was very reassuring. But most of all I remember the lovely feeling I had all the time I was in the tunnel.''

Just after Christmas 1992 Joyce suffered a heart attack, and she is now registered as disabled. "I cheated death again, but this time I had no similar experience. But when it happened and I was waiting for the ambulance to come, I felt very relaxed and peaceful. I feel sure that when I do eventually die I will go very happily."

Joyce believes her NDE changed her attitudes to life: "I feel more upset about the horrible things that happen in the world, especially when I read about human beings hurting other human beings. I think I am more sensitive about other people, more caring. And I appreciate life more."

Una Wolliston also met her father when she had her brush with death—and the encounter brought her a great feeling of happiness, because he had died only a month before, and she was relieved to see him so happy and well. But it took a very dangerous medical condition to bring about their reunion.

Una was expecting her third baby in 1980, when she was thirty-two years old, and went into the hospital for a checkup. The gynecologist who examined her explained that a lump on her stomach was not the result of her pregnancy, but that she also had fibroids in her womb, and this would probably mean a difficult birth.

At first everything went well: the labor was short, Una did not need any pain-controlling drugs, and her son Kenneth was a healthy seven-pounder. But within minutes of the delivery Una began to hemorrhage, and she heard one of the nurses telling another that something was wrong. An emergency button was pressed, and the delivery room was soon filled with medical staff—but Una was unaware of what was going on around her.

She remembers someone telling her to open her eyes, but she felt a lovely floating feeling that was carrying her away from all her pain. "I did not go through a tunnel, I just floated away to a beautiful land. The grass was so clean and green, and there were four great white marble palaces with columns in front of them.

"The white color was dazzling, yet there was a soft mist and there were people walking around wearing long white robes. I was overwhelmed by the beauty and the peace, I forgot everything else. I wanted to stay there for ever.

"Then I heard a voice calling me. He said 'Glo,' which was a name my close family used for me, and when I looked around there was my father. He looked so happy. In life he was always a happy person, but he looked so calm and peaceful as well. But he told me to go back because, he said, my children needed me. He said it was not my time to go to that place, but I did not want to leave. The next second I was back in the hospital, waking up with the doctors crowded round me. One of them said, 'Welcome back.' The pain came back then, and I was whisked off into intensive care for three days."

A year later Una, who lives in Milton Keynes, had to go back into the hospital for a full hysterectomy, but she did not have a repeat NDE.

"I have told people about what happened to me, and some believe and some look at me as though I am odd. I'm a shy person, so I don't go round telling everybody. I was already a Christian, and I always knew there was a life after death. I didn't expect to see it while I was still alive, though."

Veronica Matthews also gave birth without any drugs to control her pain, which means that she knows her NDE was not a hallucination induced by medication. Veronica, from Liverpool, was having her third baby in March 1984, when she was thirty-eight. Her two older children were both teenagers at the time, and Veronica was nervous about having another birth after a thirteen-year gap. She went into the hospital late in the evening, and within a quarter of an hour had given birth to Thomas, a healthy seven-and-a-half-pound baby. But what seemed like a quick and easy birth abruptly turned into a medical emergency, as the nurses around Veronica began to panic.

"I felt as if my stomach was leaving me. An emergency bell was rung and a lady doctor came in, running. It felt to me as though she was trying to push my stomach back into me, and I heard her say, 'I can't get the uterus back.' I saw my sister, who had been with me through the birth and was sitting next to me holding my baby. The pain was awful, worse than having ten babies. But then I suddenly floated away from it. I floated up to the ceiling in the right-hand corner of the room, so close I could almost touch the ceiling, and found I could look down on what was happening below. Everything was bathed in an incredibly bright light. I could still see my sister and my baby, but now I was looking at them from above. I could see the doctor next to my body, which had a green sheet draped over it. She was wearing white Wellingtons, and they were spattered with blood. Everybody seemed to be incredibly busy, but I felt very calm and relaxed. There was no pain.

"Then suddenly my body started to move forward. The light was becoming brighter still. I was moving towards the wall, with a sensation that was like floating on an air bed, but with nothing under me. I had the strong feeling that I could float away completely, from everything. Then I caught sight of my baby, and I thought about my daughter Shirley, who was seventeen at the time, and my son Joe, who was thirteen. I'm a single parent, and I began to panic about who would look after them if I was not there. The feeling of moving was getting stronger; I felt as though I was being swept away. It was not unpleasant, in fact it was a fantastic feeling and there was no pain, but I felt desperate to be back with my children. I said, 'God, please God, don't leave my kids without a mum.'

"At that moment, the feeling of moving went and I felt a jolt followed by an enormous pain, the worst pain I have ever experienced. The doctor was stitching me up and apologizing to me for having to do it without painkillers. The sensation of floating away came and went, but I didn't again have the feeling of rushing away from everything."

Back on the ward that night, Veronica continued to float up to the ceiling. "I drifted up and back again, always going to the right-hand side. I was able to look down on the patients in the other beds. I could see that a woman in a bed opposite mine had a baby girl's pink dress hanging at the back of her bed: I could not have seen that from my own bed."

The following day Veronica was told that the doctor had only just managed to save her from needing an operation that night, and that it had been a very close thing. When her sister came to visit, Veronica was able to tell her about the doctor's blood-spattered Wellies, which she would not have been able to see had she not floated above the bed.

Veronica has since talked about her NDE to several people, with mixed reactions: "Some of them give you a very odd look, as though you are not quite right in the head. But many of them believe me, and I hope it helps them. When my brother was dying of lung cancer recently, I was sitting with him when he told me that he had been towards the gates of heaven ten times, only to come back. I knew what he meant, because although I did not get that far I knew that was where I would have gone if I had carried on floating away.

"I would still be very upset at leaving my family, but apart from that I know that there is nothing to fear in death. It will be lovely: no pain, no worries, and everyone reunited."

• • •

Daphne Richardson's experience involved floating down a tunnel, and like Jennifer Mallett she came around when she heard her own name being called. But, tragically, Daphne's experience happened after she lost the baby she had been carrying for three months.

One common factor in all NDEs is that, no matter how long ago they occurred, the memory of them never seems to fade. Daphne, from Hove, in Sussex, had hers in 1947, when she was twenty-eight years old and had been expecting her third baby. Her other two children were two-and-a-half years and twelve months old at the time, and Daphne and her husband were living with Daphne's parents.

After she miscarried her baby at her mom and dad's home, the "very ancient" doctor who was called out to see her ordered that she should spend a week in bed. The following day she felt ill, but did not complain as she thought that was the natural aftermath of a miscarriage. In the afternoon her mother and sister took her other two children out to the park, leaving Daphne at home on her own. When her father came in she was so ill she could barely speak, but whispered to him to get help.

When the doctor arrived, he discovered that part of the afterbirth had failed to come away during the miscarriage. He was able to remove it. Daphne's condition was so critical that the doctor suggested her husband should be brought home from work to be with her. When he had done as much for her as he could, the doctor left her to sleep, warning her mother that because of the amount of blood she had lost she would be very weak.

"I was conscious up to that point, but then, when there was just my mother in the room with me, I felt a strange sensation of floating away, floating dreamily down a tunnel. I could see a light at the end of it, and I knew I was dying. I remember thinking about my other two children, and then reassuring myself that my mother would look after them. I was very comfortable, and quite unafraid. I wanted to go. The thoughts about my family were the things that seemed unreal, not the tunnel or the sensation of floating.

"Then I heard my mother calling my name. She kept on calling it. I felt irritated, I thought, 'Let me go,' but she persisted. I was annoyed, but the calling seemed to drag me back. The tunnel vanished and the peaceful floating feeling went away, and I was lying in bed again feeling exhausted and dreadfully ill."

Daphne's mother gave her a sip of brandy and the doctor, who had been called back, reappeared. He debated whether or not to get Daphne into the hospital, but by then the crisis had passed and she was able to recover at home.

"My mother's voice brought me back from dying," says Daphne. "But the experience taught me that death is not unpleasant. I was not at all frightened and all my pain had gone away: it was a lovely feeling."

Five years later Daphne successfully gave birth to a third child, a daughter.

Doreen Carter's experience was also a long time ago, in 1954, when she was twenty-six. Her NDE was short and did not involve the tunnel experience, only the sensation of pain-free peace and the presence of a bright and soothing light. Doreen was in the hospital giving birth to her only son, Stephen. It was a difficult labor, and she was not aware of what was going on around her for much of the time. But she was conscious of a doctor being called.

"I heard him ask, 'What have you done so far?' and somebody replied, 'Everything except dance on her chest with hobnail boots.' Immediately after that the pain disappeared and I saw a bright silvery light, blurred as though I was looking at it through a frosted glass window, and in one corner of the room there were three dense patches of light. I felt very calm, very happy and there was a sensation of floating. Then I heard a voice, which seemed to come from the dense light, and said, 'It's pure white, I've never seen anything like it.'

"Then all the pain rushed back in again and I was in agony. I remember thinking that I would scream with it, and then, being a logical person, I told myself that it could not get any worse. Once again, calm swept over me and I felt peaceful and pain free. The next thing I remember was someone patting my face, telling me to wake up."

Doreen's mother and grandmother had been brought into the delivery room while the medical staff worked on her, and they had been warned that her life hung in the balance.

The following day, when Doreen was back on the ward with her baby son, happy and healthy, a nurse looked in twice and was about to walk out again when Doreen asked who she was looking for. The nurse replied that she wanted a Mrs. Carter, who had given birth to a son the previous day.

"When I said I was Mrs. Carter she did not believe me at first. She said, 'You can't be—we as good as lost you yesterday, yet you look beautiful today.' That confirmed that I had been very close to death. All I know is that if that is what it is like, there is nothing to be frightened of. There's nothing to it—if you don't come back, you don't come back. If I died tomorrow I would be sad not to see my family again, I'd like to see my granddaughter growing up. But I would not worry for myself."

Doreen's husband William died in 1981, and she misses him greatly. "But I am comforted by the knowledge that he did not suffer in death," said Doreen, who comes from Eastbourne, Sussex.

Wendy Carter's experience was not a classic NDE: there was no tunnel and no bright light. But it was an exceptional experience that carries within it all the core symbolism of an NDE, and even though it is more than thirty years since it happened Wendy, like all other NDEers, recalls it as vividly as if it were yesterday.

Wendy, who was a familiar face on television in the sixties and seventies, when she appeared in dramas like *Doomwatch* alongside the actor Robert Powell, was warned before the birth of her first child, Sheryl, in 1964 that it was going to be a difficult labor and birth.

The baby's head was the wrong way around, and the birth was what is medically termed an "extended breech." Wendy was given painkilling medication—she does not know what it was—and she vividly remembers a feeling of floating away from the pain, and no longer being aware of where she was or what was happening. It was only afterwards that her TV-producer husband David told her that the doctor present had warned him that both she and the baby were in very real danger, and that one of them might not survive.

"The pain of the labor went, and I felt myself floating away from everything. It was as though my spirit was above, looking down on my physical self. I was at the bottom of a hill, which was a cobbled street lined with old terraced houses, and in the doorways of the houses were a few very old people, sitting and watching. I didn't recognize any of them. There were many people coming down the hill, and a few going up, pushing their way through the ones coming down. They were rather like figures in an L. S. Lowry painting, the matchstick men pictures he drew where all the people seemed to be leaning forward and in a hurry, and rather careworn looking. They did not look quite real, and yet I knew they were real. The whole scene was totally real to me.

"I was at the bottom of the hill, looking up, and at the top I could see a small humpbacked bridge. Across the bridge was the most wonderful, cool, lush green grass, which stretched away as far as my eyes could see. I knew that if I could get to that grass it would feel spongy to my feet and I could sleep forever in peace on it. It would be soft, cool and beautiful, and I would never have to leave it.

"I vividly remember my struggle to get up the hill. I pushed up and seemed to be pushed down again by the crush of the crowd all the time. In the middle of all the matchstick figures I saw a very real-looking little girl, swinging easily down the hill. She had plaits, a bright smile, and her clothes were more colorful than anyone else's. She was almost dancing down.

"Against all odds I managed to get to the top, where there were plenty more people milling about. To my horror I found that in order to get to the bridge I had to walk over a stretch of land covered with bramble bushes and debris. I somehow struggled over it, and was finally at the bottom of the small bridge. I knew that I only had to take a few more steps and I could plunge into the peace of that grass that was waiting for me. I tried to walk, but I could not move my foot, and as I struggled to take a step a voice told me that I had to go back down again. It was a strong voice, probably male, but I do not know where it came from—it was almost just a feeling inside me, more than an actual voice.

"I felt very sad as I turned away from the peace of that lovely grass. I wanted to go there, and I also did not want to face having to make my way down through all the people who were struggling up. As I went down I had to push and push: I realized afterwards that this was probably the point at which I was pushing out my baby, which I have no memory of doing.

"The next thing I remember is the scene fading and I was back in the hospital, and Sheryl was born. If it was a dream, it was strangely significant—and I had dreamt through the acute stages of labor and childbirth, without being given a general anesthetic.''

After Sheryl's birth, Wendy, from Welwyn Garden City, was warned that she might have similar health problems if she had a second baby. At first, she was so delighted to have managed to have one healthy baby daughter that she agreed that it was a good idea not to have a second child. But gradually, over the next few years, she began to have dreams.

''I dreamt of a tiny baby boy, in the middle of the most beautiful garden. I dreamt the same dream five times, but each time the child was bigger, just like a baby developing. Eventually, by the time he was toddling, he turned to me and said, 'Don't worry, Mum, I've waited all this time.' ''

Eleven years after Sheryl was born, Wendy became pregnant again and gave birth to a son, Matthew. The birth was straightforward: both she and Matthew were perfectly healthy.

''These dreams, like the experience I had when giving birth to Sheryl, are still so vivid and clear to me,'' she says.

Jenny Simmans's fourth pregnancy nearly killed her. Jenny, who has three sons, was early in her fourth pregnancy when she became very ill—the pregnancy was ectopic, and when it ruptured Jenny came close to death. An ectopic pregnancy means that the baby is conceived outside the womb, usually in one of the tubes connecting it to the ovaries. For a few days the tube is able to stretch to accommodate the growing baby, but eventually it splits, or ruptures. A ruptured ectopic pregnancy is recognized as an acute emergency, needing immediate surgery if the mother's life is to be saved.

On the day it happened, Jenny had been to the hospital to confirm that she was pregnant. That evening she was in pain, but it was midnight before she was seen by a local doctor who was called to her home. By this time she was gray, her body was very cold to touch, and she was delirious. An ambulance rushed her to the hospital, where she was found to have a blood pressure of 70 over 30 (a healthy average is 120 over 80), and her temperature was so low that it would not register on a normal hospital thermometer.

The problem was accurately diagnosed straightaway, and she was rushed to the operating theater. One of the last things she remembers hearing was the anesthetist saying that her veins had collapsed.

"The next thing I remember was suddenly being lovely and warm: I had been so cold before. I was probably under anesthetic when it happened, but I remember it so clearly, even though it happened in 1983, that I do not believe it was a dream or a hallucination. There was a very bright light, and I was moving towards it and getting warmer and warmer. It felt wonderful. The light was shining from the end of a tunnel. It was like bright sunshine, and as I got nearer to it I could see my Uncle Bill, my mother's brother, standing there, beckoning me to join him. He told me everything would be okay, and that where I was going was a lovely place. I felt secure, cozy, happy, but at the same time I was able to tell him—and we seemed to communicate without actually speaking—that I was frightened to go any farther. He told me that it was my choice, that I had to make the decision. As soon as he said that I was cold again, in pain and angry. The warmth, the light and my uncle all faded, and the last I saw of him he was waving to me. I heard him tell me that I would see him again, and then all I could feel was a horrendous pain in my chest."

Afterwards Jenny was told that her heart had stopped twice on the operating table, and that she had been resuscitated with electrical charges applied to her chest. The first time, it had taken ninety seconds to get her heart beating again.

Jenny's uncle had died two years before she had her NDE. He was only forty-nine when he died, from cancer. The last few months of his life had been traumatic, and Jenny's last living memory of him was as a very sick man. She had always been close to him, having been brought up for some years by her grandparents.

"Bill was always around, because my nan and granddad were his parents. I saw a lot of him for the first seven years of my life. It was so lovely to see him again, free of pain and looking young and happy."

Jenny has seen her Uncle Bill twice more, each time when her own health has been in crisis. The first occasion happened a year after her ectopic pregnancy, when Jenny, who lives near Salisbury, was in hospital for a hysterectomy.

"I was frightened, because although I now know that death is easy and pleasant, I did not want to leave my children. After the ectopic pregnancy operation the doctors had discovered that I had some abnormal cells in my womb, and they advised me to have it removed. I'm an asthmatic, so I was feeling nervous about having an anesthetic.

"The night before the operation, I was lying in my hospital bed when I looked up and saw my uncle sitting on the end of the bed. I was wide awake and fully conscious. It seemed the most natural thing in the world to see him sitting there, but we did not speak and within a few seconds he was gone. It reassured me, and I feel he came to remind me that whatever happened to me during the operation, life after death would be happy."

The next time she saw him was after another operation, this time on her jaw. As she was coming around from the anesthetic she had an asthma attack, caused by an allergic reaction to the anesthetic. She was choking on a blood clot.

"As I panicked, my uncle appeared and said hello and good-bye, then waved at me and disappeared. Nothing more than that, but it was enough to let me know that I was going to be all right, which I was.''

Jenny believes that seeing her uncle, and the knowledge that it has given her about life after death, has helped her get as much happiness as possible out of her life. Her first marriage has ended, and in September 1994, at the age of thirty-seven, she married her second husband Bryan, a professional soldier.

"I've talked to him about my experiences, and it has helped him come to terms with the idea of death which, as a soldier, he has to be prepared to face. I have made a pledge to him that I will stay at the same weight that I am now, so that when I die I can be buried in the dress I wore to marry him.''

Jenny has worked as a care assistant in a nursing home, and has seen several of the people of whom she was fond die.

"When I sit with them at the end of their lives, I can comfort them. I don't tell them what happened to me, because I think we all have our own personal experiences. But the fact that I am relaxed and accepting about death helps them, I think. I tell them to go with the flow, not to fight it, and I reassure them that everything is going to be all right. It helps me to remember how warm and comforting that feeling was, how cozy and secure I felt, because I know that is what they are going to. I grieve because I miss them, but I know that the grief is for my sake and the sake of those left behind: they do not need our pity.''

Carol Amodt also had her NDE as the result of an ectopic pregnancy rupturing. Carol, of Salt Lake City, Utah, had no idea that she was pregnant. She doubled up suddenly with stomach cramps as she was trying to get from her bed to the bathroom. Her husband Bob called for an ambulance and she was rushed to the hospital. She found out afterwards that she was clinically dead for seven minutes, while doctors worked to revive her with electric paddles applied to her chest.

Carol, who already had four children, remembers the horrific pain before she reached the hospital, and the panic as frantic nurses and doctors rushed around her bedside. But after that she was overtaken by a feeling of peace and tranquillity, and she floated away from all the activity around her body.

"I felt so good," she said. "I thought, 'This is a beautiful place.' The pain was all gone, and I really enjoyed the feeling. There was a bright glow all around me—not around my body, which was below on the bed, but around 'me,' which was floating away, as though I was in a bubble.

"Then I saw my kids. They had been taken to my parents' house, and they were running around, laughing. Then my oldest daughter was running towards me and I reached out to hold on to her and she ran right through me. I tried to hold her and I couldn't. I was very focused on the children and I knew that because of them I had to go back. Then suddenly I was in my body again, in the hospital, and in great pain. I was screaming with pain, and all I wanted then was to be back in that place.

"I heard people say that there is no such thing as life after death, but after my experience I know that there is. And the place we go to is a lot more beautiful than here. It felt so good to be there."

Carol has never had any problem sharing her experience with her husband. Bob, who is a year older than his wife, had his own NDE in 1980, when he was twenty-one. He was riding his motorbike when he crashed into a school bus. As soon as the impact occurred Bob, a custom-car refinisher, was aware of floating above his body, looking down on what was happening.

"I saw my motorcycle come out from the back wheel of

the bus. Everything was quiet and I didn't feel any pain. It was really very peaceful and pleasant. All of a sudden I was back in my body and I realized that somehow I had come out on the other side of the bus virtually unscathed. The medics could not understand how I lived, as they reckoned I must have hit the bus at 66 mph.''

Bob and Carol are now both very relaxed about the prospect of death, saying that, although they do not want to die, when the time comes they will welcome it, knowing that it will be a pleasant experience. At first they were reticent about talking of their experiences, but as more and more people in the United States have come forward with their stories, they have realized that they are not alone. They now say they do not care whether people believe them or not. ''We've been there, we've seen it, we know,'' said Bob.

Chapter 7

AFFAIRS OF THE HEART

Heart attacks are the biggest single cause of death in Britain and the rest of the developed world, so they are an obvious area for medical science to be hard at work improving every patient's chances of survival. Modern medical techniques mean that hearts can be restarted by applying an electrical charge to the chest, bringing a patient who has "died" back to life again. From among the ranks of these people who have so narrowly cheated death come a great many accounts of near-death experiences.

Arthur Carr's brush with death changed his life completely: not only did he experience the first stages of an NDE, he was so profoundly affected by it that he believes it has made him psychically sensitive. In the years since his illness he has been involved in a number of paranormal happenings, which he feels have happened to him because of the increased sensitivity his NDE has given him.

Arthur, from South Ockendon in Essex, had his heart attack in 1982, when he was forty-three. He felt pains in his chest and was taken to the hospital, but after three days everything appeared to be much better and he was told he could go home. He walked to the ward telephone to call his wife Glenda to ask her to drive over and pick him up, but as he put the phone down he felt a pain in his chest as if he had been hit by a sledgehammer. He managed to stagger back to his bed and asked the patient in the adjoining bed to summon help. Within seconds he was surrounded by medical staff.

"The pain was like a knife going into my chest very, very slowly. It seemed to get worse and worse, and then all of a sudden I was thirty to forty feet above, looking down on my body and the doctors and nurses. I can't remember any feeling of getting there: I was just there. I heard a doctor say, 'Put the needle in his arm,' and the nurse replied, 'I haven't done arms, I've only done legs.' The doctor said, 'He won't feel anything.'

"As I was watching all this from up above, I suddenly realized I was alive, that the real me was up there, not the body down below. I wasn't interested at all in the body down there that I occupied, I had no affection for it at all, I was extremely free. It was a very, very nice feeling.

"Then a thought crossed my mind: why, if this is true, why didn't my mum and dad and nanny and granddad tell me about this, why wasn't I told before that life continues after death? Then I remember thinking that it had obviously eluded them as well, they hadn't been let in on the secret. I was ecstatic about this new knowledge of an afterlife.

"Then I looked down at my own color. It was an awful gray. It seemed very embarrassing, far more important at that moment than the realization that life goes on after death. I felt really upset about it. It was like standing in the middle of a crossroads with no clothes on and lots of people looking at you. It was so embarrassing I didn't know what to do. I couldn't wipe the color off, I wondered how I got this color.

"As I was thinking this, a voice from behind me, which had apparently been listening to me, said, 'You are gray because you have done nothing to improve yourself. You haven't done anything about it, have you? You haven't been you. You must be you, be a good individual.'

"The next moment I was back in my body. My body was very wet through perspiration because of the pain, but my mind was ecstatic about the happiness I had experienced. The feeling was so lovely. My body was really weak but I felt I wanted to shout out and tell everybody of the really wonderful thing that had happened to me. The memory of it helped me get through my stay in hospital. I'd been given knowledge to show that after death we move on. I felt I couldn't tell anyone because there was no proof, and I felt frustrated because I wanted to share it, but I couldn't. This realization, this knowledge, seemed to just be for me.''

Arthur's heart condition was serious, and did not improve. He was unable to go back to his job as a driving instructor, and after eighteen months off work he had to face up to the fact that he might never work again. He was surviving on a daily diet of pills. As the weeks slipped by, he became more and more depressed. The highlight of his day was his early morning walk with his dog, Sheba. He began to feel that life was not worth living.

''One day I woke up feeling very depressed. I felt like a rotten old cabbage, no use to anybody, particularly my family. I went to the woods with the dog, looked up to the heavens and got very angry with God and Jesus. I swore all the swear words I could think of. Why hadn't I died? I asked them. I couldn't work, couldn't support my family. I was useless. I told God and Jesus I wanted nothing more to do with them, they were no use. That night I had a very clear dream telling me I'd find a golf ball on my left-hand side, and I wouldn't have to look for it. It happened the next morning while I was out with the dog—I'd forgotten about the dream but as I was walking I recalled it, and at that moment I looked down, and there was the ball. I felt a lovely shimmering feeling through my left arm when I bent to pick it up, a warm, tingly, relaxing feeling. The rest of the day I was really happy.

''The next night my dream said I would find a brown

golf ball—you don't normally get brown balls in golf. But once again, towards the end of my walk when I pass near a golf course, there was a brown golf ball. I felt I was being given these signs in order to renew my faith, and it made me feel twice as strong, and the depression was plucked out of my heart. I picked up the ball, and I felt the sensation of being cuddled, I felt my hair being smoothed down, and I could feel rather than hear a voice saying, 'Let's have another go at this life.' I shouted out, 'Who are you? I know you are there.' There was no reply. A couple of golfers who were enjoying a round nearby must have thought I was mad.''

From that time on, Arthur believes his life started to improve. He had more predictive dreams, some of them practically rather than spiritually rewarding: once he was told that he would find a £10 note, another time that he would find £20. On another occasion, when he was staying with his sister, they visited a casino and he was told to put his chips on red eighteen on the roulette wheel: he won "quite a few pounds.''

One night he dreamed he met his father, who handed him two golf balls, one dirty and one clean. The following day the head green keeper at the golf course, who knew Arthur was looking for work, came up and offered him a job helping to look after the greens. "It was exactly the sort of job I needed, and I've loved doing it ever since.''

He was still taking a lot of pills every day, and whenever he went for a checkup he was told he must continue with them. But soon after starting his new job Arthur felt a very strong message, telling him to wean himself off the pills. He gradually cut down over two weeks until he was not taking any and he immediately began to feel better.

''I was very nervous the first day without any, but then it went to a second day, then a third, and I realized that I

was feeling so much more like my old self. I'd obeyed my
own body, which had instinctively known that it could do
without the pills.''

Arthur also believes he was visited by the spirit of his
grandson Darren, nine months before Darren was born. It
happened in April 1984, when Arthur was preparing to play
chess. ''As I got the chessboard out a golden light came
beside me, then gradually expanded and covered all the
room, creeping round everywhere, all over me. It seemed
to be separate units of gold light, and the only way I can
describe it is that it was like the light you imagine follows
angels. I could not move: I felt as though I was being held.
After eight or ten seconds the light appeared to go through
the wall, and I was released from the gentle grip. In December my grandson Darren was born. A few weeks later,
when I was on my own, I asked out loud who the light
was, and a voice said in a matter of fact way that it was
Darren.''

Since then, Arthur believes there has been an especially
close bond between him and the grandson he loves. He has
also experimented with spiritual healing, trying to help his
brother Bernie, who suffers from spondylitis of the spine,
a painful and crippling condition in which the joints of the
spine fuse together. Bernie was given six weeks remission
from pain after Arthur stood over him, asking for the power
to heal him. When the pain came back, the brothers were
both very disappointed, but the voice that Arthur hears told
them that pain is a means for spiritual growth.

The voice also told Arthur to share what had been happening to him with his local vicar. Arthur admits that he
has never been very involved in organized religion, although he's a Christian, but he tracked down the vicar, who
listened attentively and told Arthur that the voice he heard
was the Holy Ghost. He asked Arthur to come to church,
to share his experiences with the congregation.

"I was nervous because I'm really a rather shy person, but I decided that all I could do was tell the truth. Several people were talking about me being touched by Jesus, but I felt my stomach churn every time I heard these high words, and I wanted to get away. It did not feel right to think of it in such elevated terms. I felt uncomfortable, and I wanted to get out of the church and get free, and when I did my voice spoke again and said, 'There is no one greater than I, and I am no greater than anyone else.' That made me bring him down to my level because, although he had so much knowledge, he was not above me, and I am not above anyone else: we are all level. So I now treat everyone as equal, no matter who they are. We are all souls, learning, and that is the most valuable piece of knowledge I have acquired since my NDE."

Arthur has taken positive steps to change his life for the better since seeing himself from above. He believes that he was warned by seeing the gray color of his body as he hovered above it. "The gray color that was in me was because I was selfish, on my own, just concerned about myself and those near me. We must all share more. We have got to do away with anger, lust, temper, and use our strength to further our knowledge. I'm a better, kinder, nicer person now than I was."

Although his marriage ended in an amicable divorce, Arthur is very close to his two daughters, Linda and Susan, his grandson Darren, and granddaughter Alex. "One thing I learnt is the importance of family. I knew it before—but after my NDE I am even more aware of it," he said.

The change for Mrs. Christa Cutt since her NDE has not been as mystical as the change in Arthur Carr, but in another way it has been equally profound. Christa now finds herself far less interested in material things than she was before. She's also become much more aware of other living creatures: she picks up ants and carries them out to the garden if she finds them in her kitchen, and she gets cross with any of her family who step on beetles or spiders. She won't even allow a wasp to be killed, and she and her husband Alec now have three dogs and a cat to share their home in Woking.

Christa's experience came in 1982, when she was fifty-two years old. She and Alec were running a grocery business, which meant working long, stressful hours. She was feeling very, very tired, and only got through the morning in the shop by holding on to the counter to stop herself fainting. By lunchtime she knew she was ill, so she phoned her doctor's office and made an appointment for later that afternoon. In the meantime she lay down on her bed.

"Suddenly I was floating under the ceiling and looking down at my body on the bed. I felt at peace and very relaxed. I remember thinking 'This is easy,' which was a surprise because I had always associated death with pain, and somehow I knew I was dying. I looked down at myself, but all I could see was a shell. I felt calm and happy, but something kept telling me that I should not be up there. It wasn't exactly a voice I could hear, more something I could feel. All of a sudden I was back inside my body and the pain was terrible."

Christa lay on the bed until she felt a little better, and later that day was able to visit her doctor. She was sent to the hospital for tests, and she was told that she had had a heart attack. She told the doctor who was carrying out the tests of her experience, prefacing it with "Don't laugh." He assured her that he was not taking it lightly, because he had heard many patients talk of similar experiences.

Christa has enjoyed much better health since the business was sold two or three years after her heart attack, and she and her husband are enjoying their retirement. "I have been completely changed by what happened. I used to be very afraid of dying, but now I don't mind at all. And I'm so much more aware of every other living creature around me—I even apologize to the flowers in my garden when I cut them.''

Bill Wheeler is another heart attack victim whose whole attitude to life has been changed by his NDE. Bill was sixty-seven and a retired fire officer at the time of his attack, in 1982. He had taken a job as a handyman and caretaker at a school, and was enjoying his work, although the breakup of his marriage after forty-two years was causing him some stress and unhappiness.

Four days before he was admitted to the hospital he was sent home from work because he was feeling ill. Pills prescribed by his doctor did not help, and the pains in his chest worsened until his doctor called an ambulance to take him into the intensive care unit of Musgrove Park Hospital, Taunton. Propped up in bed with pillows, Bill suddenly felt his head drop down "as if all the blood was passing down to my legs." All his pain melted away, he felt calm and relaxed.

"I saw my own body floating on a channel of air. It was going through a tunnel, feet first, towards a pinpoint of very bright light. I could watch it, as though it was nothing to do with me. Then I felt myself being lifted off the bed, and in the very far distance I heard a voice saying, 'He's a tough old b. . . .' I replied, 'I heard that,' and then I opened my eyes and I was surrounded by doctors and nurses, and the curtains were drawn around my bed."

Bill was told that he had had a heart attack, and that electric-shock treatment had been used to restart his heart. The doctor who carried out the resuscitation asked Bill what he remembered, and when Bill recounted his story the doctor showed no surprise. "You've been there, my lad. Behave yourself!" was his comment.

"Since then I have been convinced that there is life after death, and that dying itself is just a lovely, contented feeling. I had a strong awareness that I was going towards a destination, and that it was somewhere that I really wanted to be. There was no fear."

Although Bill's whole working life had been spent helping others, his NDE left him with a strong feeling that he had not done enough good work on earth. "I feel as though I have a debt to someone, and the only way to pay it is to help others. I've also started praying, both morning and night, and I have found that very satisfying."

Although he himself is long past retiring age, Bill now spends his days looking after two other old people, cooking for them, doing the laundry, decorating, gardening, and chauffeuring them around. Gardening has become a passion, and although he gets a lot of personal satisfaction out of winning prizes for his flowers, he also sees growing them as a way to bring some cheer into the wards of his local hospital in Cornwall, where he now lives. All through the summer he supplies flowers, and when he's delivering them he makes a point of talking with the patients.

"Somehow it now seems easier to see other people's problems, and it seems to be no trouble at all to share a chat and a bit of sympathy with them, whereas at one time I would have felt I was too busy. My NDE made me feel so good, and I can still recall that wonderful feeling of peace. I'd like to be able to share it with everyone else, but I realize that unless you experience it personally it is hard to appreciate it. So I do my bit in other ways, supporting lots of charitable causes and finding time for people.

"I don't think I was especially selfish before. But it took the NDE to make me know the pure joy of sharing and helping for its own sake. It made me a better person."

• • •

"I was sitting in an armchair one minute; the next I was running through a beautiful field, and at the side of me were lots of little children, and they were all running, too. I was sure that I was leading them somewhere, yet nobody told me to do it. There was a sense of urgency, as though we had to get somewhere before a door or a gate closed, although I did not see anything like an entrance to the field.

"The colors were all faint, and I could not see the faces of any of the children. I was wearing a summer dress, very light and with a full skirt that billowed behind me, and my hair was longer than it is now. I could feel it bouncing on my back.

"I felt so peaceful, so happy, so relaxed, yet in my heart of hearts I knew I was dying."

When Mrs. Margaret Miles recovered from the two heart attacks that she suffered within minutes of each other in 1991, her husband John told her how worried he had been because she had been so close to death. "You would have been the sad one, not me, if I had died," Margaret was able to tell him, after her "wonderful" NDE.

Margaret had her heart attacks while she was on a hospital waiting list to have a bypass operation and a new valve installed in her heart. She was at home in Larkfield, Kent, and was feeling better than she had felt for some time.

"I had been told to take life easily, but on that particular day I have never felt healthier. I went to the local newsagent's shop and the staff there commented on how well I looked, and I told them I felt I had the energy to spring clean the house. Later on I was at a neighbor's for coffee, and I was sitting in an armchair, listening to her talking about the local scouts, when I suddenly had a terrific pain in my chest.

"Straightaway I was in the field, with the children. Not

a word was spoken but I felt such a glorious, natural peace. I was running in slow motion and I knew I did not want to go back.''

But return she did: within minutes Margaret was back in the armchair in her neighbor's house, with ambulance personnel in attendance. Her first words were to ask where she was, and where had the field gone. They were telling her that there was no field when she had a second attack—but this time she did not have an NDE.

Margaret, who was fifty-five when she had her heart attacks, was very excited by what had happened to her, and when she came out of the hospital she told all her five children and her ten grandchildren what she had experienced.

''I wanted to share the joy of it with everyone, the whole world. It was wonderful. I now know that death is peaceful and the afterlife is beautiful. I know it is a happy place to be—I know those small children who were following me were as happy as I was to be there. It has changed my whole attitude to life and death: it is the people left behind who suffer when there is a death, not the person who dies.''

Margaret believes that one explanation for her running with the children was that her spirit had been chosen to lead the spirits of little children who had died at the same time to heaven. She is confident that when she returned to her earthly body somebody else would have taken over her role as leader, and that the children would happily get to the gate or door that she felt she was heading towards.

''I had this strong feeling that I had to get the children to their destination, but I don't believe that without me they would not make it. Someone else would take them. Although there was an urgency about us running, there was no sense of panic, or tiredness, or breathlessness. There was nothing to mar it: it was such a perfect experience.''

. . .

Joan Whalley's experience happened in the early sixties, but the memory of it is as fresh as if it happened yesterday. Joan's was an embryo NDE, which did not take her any farther than out of her body and above the hospital room where medical staff were battling to save her life, but she can vividly recall the sense of peace and fulfillment that it brought.

She was in the hospital recovering from an operation when a blood clot moved so close to her heart that her husband was told she had only a 50 percent chance of surviving. He slept next to her hospital bed that night, anxious not to leave her in case her condition deteriorated. Joan was in intensive care and can remember very little before her NDE, when she found herself floating on a peach satin cushion in the top left-hand corner of the room.

"I could look down and see the specialist and other doctors and nurses all crowded around me. I recognized them all, except one man who came in later. I didn't feel worried, I felt very happy and peaceful, and the cushion was the most beautiful thing I have ever seen in my life," said Joan, from Crawley, West Sussex.

The following morning, Joan told her husband that she had had a strange dream. She had no memory of being taken very ill during the night, but when she explained her dream to her husband he was amazed: she was able to describe accurately what had been happening to her. The man she did not recognize was another specialist, brought in to help with her case. When she later mentioned her experience to her own specialist, he told her that many patients close to death experienced something similar.

"There were no bright lights, no tunnel, and I did not meet any of my dead relatives, but I know what the sense of peace and happiness is that other NDEers talk about. Since that day I have felt an inner calm, I have been less worried about life, I have stopped being afraid of death. It was the most lovely experience I have ever had, and even though I had to stay in hospital for another seven weeks, it was well worth it for the privilege of being on that cushion. Whenever I look at the top left-hand corner of a room, I can feel the same lovely feelings as I had then, and it all comes back so clearly. If it had been a dream it would have been forgotten long ago.''

Like Joan, Al Sullivan found himself looking down on the medical team who saved his life during emergency heart surgery—but for Al his vantage point was the upper right-hand corner of the room, not the left.

Al, a dispatcher from Connecticut, was later able to describe the operation accurately, despite having watched the surgeon put tape over his eyes. He saw the callipers which held his chest open, and his heart, ''a purplish white,'' outside his body.

''Then I saw the doctors working on me,'' said Al, who had the operation in 1987, when he was fifty-six years old. ''I didn't know what they were doing, and I didn't care. I knew I was dead, but it was all right. Through the smoky darkness I noticed a shadowy figure, skeletal and draped in a cloak. He was beckoning me towards him, but I would not go. Instead I was drawn towards an incredible, brilliant light, the most beautiful thing I'd ever set eyes on.''

Al met a woman he had known who had died of a brain tumor, who asked him to tell her parents not to grieve: ''I couldn't. How can you tell somebody that while you were dead you met their daughter?''

He also saw his brother-in-law, whom he had never liked, so the experience was less than the perfection described by so many other NDEers. Finally he saw his mother, who had died when he was a seven-year-old child, and she told him to return because it was not his time.

''But I didn't want to go back to the real world, because

there was so much love, warmth, and peace where I was. Then I saw my mother move the surgeon's scalpel, and the next thing I knew I was back in my body. When I told the surgeon later he thought I had been hallucinating, but he was amazed when I described the details of the operation. He admitted that the heart-lung machine had glitched, showing I had flatlined (been clinically dead) for a split second.''

The experience changed Al: ''I am no longer afraid of death. In fact, I'd welcome it with open arms, because I know it is wonderful on the other side.''

As the bus rattled through the suburbs of Birmingham, Charlie Hughes felt the pain across his chest begin to tighten. Within a couple of minutes he felt as if he were being held in a vice. Beads of sweat broke out on his forehead and his eyes began to swim. Charlie, a carpenter with the city's council, had been feeling unwell for a few days with slight pains in his chest, but this was worse than anything he had ever known. He was on his way home, and as the pain continued to get worse he realized he was probably not going to get there. He also realized that he had nothing in his pockets to say who he was, if he lost consciousness.

He leaned forward and tapped the shoulder of one of the two elderly women in the seat in front. She turned around, startled, and Charlie told her he was ill and recited his address to her a couple of times. The pain in his chest increased, his arms felt like deadweights, and, still muttering his address over and over, Charlie passed out.

''I felt as though a great blackness crept up all over me, and then I was gone,'' said Charlie, who was thirty-five when the attack happened, in 1976.

But although Charlie appeared unconscious to the other passengers—who quickly raised the alarm—he was able to see everything that happened in the next few, crucial minutes. He had left his body, and was watching from just below the ceiling of the bus.

"I saw two men in blue uniforms come on to the bus, then a nurse. I was told afterwards that the bus driver drove into the gates of a factory near where my attack happened, and the two security men sent for the company nurse. I was able to look down and see everything that happened. I saw myself with blue lips, a white face, and looking very scruffy—I was on my way home from work in my rough clothes. I saw the nurse rip my shirt open, and she began slapping my face, but I could feel nothing. I heard the man in the seat behind mine turn to the woman with him and say, 'He must be drunk.' I wanted to shout out that I wasn't, but I couldn't speak.

"I felt very peaceful and comfortable on the ceiling. I wasn't aware of having any body up there: it was just as if I was nothing more than a pair of eyes and pair of ears. All the pain had gone completely. I heard the nurse say to one of the security guards, 'He's sinking fast, there's no pulse. Use our ambulance; it will be too late if we wait for the hospital ambulance.'

"I didn't feel at all panicked by what she said. I could hardly believe that the man with the gray-white face was me, because I was feeling so well, so healthy. I didn't care what happened to me. The nurse started to slap my face again, and then I had a feeling of being drawn back into my own body. It was like a magnet pulling me back, and I descended slowly from the ceiling and went into myself. I could feel the slaps on my face, so I knew I was back."

Charlie, an ex-professional soldier who spent twelve years in the Third Battalion of the Royal Green Jackets, was carried into the ambulance and an oxygen mask was put over his face. He started muttering, and the nurse pulled the mask away to hear what he was saying.

"I was saying, 'That's nice, that's nice,' over and over again. The cool air was reaching my lungs. I did regret losing the lovely feeling I had had when I was floating above myself, but I also started to think about my wife and my children—I had three at that time—and I was very glad I had come back into myself."

At the hospital Charlie was told that he had suffered a heart attack, and that if he had been fatter, older, or less fit he might not have survived. He was in the hospital for ten days, and had to take five months off work.

Three weeks after the attack, he and his wife Doreen and their three children Sandra, who was twelve, Dean, who was five and Emma, four, returned to the factory where the bus had stopped and where the nurse had worked so hard to save Charlie's life. They presented her with a large bouquet of flowers—and found themselves local celebrities when the story appeared on the front page of the local newspaper. Three years after Charlie's heart attack, he and Doreen had another son, Anthony.

"At first I only told my wife about the sensation of being outside my own body, because I thought everyone would think I was a crank," said Charlie. "But now I realize that others have very similar experiences. I have been puzzled, over the years, as to what would have happened had I not been inside the bus: how high above myself would I have floated?"

Charlie was brought up in the Catholic faith and has never had any doubt about there being a life after death, but the experience has strengthened his belief and made it more real. "I always knew in theory that there was something to come: now I actually know what it will feel like. It was such a good feeling that I have no fear of dying. I don't know how these things are worked out, but I do know that I have had a wonderful life since I was spared that day. Before that, when I first came out of the army, I

had been very unsettled. But now I love my job, I have a
marvelous family, and I am very happy.

"Perhaps it was something to do with that experience,
but I do feel it is important to help others. I've been in the
Royal British Legion for some time, and I am a spokesman
for the local branch."

Many NDEers feel that their psychic abilities are en-
hanced by the experience, but Charlie believes his were
already quite well developed. He shared telepathy with his
mother, and from time to time in his life has been able to
predict events accurately.

"It is not something I can use to pick the winners in a
race, because it does not happen often and I can't choose
to make it happen. Sometimes it is very alarming. I remember one occasion when I was serving in the army in Borneo
in 1964, when one of my mates was telling me how after
his next op he was being transferred out of the active-
service zone. As he said the words I looked at him, and I
knew with certainty that he was going on his last op: I knew
he would die. He did, the following day. I felt dreadful, but
there was nothing I could have done to prevent it.

"My NDE has simply confirmed to me that there is a
lot more to this life than the bits we can see in our everyday
business."

Chapter 8

THE BRAIN

Any serious medical condition is worrying, but strokes and brain tumors are more frightening than most, as the brain is an area that doctors are only just beginning to understand. The people in this chapter found comfort and reassurance from the near-death experiences that accompanied their illnesses.

Barbara Hoyles has been widowed twice, so she was surprised when she had her NDE in 1987 that it was her parents who were waiting to meet her at the end of the tunnel, not her husbands. "I was on excellent terms with both of my husbands, and I do look forward to seeing them again. But at the time it happened it seemed perfectly natural that it was my mother and father. They looked young, as I remembered them from my childhood, not as they were when they died," said Barbara, who lives in Brigg, in Yorkshire.

She was sixty-four when she had her glimpse of the afterlife. She had been for a walk with her dog and remembers not feeling very well. When she got back to the pensioner's bungalow where she lives, she felt she wanted to sit down.

"I can remember thinking that I'd get my coat off before I sat down, but after that it is all a blank. I was later told that my next-door neighbor called round, and when I did not answer the door she let herself in, because it was not locked. She found me slumped in a chair, so she rang my son and daughter-in-law, who live fifteen miles away. The doctor was called, and I was taken to hospital. I was conscious by this stage, but muddled, and I still cannot remember any of it.''

After an examination, Barbara was allowed to go home with her son, whose wife is a nurse. But the next day it was obvious she was still ill, and she was taken back to Scunthorpe General Hospital. After a week the medical staff were still unable to find out what was wrong, so Barbara was transferred to a hospital in Hull to see a neurosurgeon. She was given a brain scan, a painless procedure, but she was feeling so poorly that she was very sick in the middle of it. The reason was soon clear: the scan revealed a tumor near her brain. Four weeks later, on December 1, Barbara was taken into the operating theater for a three-hour operation to remove the tumor.

''I can remember the day before the op, and I can remember having my head shaved before I went into theater. I was dozy with the anesthetic by then, so I wasn't upset about losing my hair.''

That afternoon she hemorrhaged heavily, and when her daughter called the hospital she was told her mother was very ill. Barbara spent the next four days in intensive care, and was then in a semiconscious state for the next few weeks—the news that a baby grandson was born on December 10 did not sink in until after the New Year. The only thing she remembers with vivid clarity from this time is her near-death experience.

''I assume that it happened sometime during the surgery, when I must have come very close to death. I felt I was dying: in fact, I was sure of it. But it was a nice feeling, an easy, drifty sort of feeling. I can't swim, but I felt that it was a swimming sort of sensation. I was moving along a tunnel, and there was a very bright light at the end of it. Although it was brighter than any light I have ever seen, it was not harsh.

"As I got nearer the end, I saw my mum and dad. I saw them as plainly as if they were here now, and when I think about the experience I can see them again. My father had died of cancer in 1962, and looked ill at the end of his life, and my mother lived until she was ninety-five. But they looked young, as they were when I was a little girl. They didn't speak. I felt excited, yet calm and peaceful at the same time, and I was really looking forward to being with them. Then something changed, I don't know what it was, but instead of traveling toward them I was going away from them. I remember feeling very disappointed."

Although Barbara's memories of the time after her operation are very hazy, the NDE stands out clearly: "It was very, very real. It was not a dream: I don't remember any dreams from that time, and despite the passage of time it has not faded."

Barbara, who made a complete recovery, believes the experience changed her personality. "I'm a different person. I know that there is nothing to fear in death, so I feel very relaxed about it. But I've also changed from being the sort of person who worried a lot about everything into someone much more easygoing. I marshaled my thoughts, worked out what's important in life, and stopped worrying about anything else. It's changed my whole outlook. If I get up in the morning with a certain number of things to do and I don't get them all done during the day, I shrug my shoulders. At one time, it would have weighed on me."

Both of Barbara's husbands died of strokes, the first, Sidney, an accountant, when he was only forty-two, and the second, Kenneth, who worked for British Steel, when he was fifty-six, after only ten years of marriage.

"I have puzzled about why neither of them was waiting for me at the end of the tunnel, but I accept that there are many things that we cannot expect to understand in this life. Perhaps we do go back to being children again at first, I really don't know. But what I do know is that I am a practical, down-to-earth sort of person, and I can say with certainty that this actually happened. I did not dream it. I was there.''

Valerie Hannah felt a very strong urge to go towards a beautiful, bright light that seemed to be beckoning her. She felt calm, relaxed, peaceful, and very happy—until she remembered that she had a husband, three children, and an elderly mother who all needed her.

''The feeling of contentment and happiness was marvelous, but then it changed when I thought about my responsibilities here on earth,'' said Valerie, who was forty-three at the time of her NDE in 1989. She was a patient in Walton Hospital, Liverpool, where she was taken after suffering a massive brain hemorrhage. She was transferred to Walton, which has a neurological department, from the local hospital near her home in Ormskirk, Lancashire. An operation was carried out to stop the bleeding and clamp off the ruptured artery, and Valerie's family were warned that she only had a 50 percent chance of survival.

''I felt so weak, and I seemed to 'know' I was near death. There was a nurse sitting by my bedside monitoring me twenty-four hours a day, and the one who was there the day I had the NDE kept saying to me, 'You are not going to die.' But I 'knew' I was, and I wanted her to leave me alone and let me go. I wasn't frightened. I really wanted to let the light pull me towards it, and I had the feeling that if I could just go into the light I would be perfectly happy forever.

''But then I thought about my mother. She had Alzheimer's disease and was living in a home, where I used to visit her several times a week. I used to feed her, and a couple of times a week my husband Raymond and I would put her in the car and take her out for a pub lunch. I felt she needed me, and that I could not leave her.

"Then I thought about Raymond and our children, Debbie who was twenty-one at the time, Stephen, who was twenty, and Gary, who was nineteen. I knew they were old enough to cope without me, but I also knew that I did not want to leave them. I wanted to see them really grown up. When I started thinking about my family, I found myself moving back from the light and then it was gone, and I was in bed again with the nurse telling me I wasn't going to die."

Valerie was in the hospital for six months, but the operation was a total success. She and her husband run a frozen-food distribution business. "I don't tell anyone except close family and friends what happened to me, because other people would probably think I am crackers. But those who know me well know that I wouldn't imagine something like this. It has had a lasting effect on me. I always did believe in God and life after death, but I now feel a deep conviction about it. I am more religious. And I am certainly not afraid of dying."

For Margaret Bampton there was no tunnel, no bright light, no sense of rising out of her own body: yet her NDE was just as reassuring and comforting as the more familiar experiences, and brought with it a similar feeling of calm. Margaret was fifty-seven when on Boxing Night in 1984 she suffered a severe stroke. She had been in bed for about an hour when she woke up to find herself paralyzed. It took time for her husband Alec to get a doctor out to her, and it was three o'clock in the morning before one arrived and ordered an ambulance to take Margaret to the hospital.

For Margaret, as for so many stroke victims, there was a tremendous sense of panic and fear. She could not understand why she could not move; she could not understand why she could no longer talk; she felt very ill. But as she lay in bed waiting for the doctor to come, she experienced something which she describes as "the most beautiful experience of my life."

Her mother, who had been dead for sixteen years, appeared at the foot of her bed, with an angel on either side of her. Her mother looked fit and young, and was wearing clothes that Margaret remembered her wearing in life, yet there was one thing different: she was leaning on a walking stick. In life she had been fit and active and had never needed help walking. The angels were traditional, with long white robes, wings, and haloes.

"My mother spoke to me, and told me that I would get well again. I felt tremendous peace just seeing her, but when she said I would recover I felt marvelous, because I had been very afraid of dying. That fear just melted away, not simply because she said I would survive but because I could see that she still existed, so that was the proof of life after death. After speaking to me she seemed to float up into the corner of the bedroom ceiling and disappear. I think the angels must have disappeared at the same time, because I do not know what happened to them. I could not take my eyes off my mother, who looked so well and happy. I wanted her to stay, but I realized that she had brought me a message, and once she had delivered it she had to go."

Before that night, Margaret did not believe in life after death, and if anyone had told her a story about seeing their mother at the foot of their bed, she would not have believed it. But the experience was so real to her that it helped her cope with the agonizing aftermath of her stroke. She was paralyzed down the right side of her body, and at first she could not speak at all. After a few weeks she developed slurred speech, which improved gradually until she can now talk normally. Her husband was warned that she would never walk again, but when Margaret heard that prediction she was determined to prove it wrong. Every day she struggled a little bit harder, until eventually she could walk.

"But I need to use a walking stick—just like the one my mother was holding when she appeared to me. I now think she was telling me that although I would recover and be well again, I would have to use a stick."

Although Margaret has recovered most of the use of her body, she still has some restricted motion in her right arm, and she walks with a limp. "But I have done better than the experts predicted I would, and I feel that is largely because my mother's appearance gave me confidence. She had told me I would get well, and I believed her rather than anyone who tried to suggest I would be in a wheelchair for the rest of my life."

Margaret's husband Alec died in 1991. Although he had cancer, he had a relatively easy death—he was in the garden of their home in Lincoln the day before he died.

"The experience I had was a great comfort to me, because I know he did not suffer. I know that he must have felt that same calm and peace that I felt, which is very reassuring. And I'm now looking forward to death, because I know we will be reunited. I don't want to leave my three sons and my two grandchildren, but when the time is right I will welcome death, whereas before I was terrified of the thought of it.

"Six months after he died I saw my husband, as plain as anything, standing in the doorway of our bedroom. I asked him what he was doing there and he said, "I've come to fetch you." Then he was gone. Again, I felt very relaxed and peaceful, not a bit afraid.

"Before my NDE I would have laughed at anyone who said they saw visions of angels and dead people: now I know that there is something wonderful to come."

For years Michael Angel felt ill. He went to work, but by the time he returned home he had no energy left for a social life. While driving he used occasionally to pass out at the wheel of the car, but never for long enough to cause an accident. He was frequently sick, always lethargic. At home he struggled to take an interest in his two young children, but could never find the energy to help his wife, Arlene, with them. Life seemed gray: he was doing no more than surviving, and there was no joy in it. From time to time he was in such intense pain that he would be reduced to tears.

When he collapsed after leaving work one day—people around him in the street thought he was drunk—he went to his doctor. But the doctor could find nothing wrong with Michael, even though he was so racked with pain that he cried while talking to her. He was referred to a hospital for tests, but the results always came back the same: the medical profession could find nothing wrong with him. He was told that his problems were psychological and that he was imagining them; he was treated for bad "nerves."

Then, in 1981, after ten days in the hospital in Manchester, Michael, who was thirty-two at the time, was once again sent home. That night he was violently sick and the pain was worse than ever, and Arlene called an ambulance. Michael fell into a coma and has no memory of being rushed to the hospital—but he knew he was there, and that he was dying, because soon after he was admitted he left his body and found himself looking down on himself as he lay on the bed.

"I stood beside my wife and a neighbor of ours, who was drinking a cup of tea. We were all looking down at me, and I felt better than I had been for years. I felt myself moving out of my own body: I seemed to become weightless and just drift away. It was a very tranquil feeling, and all the terrible pain in my head had gone. I looked down, but the body on the bed did not seem to be the real me, although I was aware who it was.''

Michael remained in a coma for a few days. When one of the medical staff realized that he had never been given a brain scan, one was ordered for him immediately. Again, although Michael was unconscious, he knows what happened to him because he stood outside his body watching it.

''I saw a room full of very sophisticated-looking equipment, and I saw myself with what looked like a bucket on my head. Although I was outside my body, and again it was a very pleasant feeling, this time I was aware of a very nasty noise in my head, like plates being rubbed together. But although I could hear it and in a sense feel it, it was still as though it was happening to someone else. It is a very hard sensation to describe: I felt I was aware of someone else's suffering, not my own.''

The brain scan showed that Michael had a tumor. After twenty-four hours spent building up his physical strength, he was operated on and the tumor, which had reached the top of the brain, was removed. Michael was warned that he might end up paralyzed, but luckily the operation went well.

It was only afterwards that Michael told his wife about his experience of seeing her and their neighbor looking down at him. Arlene was surprised: the neighbor's wife was, by coincidence, in the hospital at the same time, and the man had popped in to see how Michael was. Arlene had forgotten all about it until Michael mentioned it, but she was able to confirm that the neighbor had been drinking a cup of tea.

When Michael went for a second brain scan he recognized the room from his previous experience—although he had been in a coma on that occasion. When he heard the unpleasant swishing noise, he knew that he really had been there before.

"I was quite happy to leave my body behind, when it happened. I felt relaxed and philosophical. I didn't seem to have any worries, all my problems slipped away and I felt a great tranquillity. I know that I was dying: I knew it at the time without being told. But there was no fear, and there was a really tremendous feeling of being free from pain."

Michael believes his experience has made him much more aware of the important priorities in life. He looks back and realizes that he saw very little of his daughter Leanne's first two years, because he was too ill to enjoy her. "She was born in 1979, and that was the stage where I was nothing more than a living robot. I look at pictures of her as a baby and feel very sad that I have no memories of that time. Darren is four years older, and so he was at the stage where a boy needs his dad to play with, yet I never had the energy. My family is wonderful, and having such a close brush with death has made me very aware that they are the most important thing in my life."

Michael, who is a color chemist in the textile industry, now has a very relaxed attitude to work: "I was made redundant, which at one time would have seemed like the end of the world. But now I know it is not worth getting depressed about, there are so many other compensations in life. When I was working, I always turned down offers to go abroad, because I did not want to be parted from my family: there's no amount of money in the world can make up for missing out with your wife and children.

"I'm now much more relaxed than I was. I take one day at a time. I help other people with similar medical problems by talking to them: they can see that, however serious the operation is, I have come through it and survived.

"I'm a happier person than I was, better company, more emotional, more ready to express my love to those around me. The experience did me good—the operation saved my life, and the NDE helped me to appreciate that life."

Chapter 9

OUT OF THE BLUE

Near-death experiences that occur at the time of accidents are one of the best proofs that they are a real happening, not something created by the imagination. When an NDE happens at the critical point of an illness, skeptics can argue that the patient is already preoccupied with death and has already started to prepare themselves for the possibility of not surviving: as a result, they may be susceptible to dreams and hallucinations about dying. That argument cannot be used, however, when NDEs occur spontaneously at the time of an accident.

Accidents come out of the blue. They can happen to anyone, and there's no time to prepare for them. There is no autosuggestion at play, because being close to death is the very farthest thing from the victim's mind. Whatever happens is totally unexpected, totally uncontrived, and therefore even stronger evidence for the validity of the experience than the more familiar NDE, which occurs on the operating table or in the intensive care unit.

Jean Allan had her NDE as the result of a horrific accident with a chain saw which she rented after friends offered her the wood from a tree they had had cut down. Using the saw to cut the trunk into logs for her fireplace, she'd successfully cut more than a ton and a half of firewood when the accident happened.

"The chain saw locked. The engine noise dropped in tone, then picked up and suddenly it reared up and hit me in the face and arm," said Jean, from Canterbury, Kent. "I was hit in the left cheek, the neck, the chest, and then it sliced through the inside of my left arm. It took fifteen seconds to run down, and that was enough to do plenty of damage to me.''

Jean was later awarded damages from the rental company, because she had been given so little advice about how to use the 44-lb. saw. She had not been told that, after long use, the finger controlling the trigger switch can become numb, a condition known as ''white finger.''

When the machine reared up, Jean had the presence of mind to hold on to it and lower it to the ground, worried that if she let go it would cause worse damage. Luckily, a friend who was with her at the time is a nurse at Canterbury Hospital. Jean was rushed to the hospital and a medical team spent three hours working on her, inserting a total of ninety-three stitches. Before the work started, though, Jean had a two-hour wait, and it was halfway through this time that she had her NDE, while she was fully conscious.

''I was suddenly above myself, looking down. I could clearly see myself on the bed, but interestingly I did not see any blood or any wounds—and there were plenty to see. It took me a second or two to realize that it was me down below on the bed. All the pain went away, and I felt very peaceful, very calm and rather sleepy. It was as though all worry had been lifted from me. I didn't see anybody else around my bed, just myself.

''I had a full conversation with myself. I asked myself what had I done, and I remember the reply, 'I don't know.' So I said, 'Well, get up, you silly bitch.' I answered myself with 'I can't.' So then I asked why, and the reply was again, 'I don't know.'

''It was a very weird conversation, because I was both sides of it. I never felt that I wasn't the person on the bed, yet I was two completely separate beings. Suddenly, without any warning, I was back in my body again. The lovely comforting warmth had gone, and all the pain came flooding back.''

The experience of being outside herself, coupled with the trauma of the accident, affected Jean profoundly. "In some ways it was good, in some ways it was not. It shook me, and for quite a long time I found it very hard to cope with life. I didn't want to be with people, I became very meek— I wouldn't argue with anyone about anything. I lost interest and pride in myself: I didn't even want to wash or keep myself tidy. I suppose I was in a depression. I'd go shopping to buy a loaf of bread and then forget to get it, and I'd make lots of excuses. I don't know whether this phase was linked to the NDE, or whether it was the trauma of the accident.''

Eventually Jean, forty-three when the accident happened in 1985, became her old self again, and it was then that she began to appreciate the beneficial aspects of the NDE: "I have always been quite aware of the fact that this life does not begin and end with what we can see and hear and touch. Since I was young I've had a few paranormal experiences, so I am not skeptical. But I'm not silly about it, either. My friends would describe me as a hard-headed person, and as a Royal Mail driving instructor I have to be very sensible and level.

"But ever since I was quite young I have experienced certain things, and I know that there is a life after death. What the NDE did was to take away the fear of the act of dying. It's given me a lot of faith.''

When Jean was only fifteen, she heard a voice calling her name when she was at her grandmother's house, shortly after her grandmother had died. She assumed it was her mother in the kitchen, but it wasn't. Another time she heard footsteps walking into the room where she was in bed, and the sound of breathing. And three times at her parents' home she heard a weird squawking noise, which she is sure was a poltergeist. Her mother heard it too, but whenever her father arrived on the scene it was quiet. "The cat was literally terrified of it. He followed the noise around with his eyes."

Many people who experience NDEs report a much greater sensitivity to the supernatural afterwards. Jean, too, believes that she has become even more receptive since her accident. She has become convinced that she has lived previous lives, at least four. Her memories of the early ones—as a noblewoman living in a drafty castle doing endless tapestry work and as a Native American—are vague, but she has quite clear memories of the latter two.

"I was a girl in Victorian times, and I died at the age of about twelve from consumption. I can remember being so poor that I used to shelter under gaslights for warmth, and peer through windows into the homes of richer folk, and envy them. I had to walk barefoot in the snow—and because of that deep memory I can never walk around now without something on my feet."

Even more recently , she believes, she was a Spitfire pilot during the last war. She has vivid memories of running to her plane, and she feels sure that she flew from Biggin Hill in Kent. "One day I took a wrong turning and ended up driving past Biggin Hill airfield, and the feeling I experienced of recognition and of having been there before was so intense. I feel I was guided to take that turning.

"I collect old RAF memorabilia, and I was in a shop in Hastings one day, asking for old RAF gold wings. The proprietor said he rarely saw them, but if he did find any he would keep them for me. Three months later I walked in again, on the very day that some gold wings came in. He was amazed at my telepathy."

Jean's NDE was unusual, but she saw a reconstruction of an accident involving a truck driver on a television program and recognized her own experience in the driver's description of what happened to him. "A stake from a fence went right through his stomach. He, too, had the sensation of being above himself, and like me he had a conversation with himself. It was very similar."

When Jean's mother died in 1994 after a long illness, she was comforted by memories of the peace and calm that had pervaded her own NDE. "I hope she had the same lovely warm feeling that I had. I also hope that she was able to look down and see us at her bedside. I'm not going to be frightened of dying when the time comes, and I wasn't frightened for her, although I miss her. A nurse offered to try to bring her round while I was sitting with her at very end, but I said not to. I did not want to bring her back from somewhere pleasant and pain-free, which is what I now know is waiting for us all."

It was a lovely summer's day in Connecticut, and artist Paul Hoffman and fiancée Jacqueline Benedetto decided to go swimming. They were with Jacqueline's brother and her cousins. They parked their car and walked for about an hour to an area famous for its "swimming holes," or deep rock pools, all of them looking forward to a pleasant afternoon relaxing in the sunshine. The area was rocky and wildly beautiful, and they settled near a waterfall to enjoy the scenery and swim.

Their possessions were scattered around them, and one of the men suddenly cursed as a pair of shorts were caught by a breeze and disappeared over the rock face above the waterfall. Paul decided to try to spot them, and see if they could be retrieved.

"I went to the top of the rock face and I slipped and went over, falling thirty-five feet to some rocks below. On the way down my head hit some other rocks," said Paul, who was twenty-seven when the accident happened, on July

Kept in the hospital for the night after his fall, Paul felt so elated by his NDE that he could not sleep. "I felt warm and very, very alive. I felt more alive than I had ever felt before. I was buzzing. I was in a ward of four beds, and one old fella opposite complained to the nurse that he could not sleep because 'there's too much energy coming from that bed over there,' meaning me. But I wasn't being noisy or moving around, so he must have been able to feel the energy I was experiencing.

"The whole healing process was remarkable, too. The doctors said it was as though it was accelerated—my bruising cleared up so fast." At the time of the accident, Paul spent a lot of his spare time running, and within two weeks he was able to go jogging again.

He has revisited the scene of his accident a couple of times, and has felt no fear or horror. "I have also relived the episode in my mind over and over: it's all so clear." Paul, who earns his living as a graphic designer but spends much of his own time painting, is at pains to stress that what happened was not born of his imagination.

"I use my imagination a lot in my creative work, so I know the difference. What happened has changed every day of my life since then, it is with me all the time, and I think as time goes on more and more memories of my conversation with my grandfather will surface."

A hit-and-run driver was arrested because of Milly Bull's NDE. Milly's car was hit so hard that it turned over three times and ended up on its roof on a cold but clear evening in December 1981. It was half past eleven at night, and Milly was returning, alone in her Vauxhall Viva, from her parents' house in Edmonton to her home in Enfield. She was driving at a sensible speed when her car was hit from behind by another car, which had been traveling at 60 mph. The driver was so drunk that he was using the white line in the middle of the road to steer by, and must have been so preoccupied with following it that he did not see Milly's car. Weather conditions were good, with no ice on the roads.

She was forced off the road, hit a tree, and her car rolled over. The other driver drove on, not waiting to see if she was all right. "All I can consciously remember was an almighty thud," said Milly, a legal secretary who was thirty-four at the time of the crash. "I have no memory of the car rolling over, although a young couple who witnessed the crash saw it turn over three times. Luckily for me, they called an ambulance straightaway."

After the thud, Milly remembers a bright, gentle light spilling out all over the scene. She then watched from above, seeing herself scrambling around in the upturned car, watching herself climb out of a window and crawl up a bank away from the wreckage. Soon afterwards she went back into her own body and can remember the arrival of the ambulance which took her to the hospital.

"It was all over in a split second, but I can remember so clearly the lovely feeling that I had as I floated above, looking down on myself. I felt no pain at all, it was very peaceful and calm and I had a strange feeling of belonging. Then I also had a feeling that it was not yet my time: I did not hear any voices or see anybody, but the feeling came into me that I had to go back. I felt I was not required, it wasn't my turn. It was really strong, and almost as soon as it came I was back in my body."

The remarkable thing about Milly floating above the scene of the crash is that she was able to see the car that hit her. She saw its make, color, and registration number—none of which she could have seen from inside the wreck of her own car, and which she had not had a chance to see before the crash. By the time she had climbed out of the window, the other car had sped on. The only explanation of her having the right information about it was that she had really been in her vantage point above the scene. With the information Milly gave them, the police were able to trace and arrest the driver, and he was subsequently prosecuted.

"It was late at night and it would, under normal circumstances, have been very difficult to see the other car clearly, even if I hadn't been rolling over in my own car at the time. But because of the light that was everywhere when I floated up, I could see it quite clearly."

When Milly was taken to the hospital she was found to have cracked the bottom of her spine. She was kept in overnight. Her husband Geoffrey (they have since divorced) was telephoned, and came to her bedside. "I told him everything that happened straightaway. The car was a write-off, but I felt so relieved to be alive, and so lucky to have escaped so lightly. I was told that lots of people die in accidents that are nowhere near as bad as mine, and that increased the feeling that I had been chosen to return, that it really wasn't my time."

Milly's children Amanda and Ian were only ten and seven at the time of the crash, and she feels that one of the reasons she was compelled to return to her body was because they obviously still needed her.

"I'm now a firm believer that there is a time for each of us, and until that time comes we will survive even if, like me, we have a close brush with death. I have changed since the crash: I'm a happier, more relaxed person. The car was a write-off, and that would have worried me at one time, but now I realize how lucky I was to escape. A car is, after all, only a lump of metal.

"I always believed in God, and that after death we went somewhere nice, but now I have a real idea of how nice it will be. When I think about that night, the peaceful feeling returns. I don't have a very good memory—I can't even remember things that happened six months ago. But that memory remains very clear, as if it happened yesterday.''

Paul Gryzinski kept his NDE to himself for twenty years. When he first told people about it, ''they thought I was sick or crazy or on drugs,'' said Paul, an interior designer from Connecticut.

Paul, who was born in 1950, was driving through a snowstorm with his girlfriend when they had a head-on collision with another car. Paul's internal bleeding was so great that doctors decided to operate immediately, without anesthetic. ''The last thing I heard was, 'We're losing him, we're losing him,' '' said Paul, who married the girl who was in the car with him at the time of the crash: they now have two teenage children.

''The next thing I was two feet above my own body, looking down at them operating, watching doctors attach catheters to my veins. I had no shape or form, but I knew I was in a tunnel and I could see an incredible light. And I heard a voice say, 'You are one with the light.' I knew the voice was God. This beautiful, warm feeling came over me. But then the voice said, 'It's not your time,' and I got very angry. I wanted to go to the light. I didn't want to go back. Then I felt this horrendous pain and heard people yelling. I was back in my body.

''When I described the details of the operation to the doctor he was astonished but just said it was a miracle I was alive. My mother, who was watching through a glass panel, confirmed what I had seen. It was the most profound thing that has ever happened to me.''

Yet when he told others, they did not believe him: ''I stopped talking about it, because of the funny reactions I got. But I never forgot it and I never doubted it.''

When NDEs began to be openly discussed, Paul joined the first support group that was launched. Now he counsels terminally ill patients, helping them to prepare for death by sharing his experience with them.

Barbara Farmer always loved motorbikes. She was married with five children, but she used a 250 cc Honda bike to get her around London, where she lives. When she wasn't riding the bike, Barbara used to bring it into the house and tinker with it. She kept it spotlessly clean, and she enjoyed working on it mechanically. But a serious—and unexplained—accident in 1982, when Barbara was thirty-one, ended her enthusiasm for bikes, and nearly cost her her life.

Quite what happened to Barbara nobody knows, least of all her. The most likely explanation is that she had an epileptic fit while riding her bike. She was on her way home late one evening after visiting friends: the next thing she knows, she was found in the road, underneath a parked car, her bike nearby. Local residents who had heard a loud bang rushed out, an ambulance was called, and the car was literally lifted off Barbara to allow her to be put on a stretcher without damaging her spine.

The road where she was found was not on her normal route home, although it was close by. Barbara believes that she may have had a premonition that a fit was imminent and pulled into the side road in order to get off her bike. Before she could do that, the fit overtook her: she collided with a parked car, and afterwards crawled beneath another car. This is all guesswork, because Barbara does not remember a thing, there were no witnesses and nothing was reported to the police. She is sure that she would not have been speeding: at the time of the accident, she had been driving her bike for about four years. "With five children of my own I was always very conscious of keeping my speed down in built-up areas. I was never a mad driver, I always preferred safety to speed."

Barbara had first been diagnosed as epileptic when she

was eleven, when she had her first fit in the middle of a road and had to be dragged clear of the traffic by an elderly passerby. But her fits were under control, and at the time of the crash she had not had one for years. Barbara is a photogenic epileptic, which means her fits are triggered by flashing lights.

"I'd learnt to avoid them by not going anywhere that I cannot control the speed of flashing lights, so I never went to discos when I was a teenager. And I knew there was one stretch of road I drove down on my way to my mother's where, on a sunny day, the light flashing through the trees at normal speed could cause me to feel a fit coming on, so I either had to break the speed limit or go slowly."

Today, Barbara has not had a fit for many years. If she feels herself likely to have one, she calms down and relaxes and manages to control it. She can only guess that on the night of the accident she was about to get off her bike because she could feel the warning signs coming on.

After the accident Barbara was rushed to St. George's Hospital, Tooting, where she remained in a coma for over a week. Her crash-helmet visor had broken and been driven into her forehead, which had caused a blood clot to migrate to her brain. She had no other physical injuries, but when she came around she had completely lost her memory: she did not even know her own name; she believed she was in the hospital after giving birth, and spent days wandering around from ward to ward looking for her baby. The staff had to pin a note to her saying her name and which ward she was from.

When her husband Anthony and her children came to visit she did not know who they were, and had to learn their names from scratch. Within two or three weeks her most important memories—like who her family were—had gradually come back, and every day there was more improvement. But it took nearly a year for Barbara to regain her memory completely and get back to a normal life, and she has never been able to recall the events leading up to the accident.

It was while she was in the coma that Barbara had three separate "dreams," which she now believes were all part of her near-death experience. Although they seem to be unrelated, and although she remembers them as if they happened on three separate occasions, the events and themes of the dreams are interrelated when viewed in retrospect. One of them is a typical NDE, but the two that preceded it are more unusual, and seem to be part of Barbara's unique encounter with death.

"In the first one I believe I was literally fighting with death, trying to escape it. I was in the dark, and there was a sinister black blob pursuing me, and I was convinced it was going to get me. I ran to the doorway of a church, and I was banging and hammering and shouting that I needed to get in, I was terrified that the blob would get me. Nobody answered the door, and at the time that seemed weird. I was thinking, 'They've got to be in, because it's late. They must be there, they must be in. I must get in before midnight.' Midnight seemed critical to me, and maybe that's because I had my accident at about eleven-thirty P.M., and was being rescued by the ambulance round about midnight. The overriding feeling of that dream was complete terror, total fear, a need to run away and be saved. Perhaps it is symbolic that it was a church I was trying to get into, although I was not a particularly religious person."

Barbara's second dream involved her riding naked on a white horse. Again, her surroundings were dark, although not pitch-black night as in the first dream. This time it was more like late evening. Swirling around the feet of the horse was a white cotton-type cloud, similar to the dry-ice mist

effects used in a theater. As she rode through it, Barbara
kept picking off bits of the cloud. Some she kept, some she
discarded.

"I can remember thinking that I wanted certain bits but
not others. I don't know how I knew which ones I wanted:
to look at, all the lumps of cloud looked the same. They
were white and fluffy, and I could actually hold them. I did
not feel frightened in this dream, although there was a sense
of urgency that I had to find all the bits I needed. The
general feeling was quite pleasant."

Looking back, Barbara believes she was collecting together pieces of her own memory, her own previous life.
As she discovered when she emerged from her coma, her
memory had been temporarily wiped completely clean, and
she believes that she was symbolically restocking it.

The third "dream" was recognizably an NDE. In this
one, Barbara was traveling up a tunnel towards a light.
There was a slight incline in the tunnel, but it was not steep
and she did not have any trouble moving up it. She felt as
though she were gliding over the floor, although her legs
were making walking movements. It was like traveling
along a moving walkway, the sort found at airports, where
passengers with long distances to move between terminals
have a choice of either standing still on the walkway and
being carried along, or walking with it, which gives a sensation of unusual speed. Barbara was traveling easily, without making any great effort, so she believes it was not just
her own walking steps which were carrying her along. At
the end of the tunnel was a bright, warm light, and she was
filled with a longing to get there.

"I just knew that if I could get into the light everything
would be fine, I would feel good, I would be 'home.' It
was a very strong feeling, and the nearer I got the better I
felt. There was a lot of excitement: I was thrilled to be

going there. But at the same time I felt great peace, more peace than I have ever felt before or since."

Just as she was getting close to the end of the tunnel and the light was beginning to fill all her vision, Barbara was suddenly no longer there. The next thing she remembers is waking up in her hospital bed.

"At first the dreams seemed to make no sense, but I now believe I was fighting off the physical effects of death in the first one. I was running away from it, and that may be why I was found under a parked car: the only explanation is that I must have crawled there, because I could not have been flung there by the accident. In the second one I was assembling my own life, either to give me some memories when I came back to life or to take with me up the tunnel to the next life. And in the final one I was going towards the afterlife."

Barbara spent two months in the hospital. She was lucky that the physical injuries from the crash were not great, but rebuilding her memory was difficult. "I gradually began to realize who I was. I accepted that I had not had another baby, although at first I was utterly convinced that was why I was in hospital. I felt terrible: I thought somebody had taken the baby away from me, and I needed to find him. When I saw my own children, they were not complete strangers to me: I knew that I knew them, but I could not remember their ages or anything about them. My youngest, Anthony, was only two at the time, and I feel very sad that I missed out on some of his early life because I was in hospital, and even when I was home it was months before I was normal.

"It was as though my memory came in and out for a while. The hospital gave me paper and pen and suggested I write things down when I remembered them. I've still got some of the pages I wrote: on some of them my writing is okay and makes sense, on others it is as though I had forgotten how to write. Some of it was very faint, and one of the hospital staff apparently had to show me literally how to put pen to paper, because I had forgotten.

"Gradually, I got flashes of memory of my own life. Important things came back to me first, and then more and more. I think I now probably have a normal amount of memories, although there are still times when people say 'Remember when . . .' and I'm left floundering, trying to recall it."

Barbara, who lives in Wandsworth, south London, had one more go on a motorbike after her recovery, just to put any fear behind her. But afterwards she decided that she had lost her enthusiasm for bikes, and she now drives a car.

A year after her accident she was able to go back to work, rejoining her old employer in a clerical job. "I had to be given an easy job, one that did not require much memory at first. People who knew me then said that although I seemed to be okay, there was a weird look in my eyes, as though I was somewhere else all the time."

Now fully recovered, Barbara works full time as the membership clerk for a trade union. Her husband Anthony has been let go, but Barbara is not too concerned: "I've got a very laid-back attitude now: I don't know whether that is because of being so close to death and having an NDE, or whether it is because the accident was so serious that I've come to appreciate life more. I know what's important now, I'm more tolerant than I was. I accept what life gives me.

"Before the accident, I was quite tough. I could tear into people verbally. I'm quieter now. I don't get so angry: I used to flare into a temper at the slightest thing. I still worry about things, but I'm not so tense. I think having to relearn everything was like a rebirth, and I have in some ways been reborn as a different person."

Barbara does not claim to be particularly psychically sensitive, but she did have one strange experience years before her accident, when she and her family were living in Brighton. The kitchen in their home was three steps down from the adjoining room, and Barbara had a strong feeling of dread whenever she had to go down the stairs. It was always there, but it became much worse after she once felt sure that she saw a female arm reaching out of the steps and trying to grab her ankle. She took to jumping down the steps—not easy with two cups of tea in your hand.

"It was only when I mentioned my feelings to the landlord that he told me that the previous tenant was an old lady who had died on those steps, after falling down them. She may have lain there for a while, dying, before being discovered. Her arm was obviously still reaching out for the help that never came.

"I was the only one who felt it or saw it, but it was very strong. I had blamed my imagination for it all until he told me about the old lady, and I now believe it was not all my imagination at all."

It was ten past five on a chilly October morning. Light was creeping up the sky over Birmingham. The streets were quiet: just a few factory workers waiting at bus stops, the odd milk truck whining slowly along the damp streets. The only lights to be seen were from newspaper shops, where weary shopkeepers were unlocking doors and taking inside the bundles of papers that had been left on their doorsteps.

It was the end of the shift for two tired traffic policemen who were patrolling the city center, an easy time, with so little traffic about. It was quite a contrast with the evening before, which had been busy for a Sunday. Both men in the police car were looking forward to getting back to the station at six, and to the two days off duty that stretched ahead of them. Constable John Priest, sitting in the passen-

ger seat, was only nineteen, and it was his first experience
of traffic patrol: he was on a two-week training assignment
with the traffic division. He should have been in the back-
seat, with the front passenger seat occupied by the driver's
regular partner, a woman police officer. She'd had a lot of
paperwork to catch up with, so she'd stayed behind at the
station and John had moved to the front.

"As we approached a bend in the road the rear of the
car began to sway from side to side and the driver shouted,
'Hang on. We're in a skid.' He was struggling with the
wheel. I glanced across at the other side of the road and I
could see a lamppost directly in our path," said John, who
had been with West Midlands police for nine years.

"The lamppost came nearer and nearer, but everything
seemed to be going at a snail's pace. It was as if life had
been switched into slow motion. Everything in front of my
eyes seemed to be flickering, like in an old black-and-white
movie. After each flicker, in which the view in front of my
eyes went from a negative to a positive image, we were
that bit nearer to the lamppost, and I knew with complete
certainty that we were going to hit. It can only have taken
a couple of seconds, but to me it seemed like ages as it
loomed closer and closer."

John braced his arms against the dashboard and waited
for the impact. "It seemed a long wait, but I don't remember being afraid, just concerned that I was ready for it. As
we hit the post I pivoted on my rigid arms and catapulted
forwards, and my head came through the windscreen. I felt
and heard the explosion of glass, and for just a second I
was in excruciating pain, and then something extraordinary
happened.

"My entire body seemed to be pulled upwards with great
force, as though I was on a giant elastic band that
somebody was tugging at. I didn't look down. I don't know
if I would have been able to see the crash below me if I

had. I didn't have time: I seemed to shoot upwards at a great speed. I stopped suddenly, and found myself face to face with an old man. He had a long white beard to match his long white robes, and all around him was a warm, bright glow of white light. He smiled at me, and straightaway shook his head.

"Instantly I shot downwards at the same kind of speed, as if I was in a lift that had gone out of control. I could feel myself plummeting down with a whoosh. Then, just as suddenly, I stopped again. I was face to face with another old man, dressed and looking exactly like the first one. He, too, was bathed in a brilliant light, so bright it was blinding me and yet at the same time it was soothing. He, too, shook his head.

"At that moment I was back in the car crash, and I became aware of blood pouring down my face. I called out for help. There was so much blood pouring into one of my eyes that I was blinded by it, and at first I thought I had lost my eye."

An ambulance arrived and rushed John and his colleague to Birmingham Accident Hospital. The driver had only minor injuries, but John's face needed 140 stitches. He had lost a lot of blood and was told that if help hadn't been so prompt he would not have survived. One side of his face swelled to the size of a football. Luckily the cuts were above and below his eye, and no permanent damage was done to his vision. He was out of work for a total of four months.

"As I lay in bed in the hospital all I could think about was the incident with the two old men. I was sure that one of them was at the gate of Heaven and the other was at the gate of Hell: I felt this at the time it was happening, and I've been sure of it ever since, even though there was no obvious difference between them and they both exuded a comforting feeling.

"What worried me at first as I lay there was that they had both shaken their heads, as if rejecting me. If neither of them wanted me, what could be the matter with me? I thought I must be a really terrible person if there was no place for me in hell. I was really upset. It was some weeks later before I was able to think about it rationally, and then I realized that the reason they had turned me down was that I was still alive."

John had to quit the police force in 1985 at the age of twenty-seven after another serious injury: his leg was shattered in a football injury while playing in a match to promote a better liaison between the public and the police. "Some of the opposition liaised a bit too well—with my leg," he said. He lives in Dudley, West Midlands, with his wife Jeannette and his daughters Hannah, who was born in 1981, and Sally, who is two years younger, He works as a writer of short stories for magazines, and as a singer.

"I missed the police when I had to give it up. I was a beat officer for most of my time with the force, and I enjoyed the opportunities that gave me for helping people, particularly the elderly. That part of the job was always more satisfying than arresting criminals."

In the course of his work John was occasionally called to the scenes of deaths. "I think my own experience helped me. I'd been brought up as a child to believe in heaven and hell, and as an adult I had never given it much thought, until that crash. After that, I have always been able to take some comfort in the knowledge that people do go on after death. My sister and my father have both died quite recently, and with only a year between their deaths. I know now that their bodies may be in the cemetery, but the real people are not: they have gone on to another life."

For Ann Miles and her family—and every other family in the country—it was an exciting morning: Christmas Day,

1970. Her children, seven-year-old Marnie and twenty-month-old Warren, had opened their presents, and then she and her husband Roger had loaded them into the car for their traditional tour of the relatives. Every year since they had married Ann and Roger had gone first to Roger's mom and dad, then made a few other calls before ending up at Ann's parents' home. This year, for the first time ever, they were doing the tour in the opposite order. Warren sat on his mom's lap in the front passenger seat, playing with a toy steering wheel he had been given that morning, which clipped on to the dashboard of the car.

1970 was an unusual Christmas for Britain: the last year on record that heavy snow fell over large areas of the country, particularly the Midlands. In Birmingham, where the Miles family live, the roads were treacherous. Roger, who runs his own small confectionery business, was driving his pride and joy, an E-type Jaguar, with extra care, because overnight fresh snow had fallen on to hard-packed ice.

They approached his parents' home down a hill, with factories on either side of the road. "We went into a skid and all I can remember is seeing a wall where there shouldn't have been a wall," said Ann. Although she cannot recall it, the car skidded, mounted the pavement, went on to a parking area in front of one of the factories where the surface was a sheet of ice, plowed into the factory wall, bounced back, and skidded around to end up wrapped around a lamppost.

The car was cut into two parts by the impact. Marnie was catapulted through the roof and was lucky to escape with some bad bruises; Roger cracked several of his ribs, and Warren escaped almost unhurt because, without consciously thinking about it, Ann had wrapped herself around him. She was not wearing a seat belt, and this probably saved her life—in a tiny minority of accidents, seat belts are a liability.

Ann's injuries were extensive. She had fractured her left arm; punctured her lung; her pelvis was shattered, with seven fractures in it; every rib in her body was cracked; the bone where her neck and shoulder join was broken; most of her internal organs were ruptured, and her internal bleeding was so great that by the time she reached the hospital her stomach was so swollen that medical staff initially thought she was nine months pregnant. She was losing blood faster than they could transfuse more into her. Things looked so bleak that, on Christmas night, her family was told it was unlikely that she would pull through.

Ann was unconscious in the hospital for three weeks, and in intensive care for a month. She has a vague memory of an ambulance man telling her she was going to be all right, and from then until she awoke in the New Year she has no memory apart from her NDE. She does not know when it happened during that time, but believes it was probably on that first critical night.

"I felt myself somersault out of my body, slowly and gently, with my feet going first. Then I floated up to the ceiling of the ward and looked down on myself. I could see doctors, nurses, tubes coming out of me, monitors, all sorts of equipment, and I remember wondering what I was doing there. I had no memory of the crash, but I knew it was me down below, even though there were so many people and things around. I was curious about how I was able to see myself, I thought it was a bit odd. But it only lasted a few seconds. I don't remember going back into my body: everything was completely blank until I regained consciousness. I don't believe it was a dream, because I can remember it so clearly, and I have no memory of any other dreams in the whole three weeks that I was out."

More than twenty years later, Ann, who was twenty-five at the time, still suffers from the aftereffects of her injuries. But the crash was not the greatest tragedy of her life: that came five years later, when her daughter Marnie, then aged twelve, was knocked down and killed by a police car as she crossed a street just a few yards from the family home. She had popped out to buy her father a newspaper. The first her parents knew was when their dog arrived home on his own, dragging his leash behind. They dashed outside and saw ambulances and police cars at the scene of the accident. Their beloved daughter died five days later without regaining consciousness. Her head injuries were terrible, her pretty face transformed into a grotesque mask.

"I knew straightaway when I saw an ambulance that it was Marnie, and I knew, deep inside me, that she was dead. I am not over the shock yet. It was the worst thing that could possibly happen to anyone."

Since then Ann has seen and spoken to Marnie three times. "It was not a dream, a hallucination, or wishful thinking—although that's what some people seem to think if I tell them about it. They seem to think I'm a neurotic, desperate for any sort of contact, even imagined. But each time she was clear and real, and I can swear that I saw her. I remember it as vividly as I remember my near-death experience.

"The first time I saw her was about a month after her death. My bedroom was decorated in lemon at the time, and Marnie's in lilac. I saw her lying in my bed, but with her own lilac bedclothes on it. Her face was as lovely as it had been before the accident, and she reached out to me and said, 'It's okay, Mum, I'm all right now. Look, I can see again, my eye is better, don't worry about me now, I'm fine. I love you.' Then she was gone, but I can so clearly remember touching her. She was warm and alive, not cold and dead as I had been seeing her in my dreams.

"I also saw her once in our spare room, and the most comforting experience I had was seeing her after my father died in 1984. Again, it was about a month after losing him. I was in bed one night and I saw a lovely green meadow, and Marnie was lying there with her beloved grandfather. They were holding hands and my dad was asleep with a lovely smile on his face. Marnie reached out to me and said, 'I'm fine now, Mum. Look, Granddad is here with me to look after me.' Then she disappeared.''

Marnie also appeared to Ann's mother-in-law, when she had an NDE. She was in the hospital for an operation on her kidneys, and in the middle of it, on the operating table, she suffered a massive heart attack. Her heart actually stopped for a minute or two. When she came around after being resuscitated the nurses asked her who Marnie was, as she had been saying "No, Marnie," at the precise moment that her heart stopped.

At first she was reluctant to tell Ann what had happened, because she did not want to upset her by reviving memories of Marnie. But eventually she told how, while unconscious, Marnie had appeared at her bedside and had asked her to go towards a lovely light, but she had said, "No, Marnie, I'm not ready to come with you yet."

"When she did tell me, I thought it was wonderful," said Ann. "It confirmed what I already knew: that Marnie is waiting for us and one day we will all be together again. My mother-in-law has since died, and it is very comforting to think that she is now with Marnie. I had always believed in an afterlife, but now I'm sure of it."

The traffic light turned to green and Laura Combs pulled her car out to cross the intersection. It was early evening and she was on her way home from a meeting, with a friend in the passenger seat next to her. They were chatting away, and Laura was looking forward to getting home and having a shower and something to eat. She doesn't remember what happened next. Afterwards she was told that a truck crossed the light on red and rammed her car broadside, on the driver's side.

"Everything went black, and I found myself floating up a transparent tunnel. I could see stars through the walls of the tunnel, although it was not a starry night," said Laura, from Columbia, Connecticut. "I could see a light at the end of the tunnel. Everything felt marvelous. I knew I was young—I felt I was about nine years old, although in 1989 when this happened I was really twenty-six. But I felt completely free of all worries and problems, my body felt great, I was relaxed and enjoying it."

As she moved up the tunnel Laura found herself walking in warm, shallow water. She could feel it splashing around her toes, which increased her feeling of being a child again—it was like paddling at the seaside. She went eagerly towards the end of the tunnel, and as she approached the light became larger. She knew that she wanted to get there.

"I did not know what was there, but it was going to be very welcoming, I could feel that. I had a real desire to be there. But then I heard a voice, a man's voice, telling me that it wasn't my time and that I had to go back. I felt a big sense of disappointment, and I tried to fight the voice and carry on towards the light. I said, 'No, I don't want to go back.' I think I said it aloud: it was more than a thought.

"But I had no choice. I was thrown back, quite hard, and I opened my eyes and I was back in the wreck of my car, with the paramedics trying to get me out. I became completely conscious, and was even able to help by telling them how they could haul me out."

Luckily, Laura was not badly injured, although her car was totaled. She could remember nothing about the accident—it took her an hour or two even to recall that she had a passenger at the time of the crash. But she could remember vividly her journey along the tunnel.

"My passenger was on the other side of the car and had only a few cuts and bruises. I was badly shaken and bruised, but I was discharged from the hospital quickly because they could find nothing wrong with me, although I have suffered from migraines ever since, and I had some problems afterward adjusting to the shock of what happened.

"I was very puzzled by my NDE. I didn't know what it was until I started a college course and did a psychology class on death and loss. I heard NDEs mentioned for the first time, and it clicked with me that that was what had happened."

Laura served in the United States Army until 1987, in a support battalion. Her job was to maintain generators, and later she was a clerk. "I had a whole lot of problems: I drank too much, I was involved in fights, I got into lots of trouble. At the time of the NDE I was out of the service and trying hard to straighten myself out: it helped me a lot. I have become a lot less materialistic, I take each day as it comes, I value my life."

Laura is now married and gave birth to twin sons, Lee and Keith, in June 1994. "I guess I am happier than I ever thought I would be. The NDE helped to make me the balanced person I am today. I want to spread the word about NDEs to other people, so that they can all know that death is not a frightening process. It changes you, but the change is good.

"I was brought up in a strict Lutheran family, and I've reacted against organized religion. But I truly believe that there is a life after death, and that going there is going to be a peaceful, enjoyable experience."

Running out of gas on the way home from a Christmas shopping trip nearly cost Lois Clark her life. She and her five children waited in their car while her husband set off to walk to a gas station in West Valley, Utah. As Lois amused the children, there was suddenly an almighty bang as a drunk driver careered out of control and slammed into the back of their car. Lois suffered massive internal injuries and several broken bones, and lost a great deal of blood.

She lost consciousness, and the next thing she remembers was hearing someone say "She's going to flatline"—the term for clinical death, when the heart-monitor graph stops going up and down and traces a flat line.

"Moments later, I'm floating in the air looking down at this woman on a table. There were all these people working around the table. Then I saw a bright light, the most beautiful light you can imagine, I've never seen anything like it. And although I couldn't hear music, I could feel it. There was a feeling of peace, beauty and love, and I felt as though this was what I had always wanted.

"I started walking towards the light, which was white and yet yellow, a very mellow soft and yet bright light. I had to look down and then blink my eyes up and then down again, because it was so bright. But as I walked towards the source of the light I was told, 'No, go back.' I saw forms, not recognizable faces, and yet I knew they were spirits. One seemed to shine with brightness while the others seemed at peace—sort of idyllic. But they were all urging me to go back, though I didn't want to."

She woke up in tremendous pain, surrounded by doctors, and was at first angry that she had been allowed to live: "The other world was so much more beautiful than this."

Lois's NDE happened in 1957, when she was twenty-seven. She realized afterwards that she was sent back because her children were small and needed her. She's now divorced, and the children have been the mainstay of her life.

In 1989 she discovered that she had breast cancer, and was admitted into a hospital to have a mastectomy, an operation to remove her breast. She was not afraid—her NDE had helped her feel happy about the idea of death. But to the astonishment of the doctors, an X ray taken on the day she was due to have the operation showed no sign of disease in her breast: the cancerous cells had spontaneously cleared up.

Librarian Gary Gillum also ended up in a hospital in critical condition after being hit by a drunk driver. Gary's accident happened when he was a young man, and he believes it was a way of preparing him for the tragedies that were to happen in his life: Gary, who was born in 1934, has been married four times, and his first two wives both died of cancer, each leaving him with three children to bring up.

Gary, who lives in Provo, Utah, was a passenger in a friend's car when it was hit head-on at a combined speed of 110 mph. He broke his back, all the bones in his face, and received multiple internal injuries.

"In the hospital they pronounced me clinically dead. But while I was dead in this world, I was alive in another: I went to a place with a lot of light. It was a yellowish-gold light, and I was in a beautiful meadow with flowers and trees everywhere. The colors of the grass and the flowers were intense, and I could feel a great wave of love enveloping me.

"I met someone who I believe was my grandfather, who had died six months earlier. He gave me a choice of whether I wanted to stay or go back, but he told me that I still had a lot of things to face on earth. I was taught that the important things in life are love and knowledge, and this has helped me cope with the death of my wives. Knowing that they were going to a far better place than this world made it much easier to bear the loss, and I can't wait to see them again, which I know I will."

Gary's third marriage ended in divorce, and he is now married for the fourth time, to a woman who has eleven children from her first marriage: "Life has not been easy, but my NDE has sustained me through all my trials and tribulations, and it has prepared me for my own death, which I know will be wonderful."

Ray Standing's story is different from the others in this book. He came very close to death, but he has no memory of it. There was no NDE that Ray can consciously recall: he, like many thousands of other people who have medical crises or accidents each year, recovered without ever being aware of anything spiritual or special having taken place.

But Ray's story is included because it typifies the comments made by many others who have not had an NDE, despite being close to death. They may not be able to recall it, but they feel sure that it did happen, because they emerge from the experience as changed personalities. Of course, the mere fact of coming so close to dying may be enough to concentrate the mind and affect attitudes to life and living, but for people like Ray it seems to be more than this.

In 1974 Ray was a sixteen-year-old window cleaner, working for a company that cleaned hotel windows in Worthing, Sussex. As one of the younger members of the team he was used to being sent up to clean the high windows, and looking back he realized that he and the others took tremendous risks, balancing along ledges to move from window to window when they should really have climbed down, moved their ladders, and climbed back up again.

Ray was cleaning the third-story windows of a hotel, standing on a two-foot-wide ledge fifty feet above the ground, when he toppled backward and fell. He hit a telegraph wire, landed on the slate roof of a shed and then fell to the tarmac in the hotel backyard. He was lucky to have had his fall broken by the wire and the shed roof, otherwise his injuries would almost certainly have been fatal. As it was, he swallowed his tongue in the accident, which could have prevented him breathing, and he was in a coma for ten days. Remarkably, no bones in his body were broken, but the muscles under one of his arms were ripped out.

When Ray emerged from his coma, his speech was slurred and he had no sense of balance. It took three months for him to relearn to walk, and it was over two years before he completely recovered his memory. His accident had caused a great stir: the local newspapers had written about him, and his family were beside themselves with worry. Even when he regained consciousness, they were worried that he might have suffered permanent brain damage.

Yet despite all this, Ray felt good. "I had a strange sensation of being safe, being secure, being looked after—not just in the way that the nurses or my family were looking after me. Something bigger than that had happened.

"I also felt carefree. I'm no longer afraid of death, and I'm not even afraid of heights. I had a strong feeling that something saved me, that it was not my time to die. Although I have no memory of an experience of peace and warmth during my coma, I certainly felt more peaceful and at one with the world when I woke up."

Ray, who runs his own welding and mechanics business, says that although he was very young when it happened, he emerged from his accident "feeling as though I know something about life, something deeper." Married with three children, he believes he is more tolerant and easy-going as a husband and father than he would have been had he not had his accident.

"I believe there is a purpose in everything, and that accident happened in order to teach me to relax more, get more enjoyment out of life, not waste my time worrying. It changed my personality, but it changed it for the better."

Chapter 10

ON THE TABLE

The operating table is the classic setting for an NDE. Stories of people who had their experiences while under anesthetic and being operated on are included in other chapters of this book, but this chapter gives a selection of those who needed surgery for a variety of different reasons, some very serious and some, ostensibly, minor.

Joyce Bennett's NDE has some of the hallmarks of a classic: there was a tunnel, there was a welcoming light, there was heaven waiting for her. But the start of her experience was very unusual.

Joyce, who was a traffic officer in Oldham for fourteen years until ill-health forced her to retire, had her NDE after being taken into the hospital for an operation to remove gallstones and her bladder. The operation apparently went well, and the following day Joyce, who was fifty-two, felt good. But the next day she was suddenly seized with unbearable pain in her stomach. Her sister was visiting her at the time, and as she walked up to the bed and placed a bunch of flowers on it, Joyce was hit by the first of many waves of pain. Within minutes she was grasping the sides of the bed and gasping for help.

The surgeon who had performed the original operation was away for the weekend. Other doctors prescribed pain-killing medication for Joyce, but when the surgeon returned on Monday he took one look at her stomach and ordered that she be taken right away to the operating theater. Peritonitis had set in, because one of her veins had not sealed

properly and was leaking fluid into the stomach cavity. It
was while under anesthetic that Joyce had her NDE.

"I could hear voices, far away and faint. And then I felt
myself floating up into the air, and when I looked down I
saw that I was floating above Frank Carson, the comedian.
He was on stage in a theater, which was packed with people
who were laughing at his jokes. He was telling his usual
sort of jokes, and I can remember him telling one about St.
Peter at the gates of heaven.

"As I looked at the audience I could see some of the
faces laughing away, but some were completely blank.
Within seconds I was being whisked away. It felt as though
I was traveling fast. I started to move through a dark tunnel,
and I felt I could see people on either side of me, people I
knew. I was saying hello to all of them, but I cannot remember who they were, and when I look back their faces,
too, were blank. But I felt I knew them—or I wouldn't
have been greeting them all, would I?

"At the end of the tunnel there was a great, bright light.
My speed slowed down and I came out of the tunnel in
front of these massive, gorgeous gates, all glowing in the
lovely light. They were very intricate, as though they were
wrought iron, but they were solid gold. I have never seen
anything so beautiful in all my life.

"Slowly they started to open. I could see a man in a
long white robe and a cloak on the other side, smiling. I
knew that it was God or Jesus. He had the most beautiful
face, with a beard, and such lovely gentle eyes, and a lovely
light, like the rays of the sun, seemed to come out from
him. He appeared to be luminous, gleaming with the light.
I moved forward to go through the gate but he put his hand
out to stop me and he said in a strong but kind voice, 'Go
back, your time has not come yet.'

"Then the gate shut, and I was no longer in that lovely
place. Instead I could hear the nurses saying, "She's over

the worst, she's going to be okay, she'll come round now."
And I opened my eyes to see all my family there, my husband Jim and my four grown-up children, Christine, Colin, Michael and Joyce, were there, and they all came over and kissed me on the forehead."

Later, when her family had gone, one of the nurses who had been at Joyce's bedside after the operation asked her where she had been. Joyce was surprised by the question, until the nurse told her that she had been saying out loud "Isn't it lovely?" over and over again. Wherever you were, the nurse told Joyce, it must have been good.

When Joyce described her experience, it was passed on to the ward sister, who introduced her to a Roman Catholic priest who was visiting the hospital. "I told him what I had seen and he did not disbelieve me. He said, 'You are one of the gifted ones,' and said that there were not many people who would see heaven and then come back to tell about it. He said that the reason I could not see the faces of some of the people in the theater audience was because they were people who had already passed on, died."

Joyce has never lost the memory of her experience, and her only sadness is that she cannot paint the beautiful scene she saw: "My son-in-law paints, but I cannot describe what I saw well enough for anyone else to capture it. I haven't got enough words to say what it was like. I can only say that it was the most beautiful thing I have ever seen or experienced."

Joyce cannot think why her NDE started with a trip to the theater to see Frank Carson. "It's not as though he is a particular favorite of mine. I've seen him on television, but I've never been to a theater to see him. He used to be on the program *The Comedians*, and I always thought he was funny, but I was never a particular fan of his or anything. I can remember thinking while I was above him in the theater that his jokes were not particularly funny, although I cannot remember afterwards what they were. But I was a bit puzzled as to why they were all laughing so much.''

When Joyce's husband Jim died two years after her operation, despite her grief she felt comforted by her own experience. ''Jim had had a cerebral hemorrhage, and I nursed him for some years before he died. Although we had been told to expect it, it was still a terrible shock when I arrived home from work to find him dead in bed. At first I was very upset, but I got a lot of help from thinking that if he was going to go down the same road that I had been down, he would be feeling good.

''I'm not at all frightened of death for myself. I love my life, but when the time comes, I'll know that I'll be going through those beautiful gates, and that He will be waiting for me. I felt I was being guided by love when I went there, and I was disappointed to be sent back, although I was back in my hospital bed so quickly I didn't have much time to think about it.''

Although Joyce does not attend church regularly, she was brought up to believe in God: ''My great-grandmother was very religious, and played the organ at St. Peter's Church in the center of Oldham, where I was brought up. I attended Sunday school regularly, but as an adult it dwindled away and I didn't spend a lot of time thinking about religion. At the back of my mind, though, I always believed—and now I have a much stronger faith.

''Before my operation I had a crisis, after losing two grandchildren in cot deaths. I questioned the existence of God then. I asked why He would do a thing like that, taking two innocent children. But now I know that they are at peace, and very happy, with Him. They were flowers soon gathered, and He must have wanted them. When they got to the gate, it was opened for them.

''I get enormous comfort from that. I visit their graves,

and I know that I should not be sad, because they are in a beautiful place. I feel very privileged to have had a glimpse of it: perhaps God just wanted me to see what a lovely place it is, so that I would not grieve for them.''

Gina Schorah and her mom Carol have both had NDEs, although of different degrees. Both were young when they had them, Carol just a month away from her sixteenth birthday and Gina when she was eleven. Their experiences were quite different, yet they have in common that they vividly remember them, even though for Carol the experience was in 1956 and Gina's was in 1970.

Carol, who comes from Southport, Merseyside, was suffering from toxemia of the thyroid gland. Doctors had been trying to control her condition with medication for two years, but without much success: her hair was thin and brittle, she had gained weight, she was permanently on edge. Eventually she was admitted to the Northern Hospital, Liverpool, for an operation to remove part of her thyroid gland. She was given the usual preoperation treatment, and went into the operating theater under a general anesthetic. In theory, she should have had no sense of where she was or what was happening.

"But I could clearly see where I was and what the surgeon was doing, because I had floated up to the ceiling and was looking down on it all. I was in a corner of the operating theater, up high, and I had no sense of having a body. I could see my body lying on the operating table, and even though I could not see the face I knew it was me, and I could see the staff in their green gowns, which were tied at the back, green hats, masks and Wellies, working on it.

"I felt no fear, and it seemed perfectly natural to be up there. I could see a great big round light with smaller disks of light inside it, beaming down on my body. That may have been the theater lighting system: I didn't have any particular sensation of being drawn to the light, or feeling of peace. The only way I can describe what I felt is that I felt nothing: it seemed normal, natural, an everyday thing for me to be looking down from a corner of the ceiling. I looked across at the wall and saw the clock: I could see that it was twenty to eleven. I remember that clock face and the time it said, today.

"Then I had a clear sense of descending slowly. The light faded and the room became less brilliantly lit, and I felt a swishing feeling, a sort of 'vroom,' as I went back into my own body. It was like slipping your hand into a glove: it was easy and it fitted perfectly. It was almost as though I was sucked back in, because the last little bit happened very fast."

When Carol came around, her family had been called to her bedside because her condition had been critical. At twenty to eleven she had been in the operating theater. "I told my mother what had happened to me, but she preferred not to know about it: she felt it was something that was best forgotten. So I never mentioned it for many years, until Gina was ill. Then other people started talking about NDEs and I felt a great relief to know that I wasn't alone in this."

Carol has three children, all of them now grown up. It was when her daughter Gina was eleven and was taken into Alder Hey Hospital in Liverpool with a burst duodenal ulcer that she, too, had an NDE. Gina's condition was serious: when a duodenal ulcer perforates it leaks acid into the stomach cavity, and peritonitis can set in. If not treated rapidly, peritonitis can be fatal.

Gina, who is divorced, has her own daughter, Tracey, born in 1982. She clearly remembers what happened to her the day she was admitted to the hospital, in terrible pain: "My mum was at my bedside and I remember going out of my body. I didn't float above myself like she did, I went straightaway into a tunnel that was totally dark at first, but then a pure lovely light began to show at the end of it. It was like a rainbow: although it was white there were other colors tingeing the edge, rainbow colors.

"I traveled along the tunnel quite quickly, and then came out of it into a field. There was a gate, with a man standing at it, and beyond the gate was a big glass building. It was all glass, not like anything I have ever seen, but without being told I just knew it was a hospital. It was in a field which seemed to go on for ever and ever, a beautiful field with lovely green grass and flowers.

"As I got nearer to the gate, which was just an ordinary wooden gate, I could see that the man was a schoolteacher, and he had an old-fashioned easel with a blackboard on it, and there were children around him. He was pointing to something on the board, but I could not see what it was. He was a tall, elderly gentleman with a kind face, and he spoke very properly, with what I would describe as a posh accent.

"I went over to a tree. At this point I was able to look down on myself sitting under the tree. The man turned to me and said, 'You are not ready yet.' I did not know what he meant, but it made me very sad. I didn't recognize him or any of the children. I started to cry, and I sat under the tree sobbing my heart out at not being ready, and then somehow—I can't remember how, it just seemed to happen—I was the other side of the gate in the field with the hospital. There was some faint but lovely music playing— I've never heard it before or since, but it was a lovely tune. Again, I don't remember how I got inside, but I was suddenly inside the glass hospital, being looked after. There was no pain, and I felt calm and peaceful, but I also felt very lonely. There did not seem to be any other people around. Then I had a very strong feeling of missing my mum. She was calling out, 'Don't leave me, come back to me.'

"As soon as I thought about her, I was jolted back into my body. This bit was the same as Mum's experience, as I remember the feeling of fitting very neatly into my own body—just like my mum describes it as slipping your fingers into a glove.

"Going up out of my body was a very nice, gentle feeling. I moved quite quickly, but not fast enough to worry me. Although I was definitely traveling along the tunnel at a good speed, there was a floating, easy feeling about the movement. Coming back was different: it was too fast. I felt it like a jolt, the moment of reentry into my body, and it was a little bit frightening."

Gina's mother was told that her daughter had come perilously close to death during the operation. When Gina came out of the theater, Carol was sitting by her bedside calling to her to help bring her around, just as Gina had heard her. When Gina regained consciousness she insisted to her mom that she had been in a glass hospital: Carol had no idea what she was talking about until a few days later, when Gina told her the whole story of her NDE.

"Mum accepted it straightaway. She didn't think I was making it up or imagining it, because she knew from her own experience that strange things can happen when you are close to death.

"On the whole it was an enjoyable experience. I can remember feeling very good, and it was lovely to be without pain. I think if it happened to me today I would not want to come back, but at the age of eleven I still had everything in front of me, and I was still very attached to my mum and my family, and I made an effort to come back. Or perhaps it was just what the man said, and not my turn.

"I'm certainly not frightened of death now. I remember the whole experience as if it was yesterday. I also remember the feelings I had: just thinking about them brings them back.''

Because she was so young when she had her NDE, Gina does not know whether it has changed her life or her personality, but she knows that she is psychically sensitive, and in the last few years has been having predictive visions.

"I don't like it, because the visions can come at any time, as clearly as though I was watching them on a television screen. I saw my Uncle Billy, who is dead, standing behind my mum one day. I never knew him, but I saw a man smoking a pipe and holding a tankard and a harmonica, and other family members confirmed that it was definitely him. I have also predicted events which have happened in the news, and silly little things like knowing the name of the district nurse who is coming to see me before she arrives.

"It is a little bit worrying, and I'd prefer it not to happen. I don't really know what to do to stop it, but I'm scared that one day I may have an important vision, something that I really ought to try to do something about.

"I don't know if there is a connection between my visions and the NDE. Perhaps because I have been so close to the afterlife I am more aware of things in this life."

Like Gina Schorah, Keith Beckett had a very full NDE, again during a dangerous operation. He was rushed to the hospital in November 1985, after he reacted severely to some tablets he was being given to help with pain in his neck. Keith, who was sixty, had been involved in a car accident, which had left him with a painful whiplash injury. An injection of cortisone into his neck had gone badly wrong, when the cortisone went solid. Doctors had to operate to remove some of it, but some was too dangerous to remove because it was close to his spine and might cause paralysis.

To ease the pain—much greater than that from the original injury—Keith was given medication. But he reacted to the tablets, all his veins became varicose and he was taken to the hospital. A few days later the veins in his stomach burst, spraying blood all over his hospital cubicle. A massive operation was necessary, in which half of Keith's stomach and half of his intestine was removed, and plastic veins were inserted in his chest, down to his pancreas and his legs. He also had to have plastic netting put around his stomach to hold it in place, a very painful operation as the netting had to be inserted into his flesh.

It was the operation on his stomach, after the veins burst, that took Keith close to death. He was told afterwards by his doctor that he had technically "died" twice during the operation, which ties in with him twice experiencing the same NDE, and he had been dead long enough for the medical staff to have started preparations to have him taken to the mortuary.

"I can see it now, so clearly," said Keith, who lives in Newbury, Berkshire. "As I went towards the operating theater, I literally passed out. The pain was enormous, and the feeling of getting away from it was one of great relief.

"I felt myself pass out, and then I came back to consciousness, only to find myself in a luminescent green tunnel, with a black spiral leading to a pinpoint of light in the very far distance. I felt myself traveling toward the light, although I can't tell how I was traveling. I wasn't aware of walking. There was a scent of lilies in the tunnel, but not that sickly sweet smell you sometimes get with lilies: this was delicate and fresh and the only words I can find to describe it are 'out of this world.' It was a nicer smell than anything I have ever known, yet it was distinctly lilies. The feeling I had was of great serenity and calm.

"The pinpoint of light became bigger and bigger, until it opened out into a large room, lit by a glowing, golden light, with a wide staircase leading off from the room. There were people standing at the edge of each stair, and the first one I could see was a friend of ours, who had died two years earlier. I didn't recognize any of the others.

"When they saw me, they all turned their backs towards me. I said, 'If you are not going to speak to me, I'm going back.' After that I was back at the very beginning of the tunnel, and I had exactly the same experience all over again, and again they turned their backs on me. After the second time, I remember nothing until I was waking up in intensive care, with my wife Eileen sitting next to me."

Eileen remembers being called urgently to return to the hospital the evening that Keith's emergency operation was carried out. She had been visiting him earlier, but received a call at 10 P.M. telling her to get back there, as he had taken a turn for the worse. She went back with their son Charles; their other son, Nicholas, and daughter Elizabeth joined them later.

"I was told that his condition was critical, that he had come very close to death," Eileen said. "It was a great relief when he recovered, and it has been a comfort to me to hear his story about his experience."

Keith, who has suffered two strokes since coming home from hospital, is adamant that his NDE was not a dream. "It was much more vivid, much more real. I don't wonder whether it happened, I know it happened. I have no fears about dying now, because I know that it will be a wonderful experience. You can't share it in words with anyone else: it is something that you have to experience for yourself. I am one of the lucky ones, I've had a preview of what it will be like."

Terry Burns went into the hospital for the same reason as Gina Schorah, a burst duodenal ulcer, but his NDE was much more similar to Gina's mother Carol's. Terry, who now lives in Fleetwood, Lancashire, was in the late 1950s living in Rochdale, and it was in Rochdale Infirmary that he had the operation.

He had been rushed in after collapsing at home. After a month of treatment, during which he was given several blood transfusions, he was sent home until he was strong enough for the operation, in which part of his stomach was to be removed. It was after the operation, before he came around from the anesthetic, that Terry had his NDE. He felt himself floating upwards, and hovering over his own bed. He was able to look down, and could see two doctors in white coats at the side of the bed.

"I knew it was me, although I could not see myself very clearly," said Terry, who was born in 1922. "I felt very relaxed, very calm, it was an entirely pleasant experience. It was like having a dream, yet it has remained very fresh in my memory ever since, and a dream would have faded a long time ago. Whatever happens in life, every so often I find myself remembering it.

"When I hear of other people seeing bright lights and tunnels, and meeting their dead relatives, I realize that mine is a rather small experience. But to me it has enormous significance. I am and always have been a Christian, so I always did believe in an afterlife. But now I have the proof that the human soul does leave the material body at the point of death."

After regaining consciousness Terry commented about his strange experience to one of the doctors, who replied, "You will never be closer to death than you were then." He told Terry that there had been a major crisis after the operation, and that for some minutes Terry's life had hung in the balance.

Barbara Prowse, who lives in Exeter in Devon, had a similar NDE to Terry's. She, too, floated above herself and looked down, and she too remembers vividly the feelings the experience engendered.

Barbara, who is a mother of six and grandmother to eight children, was in the hospital in 1980, after two miserable years of illness. She was suffering from gallstones, but because of a bad attack of jaundice the date for her operation had to be postponed. In the hospital she was nicknamed the Yellow Lady, because her skin was so jaundiced that it coordinated with her yellow dressing gown.

After going into the operating theater, Barbara experienced a feeling of euphoria. Her pain lifted away from her, and she felt herself get lighter and lighter until she floated up to the ceiling, where she hovered on a comfortable and all-embracing cloud of white light.

"I saw the doctors and nurses trying to resuscitate me with electric paddles, and even putting an injection into my heart (I still have the marks today). I didn't feel at all squeamish watching them do it, although I knew it was me they were working on. I felt so wonderful, with no worries or cares in the world. I saw a nurse running out of the room shouting 'We've lost her,' and I was trying to tell the staff that I was up on the ceiling, that I felt fine and that I didn't want to come back. I really didn't want to return, but suddenly my lovely time was all over and I was back in my own body.

"The nurses told me afterwards that as I was coming round I kept murmuring, 'I don't want to come back,' over and over again. They asked me where I had been. I told them about my cloud, and I astonished the nurse who had run out of the room by describing in detail what she had done.

"The amazing thing is that I felt no fear. I was as happy as could be up on the ceiling, and the light that I was floating on was gentle and soft, so beautiful."

Since then Barbara has had no fear of dying, although

she is not looking forward to being separated from her close family.

Laurel Glass can conjure up the sights she saw during her NDE as clearly as if she was taking out a photograph and studying it. Laurel, an American physiotherapist, went into the hospital for what should have been a minor abdominal operation in 1982, when she was only twenty and was planning a career as a professional tennis player. But during the operation Laurel's heart failed for a few seconds and she was told afterwards, she had been clinically dead.

"I found myself floating above my body watching the medical team trying to revive this lifeless form. There was red everywhere, spattered on their gowns, on the floor, and I could see a bright pool of red blood in the open abdominal cavity of the person below, which was me.

"Then I saw a horizon of whitish yellow light, but it was far away and I did not get any closer to it because I felt a presence on my right side—it was my brother-in-law, who died seven months earlier. He told me to tell my sister that he was fine. Then I felt myself slam back into my body, and I lost consciousness again."

Chapter 11

A MIXED BAG

It is impossible to categorize all NDEs by the type of illness or accident that gives rise to them. There are hundreds of different serious medical conditions, any one of which can take people to the brink of death and back. The stories in this chapter illustrate how any life-threatening illness can give rise to a life-enhancing NDE.

With six children to look after, Gabrielle Keller was always on the go. When her youngest child, her daughter Julie, was only nine months old, Gabrielle took a much-needed vacation in Suffolk with her sister. She took the four youngest children with her, their ages ranging from fourteen down to the baby. It was at the end of a happy afternoon splashing around at the local swimming pool that Gabrielle had her NDE, after she collapsed in the changing rooms.

It happened in May 1972, when Gabrielle was thirty-seven. She was, she thought, in perfect health—and even after her collapse, doctors were unable to find anything wrong with her. After swimming in the pool, Gabrielle left baby Julie in the charge of fourteen-year-old Sheila, while she went back to the changing rooms. She was intending to get her own clothes on, and then see to the children getting dressed.

In the changing-room cubicle, Gabrielle had just pulled her black swimsuit halfway down when she felt her head beginning to swim, and she collapsed. She blacked out completely, and was only found when Sheila, getting worried about the length of time her mother was taking, went to the changing rooms. When she saw her mother she screamed, and attendants came running.

At this point Gabrielle was drifting in and out of consciousness. "I can remember people running around, and someone putting something on to my face. I was put on to a stretcher and although I don't remember being taken to the ambulance, I could hear the bell and I can remember snatches of being rushed through the town."

When they arrived at the hospital, Gabrielle was aware of a great commotion around her. She heard a doctor saying urgently: "There's no pulse, no heartbeat." It was at this point that Gabrielle floated away.

"I drifted upwards, completely weightless, through a dark tunnel with little specks of gold along its walls. It was a lovely, dreamy feeling. I felt completely relaxed and at peace.

"At the top of the tunnel were some white gates surrounded by a lovely bright light. There was a man dressed in long white robes and with a gold hat, similar to a bishop's mitre, on his head. He was shimmering with light, and there was light all across his face, so that I could not make out his features. He was looking at me and he said, 'You must go back. It is not your time yet. You must return and look after Anthony and Julie.' "

Instantaneously, Gabrielle woke up. She had no sensation of going down the tunnel or returning to her body, but she felt a jerk as though she had just landed on the bed: then she was simply awake.

As she opened her eyes she saw a worried-looking doctor bending over her. He was confirming to his colleague that she had no pulse, and she heard him say that she was clinically dead.

"What are you on about? I'm all right," Gabrielle said, sitting up and seeing an expression of disbelief on both doctors' faces. Gabrielle, who comes from Liversedge,

Yorkshire, asked for a cup of tea, and explained that she felt perfectly okay. The doctors gave her a thorough examination, and after a couple of hours agreed to let her go home with her brother-in-law.

"They told me to have a checkup with my doctor when I got back to Yorkshire, but as far as they could see there was nothing wrong with me. I felt perfectly normal, not even a bit weak. I was annoyed that I had not been able to stay: I remember waking up with a feeling of disappointment that I was back, although as soon as I thought about it I was really glad not to have left my family. But I could still feel the happiness that I had experienced standing in front of that gate, and I knew it was a feeling I would not get again in this life."

The only conclusion that her own doctor could come to about the sudden collapse was that Gabrielle has poor circulation, and she was warned that she was at risk of thrombosis. Fortunately she has had no health problems since.

Gabrielle told her sister Joan about her NDE: "I knew I had not imagined it. It was very real. It definitely happened. My sister said I was a silly devil, but she accepted that I was not making it up. We just did not know what to make of it. We are very practical people: I was brought up on a farm. I'm not given to imagining things, and I'm certainly not psychic in any way. The bit about going back to take care of Anthony and Julie did not make sense at the time, because although they were the two youngest, the oldest of the six was only eighteen, and they all still needed me."

Years later, Gabrielle, who was widowed when her husband Peter died in 1989, understands the message. All her children have left home, except two: Anthony and Julie. Anthony, who is in his late twenties, moved out to live with a girlfriend but moved back home after nine months, and Julie, in her early twenties, has not left.

"I'm still looking after them both, all these years on.

Julie has really needed me, because at one time she tried to commit suicide, after she had been drinking, and I cared for her after that. I can't bear to think what would have happened to any of my children if I had died, but I can now see that I was particularly needed for Anthony and Julie.''

Gabrielle, who now has sixteen grandchildren, has had her religious beliefs strengthened by the experience. She has always believed in God, and converted to Roman Catholicism when she married: ''I believed in life after death, but now I know what it is going to be like, and I have no fear of death. My family have all benefited from my experience, too, because I'm able to tell them what a wonderful place is waiting for them one day.''

Gabrielle Keller's experience came completely out of the blue, when she felt she was in perfect health. Arnold Haworth's also came when he was in no particular health crisis, but for Arnold perfect health is only a dim memory: for more than twenty years he has been crippled with rheumatoid arthritis. At the time of his NDE he was in a great deal of pain, but it was a level of pain that he had learned to accept as normal. There was nothing particularly severe on that evening.

At about midnight, his usual time, Arnold went to bed. The pain made it difficult for him to get comfortable and go to sleep, and he was expecting to lie awake in agony as he normally did each night. But suddenly, he felt himself leaving his body, and leaving behind all the pain.

''At first I thought it was a dream, but it was too real, and although it happened years ago I can remember it very clearly. I suddenly found myself floating in a different— and very beautiful—world. It was exhilarating because my body felt whole and free of pain, for the first time in years.

There was no restriction on my movement, and I felt peaceful and relaxed.

"I was floating over green fields and rolling hills which were full of trees, small animals, and birds. The scenery was lovely, the sky was blue and cloudless, the sun was shining and there were no people around, so I could float about looking at whatever I wanted to see. The floating sensation was amazing—if I wanted to go somewhere all I did was think about it and I drifted across, without having to make any effort.

"There was a hole in the ground, like a well or a shaft, which was filled with a bright light, and every so often I felt compelled to go over and look down it. At the bottom of the shaft I could see my own body on my bed, asleep. I knew that I had to make sure my body was still there, that if it was moved I would never be able to return to it. I felt slightly anxious about this, but not enough to spoil the whole experience. Every time I looked, the body was there, so it was okay.

"In the distance I could see a lovely cottage, the sort you see in a children's storybook. I wanted to go to it, but something inside me told me that I must not. I felt that if I went there, I would not come back. Then I knew, without anyone telling me, that it was time to go back into my own body, and I traveled fast down the shaft and back into myself. I woke up at that instant, able to remember everything clearly, and with that lovely feeling of warmth and peace still inside me."

Arnold, who lives in Darwen, Lancashire, tried to convince himself that the whole experience had been a dream, although he knew that it was very different from any dream he had known. It was only when, in the hospital, he heard another patient describing an NDE that he realized what it was.

"I now feel honored, because I have been privileged to have a glimpse of something that not many people see. I think it may have been done to help me cope with my pain, or perhaps I really was near death that night. The fact that I knew I had to come back, had to keep checking that my body was still there so I could come back, makes me think that it was never planned for me to die that night. But there must have been something special happening, to have allowed me a visit like that."

Arnold, who was born in 1929, has not been able to work for nearly twenty years because of his condition. He has told his wife and daughter about his NDE, and they both take it seriously.

"I've had one or two other unusual experiences since then. I visited my uncle two days before he died, and he told me he had a visit from a woman the night before and that she had told him not to worry because he would like the place where he was going. Although there were other people in the room he turned to me, and specifically addressed me: 'Arnold, never be afraid of dying,' he said. I believe he must have had an experience similar to mine, and was prepared for what was coming.

"On another occasion I visited my father in hospital when he was very ill. Afterwards I called at his house to collect some things, and I was standing in front of his fireplace. Suddenly the light, which was switched on, flared very brightly, and then went out. The temperature in the room dropped several degrees and became very cold. Then I took a phone call from the hospital to say that he had died, and the time of his death was the exact moment the light flared and the temperature changed."

Arnold believes there is life after death, and like most NDEers he has no fear of dying.

•   •   •

Steve Price's life was profoundly changed by his NDE. In 1965, when he was twenty-one, heavily tattooed Steve was serving as a U.S. Marine in Vietnam. He was behind enemy lines when he was hit by mortar fire.

"Some shrapnel lodged in my chest, puncturing my lungs. As I sat in a foxhole trying to stay alive, my life flashed before me. Three days later I was in a military hospital waiting for an operation when I suddenly detached from my body and I was looking down at myself. Then I was facing a brick wall when it suddenly turned into this beautiful and loving light. It seemed to encompass me, and I loved it there.

"Across a stream I saw my grandfather, who I was close to and who had died when I was young. But then it was as if somebody turned out the light, and I was suddenly back in my body and in my bed. I was very angry at being pulled back."

When Steve recovered he went back to the battlefront, but he found his whole attitude to being a soldier had changed: "Although I'd been trained to kill, I couldn't do it anymore. I couldn't even fire my gun. I was a danger to my platoon, so I quit."

Steve now devotes his free time to helping terminally ill patients prepare for death: "I tell them that there is nothing to be afraid of, that the place they are going to is beautiful."

"I look forward to the day I go to the other side in the same way that you look forward to a fantastic holiday. Although I have a wonderful husband, three of the best children in the world, and lovely grandchildren who I would hate to leave, the pull from the other side is very strong and very welcoming."

Ann Joyce believes she knows what is waiting for her on the other side because she has already been there. Her

NDE happened in 1985, when she was forty-four. At the time, she was seriously ill with pernicious anemia, but the disease had not been diagnosed and she did not know why she felt so tired and unwell all the time.

"I went to bed at my normal time, feeling exhausted. I lay there feeling awful, lifeless. The next moment I floated away above myself. I was hovering, swaying a little bit, just like the feeling you might get in a hammock. Then I started to move, feet first, down a long dark tunnel. It seemed to go on for ages, but gradually I got nearer and nearer to a glorious light at the end. I dropped down, on to my feet, as I came through the end of the tunnel.

"The colors and scenery around me were beyond description. There were animals, flowers, trees, waterfalls: it was everything you could wish for if you were trying to imagine heaven. The feeling of wonder and peace that I had was something I have never experienced before or since. A group of people met me, walking up to me with their arms outstretched. I had never seen any of them before, but somehow they were familiar. They didn't speak, but I knew they were welcoming me and they wanted me to stay.

"I was aware that there was a presence on the right-hand side of me, and when I turned I saw a brilliant, glowing, white light, with an aura shimmering around it. I knew it was God. I didn't see Him as much as feel Him, a glorious feeling of love and warmth. Nobody spoke, but I felt so complete and content.

"But after a little while I knew that I must come back. It wasn't so much a decision as a knowledge that it would happen, I must do it. I felt I was being told, although again nobody spoke, that I had work to do here on earth. No sooner had that thought come into my head than I was back at home, in my own bed."

A few days later, Ann's life-threatening condition was

diagnosed, and she now has regular injections to control it. Left untreated, she would have soon been dead.

"I have been profoundly changed by the whole experience. I feel so much closer to nature than I ever was, and I feel more love towards the rest of the human race. I see things in a different way, always seeing the good in a situation, not the bad. And I have premonitions that come true. I think my sensitivity has been heightened, I'm more aware of things. I predicted the thinning of the ozone layer, although I know nothing about the science of it. I worry a little about the premonitions, because I do not know how I will react if I have one where I might be able to change things. I also worry far more about the environment and the damage that is being done to it, even though I know I can do very little to save it."

Ann and her husband Keith, who is retired, live in Swadlincote in Derbyshire. Keith accepts Ann's experience as real: "But nobody can properly appreciate it unless they have been there, because there just aren't words in the English language to describe it."

Since having her NDE Ann has told a lot of people about it, particularly people who are facing death. She shared it with her mother and with her younger sister, who died of cancer. "My mother was very ill and she knew she was not going to get better. I told her what had happened to me and it helped her to relax and not be afraid. My sister was terrified, and I think it brought her some peace. Since then I have spread the word to many more people, and I'm now convinced that this is the work I was sent back to do. I am, in a way, a disciple."

Like most NDEers, Ann can recall the place she visited with great clarity: "When I think about it, it is almost as though I am back there, although I don't get quite the same feeling of tranquillity and peace. I am looking forward to the day I can return."

• • •

The isolation ward in Edinburgh Royal Infirmary was very quiet in the early hours of Monday, February 28, 1994. Douglas Goodfellow dozed peacefully in his bed, feeling content and relaxed. Douglas was there fighting off a bout of flu, a dangerous infection because he was in the middle of a course of chemotherapy for leukemia. At two A.M. he was vaguely aware of the routine hourly visit of the nurse to check on his condition—and within seconds the space around his bed was crowded with medical staff, as two doctors and the nurse battled to revive him.

"Apparently the nurse had found me stone cold, and she'd sent immediately for the receptionist and another doctor. I remember them rushing up to my bedside, and the receptionist tapping at my face. Then I felt myself floating away from it all," said Douglas, who was an operator for British Telecom for twenty-three years before ill health forced him to retire.

"I didn't leave the hospital room: I could look down and see them pumping antibiotics into me through a drip. But up at the top of the room were three people who I think of as angels, even though they did not have wings. They were all wearing long white robes, and they were hovering in a shimmering, lovely light. They were looking down on me as I lay on the bed.

"The middle one was a man with gray hair, and there was a woman on either side of him, one with dark hair and another, smaller one, with fair hair. This one was very young, perhaps only a teenager. They didn't speak, but the look that was in their eyes was full of compassion and love. They were only there for a few seconds, and then they faded away. They all went at once, and while they were fading the lovely light around them became full of all the colors of the rainbow."

Douglas, who was sixty-one at the time, remembers

nothing more until he woke up the following morning. He knew immediately that what had happened in the night was not a dream, and when one of the nurses came into his room she confirmed that he had been very ill in the early hours of the morning, and that the medical team had worked hard to revive him.

"I did not feel any fear during the whole experience: I knew that these three beings were there to help me. I did not recognize any of them, but there was a very comforting, familiar feeling about them."

Even at the time it was happening, Douglas "knew" he was not going to die: "I did not feel that they had come to take me. I know it sounds silly, but I thought afterwards that if they had intended me to go with them they would have had wings—I don't really know why. I knew I would survive."

It was not only the feeling that came from his three visitors that made Douglas sure that he would live: he had had an earlier experience in 1990. "It was before my leukemia was diagnosed. I was ill with a virus, and my doctor could not find out what was wrong with me. I had tests at the hospital, but they were inconclusive. I was feeling really rotten."

Lying in bed at his home in Edinburgh, Douglas was unable to sleep. Suddenly his bedroom was filled with a diffuse light, and he saw himself, dressed in his usual clothes, walk across the room towards the bed.

"I knew straightaway it was myself. I was wearing a very familiar outfit: brown slacks, a brown polo-neck sweater, and a jerkin. The light, which was bluish-white, was going stronger and weaker—not exactly flashing, but changing in intensity. I saw this figure of myself walk straight over to my bed and stand there, and then it spoke, telling me that I was going to be very ill but that I was not to worry about it, as I would recover.

"I felt very calm while this was happening, and it did not seem at all strange until afterwards. The light faded and the figure went away, and I found I was soaking wet with perspiration, so much so that the bedclothes were wet, as if I had a very high fever, or as if I had just stepped out of the bath."

Douglas's illness persisted: he was off work for sixteen weeks with bronchitis, asthma, and angina. He assumed this was what the figure of himself who visited his bedside had been referring to. But in 1992 he found a small lump beneath his groin which did not respond to ten days of antibiotic treatment. When it was surgically removed it was discovered to be malignant, and non-Hodgkin's lymphoma was diagnosed. The first attempt to treat it was not successful, but the second series of chemotherapy treatment has worked, and Douglas has been given the all clear. It was during this second course of treatment that he floated away from his body and saw the three beings.

Douglas, who has never been married, is not afraid of death: "I believe there is another life after death. I was very close to my mother, who died in 1957, and I look forward to being reunited with her. She was psychic: she was very sensitive to things, she had premonitions that came true and she had telepathy with me. Although I've never seen her since she died, I've sensed her presence, particularly when I have been very ill.

"I think the beings who appeared to me were sent to give me the courage to keep on with the struggle against my illness. Since then I have learnt to appreciate life more: I take every day as it comes, and I'm grateful to have so many good friends."

David Tobin had a really bad sore throat. He'd been feeling completely under the weather, coughing, shivering, and sneezing, but it was his throat that was causing the most

problems. It was red raw and sore: he couldn't eat and
could only sip warm liquids. But, like most addicted smok-
ers, he didn't give up cigarettes—and it was nearly the
death of him.

"Apparently the lining of my throat had come away,
leaving it open and red raw. The nicotine from the cigarettes was able to get into my bloodstream, and nicotine
poisoning can be fatal. I was later told that I was within a
few minutes of death by the time the ambulance got me to
hospital, where they gave me a blood transfusion."

David, who was forty-six when he was taken ill in 1992,
was then living with his girlfriend Sue, now his wife. When
he became very ill she called the doctor.

"I have been ill before, but on this occasion I knew, deep
down, that I was very, very ill. I sensed that I was close to
death. The doctor was puzzled about what was causing it,
but he knew I was in a dangerous condition and he went
downstairs to call an ambulance. While he was away Sue
sat on my bed, holding my tongue down to stop me choking
on it. I could hear her talking about what the doctor was
doing, and, strangely, I could hear my own heart beating,
although I could not feel it. Suddenly I found myself surrounded by mist, and I was way up high, looking down on
myself on the bed, with Sue sitting there. There was no
sensation of floating away: I was just transported to this
place, and I knew I was way above where the ceiling would
be, although I had no feeling of passing through it. I was
about fifteen feet higher than the ceiling, so I was well over
twenty feet above the bed. There was mist all around, and
I could not see anything except the bed below, with a very
small figure on it, and another sitting on it.

"Then I saw a tunnel that seemed to run from the bedroom wall, above the bed, on to a great distance. It was
like looking down a single hair that has been magnified
millions of times: very rough but not jagged. The only other

comparison I can think of is looking down a vacuum-cleaner tube. There was a light at the end of it, which I sensed was a long way off. It was very bright but it did not hurt my eyes.

"Just inside the tunnel, as I started to pass through it, was my mum, who had been dead for two years at the time. She was telling me not to go towards the light, as it was too early for me. She was telling me to fight hard and go back, because I had lots to do yet. But I wanted to go to the light, and most of all I wanted to go to my mum, because I really miss her. I started to move down the tunnel very fast, at I would guess over one hundred miles per hour. But she was moving away from me even faster, facing me and still talking to me. I got close enough to the end of the tunnel to see a gate, a steel-bar gate, which I knew was a barrier between this time and somewhere else. The image of my mum began to fade into the light and eventually I could not see her anymore, and I remember feeling very sad.

"But then, almost with a click, I was back in the bed, clinging to Sue and crying like a baby. I was fighting for breath, yet I felt happy and sad at the same time. Seeing Sue was like being reunited with someone you love after you haven't seen them for years, although I'd only been unconscious for a few seconds. I was later told that I 'died' twice, when my heart stopped beating, each time for just a few seconds. I rushed into hospital in an ambulance with the blue light flashing and the siren going."

Since his NDE, David feels even closer to his mother than he did before. When she was alive, he believes she was psychically linked to him: when he was serving in the RAF in Malaya he was badly wounded, and his mother had rung his CO and astonished the officer by asking what was wrong with him before he had even been brought back into camp, and before details of his wounds were known.

"At any time of trouble, from being a child onwards, I always thought of my mother, and I think she was able to know when I was thinking of her. I have sensed her presence near me many times since her death. My father died two years before she did, yet I have never felt him come back to me—even though I loved him just as much."

David is a keen photographer, and spends hours setting his pictures up to get them right. Two months before his father died, he asked his dad to give his mom a hug, and took an instant shot without any preparation. It turned out to be the best photograph he has ever taken.

"I normally check the light, pose everybody, take it seriously. But it was always difficult to get Dad and Mum in pictures, so I seized the opportunity, clicked off one frame, and when it was developed it was so sharp you could see every thread in Dad's pullover. I have it in my bedroom in a frame, it's a perfect picture. It's as though I was meant to have one of them."

David believes that seeing his mother in the tunnel was a sign that she approved of his relationship with Sue, who is a bar manager. The two of them had been boyfriend and girlfriend in their teenage years, but had split up and both married other people. When their marriages ended they bumped into each other again, and thirty years after their first relationship ended, they married.

"I love Sue dearly, and now I feel that I have Mum's blessing," said David, a delivery driver. Between them the couple, who live in Ipswich, have five children and several grandchildren. "I now understand why she was sending me back: it was so that I could find happiness with Sue. At the time I did not know what she meant about me having more to do, but I now feel it was for Sue. I feel Mum saying, 'Yes, she is good for you.'

"If death comes to me tomorrow I will not be afraid, although I will be sad to leave Sue. But I had such a strong feeling that beyond that gate was something beautiful, and that my mum was there. I shall be quite happy to go.''

Nella Parminter's youngest son was given his name, Simon Peter, as a result of her NDE. Nella, from Dunster, Somerset, was pregnant when she went to a dentist—not her regular one—to have a broken tooth removed.

She was given gas as an anesthetic, and went to sleep easily enough. Suddenly she found herself floating up a tunnel. It was dark, but there was just enough faint light for her to see the tunnel walls as she moved along. She felt happy and relaxed and towards the end of the tunnel on her right side she could see a light. It looked to Nella like a large, well-lit doorway, and the feeling coming from it was warm and attractive.

But on her left side she saw something else entirely, something that she found quite frightening. There were twelve or more people, all wearing long black robes, standing around a table, their heads bent over it. She could not see their faces, nor could she see what was on the table, but she knew without being told that they were there to judge her life. She was sure they were a court, meeting to decide what would happen to her.

But before she could get to the table a white figure emerged from the hazy light on her right. He was also wearing long robes, but his were pure white. He was not close enough for Nella to make out his features, but she could sense he was a compassionate person. He spoke to her and he sounded slightly angry, as though he had not expected her to be there: ''Your time has not yet come. You go back there and tell them,'' he said.

Immediately Nella felt herself ''popping'' back into her own body. She felt a slight bump, nothing uncomfortable, but a definite feeling of going into herself again. She opened her eyes, and looked up into the faces of the dentist and his assistant.

"Apparently I had stopped breathing and my heart had stopped for a few seconds," said Nella, a widow with ten children. "The nurse asked me if I had a name for my baby, and at that moment I decided to call him Simon Peter. I do not know whether or not it was St. Peter who sent me back, but the name seemed right."

Nella, who was born in 1925, remembers the experience vividly, and although she found the presence of the black figures frightening, she was comforted by the peace and happiness she felt while she was floating in the tunnel: "Although it had one aspect that worried me, the rest of the experience was so lovely that I am not afraid of dying."

From the age of thirteen Frances Montague has had to cope with severe asthma attacks. She has to go to the hospital on average twice a year, and has several times found herself in the intensive care unit. The attacks used to worry her a great deal, but since having one particularly bad one in 1989, when she was thirty-five, Frances has learned to accept them.

The difference between this attack and the other acute ones she has suffered was the near-death experience she had, an experience which has changed her attitude to life and death. Frances, who is a part-time auxiliary nurse, had had a "flu" injection twenty-four hours earlier, and she believes this may have made the attack more aggressive than normal. When she was taken ill she followed her usual routine, but it was clear that she was not going to recover spontaneously and she was rushed into Torbay Hospital by her husband Gerald, a driver. The couple, who live in Brixham, have two grown-up children.

"All I remember is a great pain, almost unbearable, in

my chest. The next thing I knew I was walking down a tunnel towards a bright light at the end. I can't describe the brilliance of the light, because there are no words for it. It is nothing like the light we see around us every day. I felt very peaceful and happy, and I had a deep longing to go into the light.

"But at the same time I could hear a voice telling me to go no further, but to turn round and go back. I said that I did not want to, I wanted to go on. I carried on towards the light, which seemed to be throwing out a feeling of love towards me. But the voice kept telling me to go back. It annoyed me. And then suddenly I felt an almighty jolt, and at the same moment I felt a tremendous pain at the back of my neck. I woke up and I was hysterical, fighting off the doctor who was trying to hold a mask over my face to help me breathe. The doctor was shouting at me to keep it on. The pain in my neck and head was terrifying, and I screamed out about it. Then I must have passed out, because my next recollection is of waking up in the intensive care unit, wired up to different machines."

The pain in Frances's neck had subsided, although from that day onwards she has felt occasional twinges in it. Despite many other emergency trips to the hospital, she has never had another NDE.

"But whenever I have been in intensive care, I have felt that there is someone with me, looking after me. I found the whole experience very comforting: I am no longer terrified of having an asthma attack. I know that all the pain will go away, and I will be able to go into that beautiful light, forever, without any worries or cares. It is something to look forward to, not to be afraid of. Perhaps because I am no longer afraid of my asthma I find it easier to handle, I can manage my attacks more successfully."

• • •

Like Frances Montague, Dorothy Frape experienced only the first stages of an NDE, but it was a powerful experience that she remembers clearly, even though it happened in 1978. Dorothy, from Swindon, was rushed into hospital with a very high temperature. She was suffering from kidney stones, and she had triggered her acute illness by lifting heavy objects at the supermarket where she worked as a supervisor.

"There were trays of dog food that had to be lifted on to the shelves, and nobody else was doing it so I got on with it," said Dorothy, who was forty-four at the time. "That weekend I was very ill, in great pain and alternating between shivering and being boiling hot."

By Monday morning Dorothy was so ill that she was taken to the hospital, where it was later discovered that she had two very large kidney stones blocking her system and causing septicemia, or blood poisoning. She was so ill on admittance that she was no longer fully aware of what was happening around her, but as her temperature soared she can remember a doctor saying that if it went up by one more degree she would be dead.

At that moment, Dorothy felt her mattress rise off the bed and float to the ceiling, carrying her on it. "I was floating towards the door, because beyond the door I could see a wonderful clear light. I was in a room on my own, and when this happened there was nobody else there. I floated up and towards the right-hand corner of the ceiling, because the door was in the right-hand corner of the room. I wanted to pass through it into the light, but instead I turned and looked down at myself. I saw myself on the bed with tubes coming out of me, and at that moment I had a strong feeling of not wanting to go. I flung my arm out to try to stop the mattress and to get back to myself."

It worked, because at that moment Dorothy found herself

back on the bed, having flung her arm out in reality, knocking over her drip and a large jug of water at the bedside. The room immediately filled with medical staff who went to work trying to reduce her temperature: she was literally packed in ice, "like something out of the Bird's Eye factory." When her temperature came down, Dorothy started to feel a little better. Her husband Graham, a gamekeeper, was told that she had been lucky to survive, and that she must be a fighter.

After a week, Dorothy was a little better and went home. She returned to have a special X ray, which showed up the stones, but doctors were unable to operate right away because she was still ill. She spent three months at home, under strict instructions not to lift anything heavy or do anything strenuous, and then she went back in to the hospital to have the stones surgically removed. Since then, Dorothy, who has two grown-up children, has been in the hospital for other operations: she has had her appendix removed, and has been operated on for breast cancer.

"But I've never had that experience again. I know that it was very pleasant, and I certainly feel more relaxed about the idea of dying now. I was enjoying it: the only thing that made me want to come back was the sight of myself looking so poorly, with all those tubes and wires coming from me. I'm sure I was on my way out that night, and I would have been able to go if I had not changed my mind about it."

Gloria Woodward's recovery from a very serious medical condition has baffled doctors, but Gloria attributes it all to an NDE she had when, blind and paralyzed, she was expecting to be dead within days. Gloria, who lives in Connecticut, had a growth on her thyroid which meant the gland had to be removed—what is medically termed a radical thyroidectomy. The operation is quite common, and the vast majority of those who have it live full, healthy lives, although they sometimes need daily doses of medication to compensate for reduced amounts of the hormone manufactured by the thyroid gland. Gloria, tragically, was one of the very few patients ever known to have an adverse reaction to the medication. The daily dosage was slowly poisoning her system, but its effects had been far-reaching by the time doctors identified the cause, six years after the operation. Then she was told that there was nothing they could do to reverse the damage: she had a degenerative condition which would inexorably work through her body, damaging the tissue, until eventually she would die.

By 1976, when she was forty years old, Gloria's condition was critical. She was confined to a wheelchair, although she could shuffle about her own home on her bottom, hauling herself to and from the bathroom when necessary. For eighteen months her temperature had been at 101 degrees Fahrenheit, defying all attempts to bring it down. She was completely blind, and spent much of her time in a catatonic state, unable to take in what was going on around her.

Her husband Charles and a friend who lived nearby did everything for her, and she was reconciled to death—even, in one of her lucid times, making the plans for her own funeral and arranging for her body to be donated to the University of Connecticut for medical research.

"The doctors used phrases like 'nonreversible condition' and 'progressive degeneration' and I would think, 'Why can't you just be honest and say the word, dying?' At the University of Connecticut Hospital, they phoned all around the world to see if any medical team anywhere had been able to help someone with my rare condition, and when the doctor came to tell me the results of this research I said, 'Tell me the truth.' He replied that nothing could be done."

One night while she was feeling very ill, Gloria opened

her eyes and, although she was blind, found herself bathed
in a beautiful light. She knew that the light was God. "I
experienced God, rather than seeing him. I felt his power
and love in that light. I gained what I can only call a know-
ingness, as though suddenly I understood everything. I became aware that God was and is everything that ever was
and is. God was in the air I was breathing, the power of
his love was everywhere around me. These things have
been said and written before, and I was brought up in the
Roman Catholic faith, so I had read my Bible and knew all
the teachings, but until that moment I had not understood
it, not at a deep down fundamental level. I had not known
God before.

"I stayed with him for maybe minutes, and he spoke to
me by name. He told me many things. He said, 'Gloria, I
can allow you to finish your life right now, or you can have
another chance. Which would you choose?' I can remember
thinking, 'Why is God giving me a choice? He is God, he
is all-powerful, why is he letting me decide?' I told him
that I accepted whatever he chose for me. Just after that I
went back into that very ill place where I had been living
so long. I felt lifted up, because of the experience, but physically I was still very bad."

From time to time Gloria would suffer from internal
bleeding, and be taken to the hospital for blood transfusions. Two weeks after her NDE she hemorrhaged at home
and was taken by ambulance to the hospital. But her usual
hospital, where she was being treated by specialists who
knew her case, was full and could not take her, so the
ambulance was diverted to another, nearer, hospital. There,
a surgeon, unaware of Gloria's medical condition, decided
to operate to stop her bleeding.

"When he opened me up, he found several tumors in my
abdomen. He removed them. When I came around from the
anesthetic it was as though I had left the twilight zone. I

actually felt better, even though I had just had major surgery, than I had felt for years. I recovered faster than the average recuperation time, which was phenomenal considering how ill I had been. The paralysis went, I was alert and conscious and, most astonishing of all, I was no longer blind. The eye specialists were baffled, because clinically I should not be able to see: the degeneration of my tissue had caused the pigment in my eyes to pile up at the back, covering the optic nerve. Yet I could see.''

Three days later, Gloria's notes arrived at the hospital giving details of her critical condition. She was sitting up at a table eating a steak when three doctors and several nurses rushed into her ward with a drip and several flasks of red blood plasma.

''I thought somebody must be very ill, and I wondered who it could be. But they rushed up to me, and told me to get back into bed. They had just discovered how ill I was. I told them how tremendous I felt, although I must say the sight of all that blood put me off my steak. They were astonished.''

A whole battery of tests was carried out on Gloria, but no explanation was ever given to her for her miraculous recovery. She was told that all the tissue disease, which had invaded almost all of her body, had cleared. Her body was also found to have normal levels of thyroxine, the hormone produced by the thyroid gland, and she no longer needed the hormone supplements which had originally proved so toxic to her. To this day she continued to have ''textbook normal'' amounts of thyroxine in her body.

While she has been given no medical explanation for her recovery, Gloria herself accepts that it was a direct result of her NDE. She believes God chose for her, and chose a continued life. For eight years she was physically well, but since 1984 she has been coping with very high blood pressure.

Immediately after the NDE, Gloria moved away from her Christian roots to a more pantheistic spiritual life, believing that God transcends all organized religion. "With my church background I would have expected to meet Jesus when I had my NDE, but it was, I think, a more universal God than that, I felt no sense that he was a God for the Christians or for any other group. He was just everything."

She was drawn towards the teachings of Sathya Sai Baba, an Indian guru who has reputedly performed miracles, and who has attracted a large following across the world and across all cultural and religious backgrounds, and conducted workshops with other followers. "I had a very powerful relationship with God for eight years, and I felt he was telling me to share what had happened to me with others, and that through me they would get spiritual healing. There was no earthly reason for my life to continue in 1976, so when God breathed life back into me it must have been for a purpose.

"Then, after eight years, I began to have health problems, and I have had trouble coming to terms with other aspects of my life: I had a very unhappy childhood. But God has never left me, and occasionally I have a strong spiritual experience when he reminds me that he is still with me."

One casualty of Gloria's rapid recovery was her relationship with Charles, and the couple are now divorced. "He looked after me so well when I was very ill, but I don't think he was prepared for my recovery, or for the change in my spirituality. It freaked him out. In the end, we had nothing left in common unless he was willing to also transform himself spiritually, and we split up."

Sue Adams was in the hospital with pneumonia, a complication of emphysema, a chronic lung condition from which she had suffered for most of her adult life. It was

1989, and Sue was forty years old. The hospital staff were so worried about her condition that they contacted her husband Alan and told him to come in right away to sit with her.

"I did not actually feel that ill," said Sue, who lives in York. "I had been in hospital so many times before, and I had felt much worse than I did this time. Alan was sitting next to me, holding my hand, but I was quite conscious.

"Suddenly I had a lovely feeling. I could breathe quite freely for the first time in ages. My chest pains vanished. I felt fitter than I had for years: I had quite forgotten what it was like to feel so good, to have normal breathing. I could feel great gulps of air going into my lungs, and I felt as though an enormous obstruction had been removed.

"I wasn't in the hospital ward any more, but on a beach looking out to sea. The sea was a beautiful blue, the sort of color you see in holiday brochures but never in real life. The horizon seemed very close, and on it there was the most lovely light, a warm, glowing white light that filled the sky. I had a strong feeling that I could walk across the water to the light: not wade through it, but walk on top of it. I could see other people standing in the light, and they appeared to be standing on top of the water, too. I could see them beckoning to me, and I wanted to go and join them. They were not close enough for me to recognize any of their faces, but I was convinced I knew them and they knew me. There was something very familiar about them, something very comforting. I really wanted to be with them. They were wearing very brightly colored clothes: the colors were vivid, and I can remember them much more than I can remember the style of the clothes, except that I know they were modern everyday styles. The light behind them made a sort of halo around them, and without being close enough to see their expressions I knew they were all happy.

"I can clearly remember saying to myself, 'This looks

lovely, shall I go?' I was about to take my first step on top
of the water when a feeling inside me said that I should
not go, that it was not right, that it was the wrong time. I
didn't hear a voice, not a human voice. It was simply a
knowledge that I had. The knowledge reminded me that I
had a husband and home, and as soon as I began to think
about those things I was instantly back in the hospital ward,
with Alan by my side, and two doctors and some nurses
crowding round putting an oxygen mask on my face and
giving me an injection. Alan told me afterwards that I had
slipped into unconsciousness and stopped breathing, but
only for a few seconds because the medical staff came very
quickly when he called them. He was later told that they
thought they had lost me, and they were apparently very
relieved when I started breathing again.

"My immediate feeling was one of great disappointment.
I wanted to be back on that lovely sunny beach, to see that
lovely scenery again, to feel the pull of that glowing light. I
lay there wondering why I had allowed myself to come back,
and I knew that if I hadn't thought about Alan and our home
I'd have been able to go. I feel absolutely confident that I
would have been able to walk across that water."

Sue has been ill several times since, but has never had a
repeat of the experience: "I am not at all frightened of
dying anymore. I used to feel afraid when my breathing
became so bad that I had to go into hospital, but now I feel
that death will be lovely, when it comes. I don't want to
leave Alan, of course, but I've been able to reassure him.
I've told him that although he will obviously be upset,
when I die he must remember that I have gone to a very
happy, lovely place.

"I'm a Christian anyway, so I always believed in heaven.
But until you have experienced something like that you
cannot really have any idea what it is like. I tell people
what happened to me, but I know that nobody can appre-

ciate it, because I do not have the words to do justice to it. Whenever I think about it I get a feeling of comfort and warmth—not as strong as when I was on that beach, but strong enough for me never to forget or underestimate what happened to me.''

Two years later Sue sat with her own mother when she died: ''Before my NDE I would not have wanted to be at a deathbed, I would have been petrified. But I felt quite at ease with it, and I think me being so relaxed perhaps helped her. She was very involved with her family and believed that none of us would manage without her, and up to a week or so before her death she was worrying about us all. But when the day finally came she seemed very happy. She was unconscious for a few hours before she died, but just before she died she opened her eyes and there was a slight smile on her face. I was thinking, 'You're all right now, Mum, you've seen what I've already seen, and you're lucky enough to be going there.' I knew all her pain and suffering would slip away. I can't say I was positively happy that she died because I miss her so much, but I know that the suffering is mine, not hers.''

One moment Pat Crossling was leaning back on the sofa, telling her husband Barry that she did not feel well. The next she was floating peacefully through a dark tunnel, all her worries and illness left behind. The tunnel was swirling around her, but she was traveling calmly and easily down the middle of it. She knew that she was going to see her father, who had died when she was a young child, and she could sense his presence all around her, although she could not see him.

''My dad was waiting for me at the end of the tunnel, and I really wanted to get there and join him,'' said Pat, who lives in Hartlepool. ''I could not see the end: there was no bright light. But I could feel it drawing nearer, and the beautiful feeling of calm and peace was growing stronger.''

Then Pat's journey down the tunnel faltered. She paused to think about her two teenage daughters, and for a few seconds she hung there, torn between going forward to her dad or back to her family. She can remember thinking that she could not leave Melanie and Cheryl, and instantly she was back on the sofa in her own living room. Melanie, who was seventeen at the time in 1989, was standing over her, shouting, ''Mum, Mum, you're going to be all right, Mum.'' Soon afterwards, an ambulance arrived to take Pat to the hospital. As the ambulance personnel were lifting her on to a stretcher trolley, Pat floated away from her body and hovered above, watching them wheeling her to the ambulance. She could see the men talking to her, but could not make out what they were saying.

Once in the ambulance the sensation of being above herself continued. She knew that one of the men was working hard trying to keep her awake. ''He kept asking the same questions over and over again, questions about whether I had taken any medication, what sort of things I had been doing that day, that sort of thing. This time I could hear him, but I could not answer because I was above myself, looking down. I felt very irritated by him, because I wanted to be allowed to go back to sleep because I really believed that I would go back down the tunnel and find my father. Although it was thoughts of my family that had brought me back, at that moment I would willingly have given anything for another chance to be there. The feeling was indescribable. It was just so incredibly peaceful.''

Pat was kept in the hospital for four days, but no real explanation was found for her passing out. She had an ear infection at the time, but that was ruled out as a cause. She had also suffered a bad migraine the day before, but that, too, was discounted. In the end, her own doctor told her that her body had probably just shut down because she was under so much stress.

"There was quite a lot of worry in my life at that time. I had two teenage daughters, and I had a responsible and stressful job as deputy matron of a residential home for the elderly. I think everything was just getting on top of me."

On the day of her NDE—a Friday the thirteenth—Pat had been feeling unwell at work. From time to time she got the sensation that she might black out, but on each occasion she was back to normal after a few seconds. "I was too busy to ring the doctor, and told myself that I probably just needed a good night's sleep. I drove home after work, but could not focus on the road properly. Luckily I reached home safely, and then fell asleep on the sofa. When I woke up I had a strange, heavy feeling in my head, and I was just telling Barry that I didn't feel well when I passed out and found myself in the tunnel.

"Barry ran to call the ambulance, and my two daughters—Cheryl was thirteen at the time—were very worried, so Melanie shouted to try and wake me up. Whether her voice made me aware of them, and think about them, and that drew me back, I don't know. If it had not been for the girls, who are the center of my life, I would not have wanted to return, I'm sure, because I knew I was going somewhere very beautiful. But I remembered how young they were, and I knew they needed me.

"Afterwards I told my mum that I had felt my dad's presence, and she believed me."

It took Pat a year to recover fully from her physical breakdown, but she believes the effects of the NDE will go with her forever: "I have a much more laid-back attitude to life. I'm so laid-back now I might fall over. I believe life's too brief to waste time worrying about trivial things. I hear friends and colleagues going on about little things and I think, 'What the heck, life's too short. You might be dead tomorrow, so what's the point of getting steamed up?' I feel more confident, too: there's nothing I would be afraid of trying to do.''

"I've changed my job. I'm working with adults who have learning difficulties, which is still stressful work, but I have fewer responsibilities. I don't have the management worries that I had before.

"I told everyone about my experience straightaway, and the majority of people believed me. The doctor looked at me as though I was mad and made no comment about it, but other people have all wanted to know. Nobody else has treated me as though I'm a crank. I believed in life after death before, but I didn't think about it much. Now I know it is there. I know my dad will be there to greet me when I do eventually die, and I find that a very comforting thought.''

Roy Shackleford's near-death experience helped him to come to terms with the tragic death of one of his daughters in a motorcycle accident. It was his own knowledge of the peaceful and pain-free process of dying that enabled him to accept the terrible loss of his thirty-nine-year-old daughter Janet.

"Death at any age comes as a shock, but when it is someone as young as Janet, and when it is unexpected, it is much harder to cope with,'' said Roy, who was sixty-nine at the time of Janet's death in July 1994. She was riding her bike with a party of other motorcycling enthusiasts in Ireland when she had the accident, and her death left three young children motherless.

Roy was comforted by the words of the vicar who, at Janet's funeral, pointed out that she died doing something she wanted to do, and that many people go through life without ever having the opportunity to do the things they would most dearly like to. He was also comforted by clear memories of his own brush with death eleven years earlier, when a severe asthma attack nearly cost him his life.

Roy had suffered from asthma all his life, but it was the shock of being laid off from his job with the local government that triggered the worst attack he had ever had. He was rushed into the hospital, where his breathing stopped.

"Suddenly the room was filled with a gentle mauve-colored mist, and I was sitting up on the rafters close to the ceiling, looking down on myself in the intensive care unit. I wondered why the nurses were around my body, and it looked very odd because there were tubes sticking out of it in several places. I was puzzled by it. But it seemed quite natural to be up near the roof looking down, and there was a wonderful feeling of peace, calm, and relaxation. All the panic of the attack had gone away, and I felt really well."

Roy does not remember any more until he woke up. He asked one of the nurses to contact his daughter—and was told that his daughter had been at his bedside several times since the attack. He also realized what the tubes were that he had seen: he was wired up to a life-support machine which was helping him breathe, a heart monitor, and other equipment, and there was a drip in his arm.

After he recovered Roy, who lives in Carlisle, Cumbria, found his whole attitude to life profoundly changed. He had been very worried about the prospect of losing his job, but he decided to make the best of his early retirement: "I became much more relaxed in my outlook, and that seemed to give me a lot more energy and enthusiasm."

He took over the development of the Cumbria Association of Youth Clubs, and upped membership from about a dozen to 130 clubs. He organized events to raise the £7,000 needed to equip a caravan with arts and crafts projects for young people, and for a couple of years was actively involved in helping to run the Duke of Edinburgh's award program. More ill health has forced him to cut back on his commitments. "But I'm still more active than I have been for years. I go dancing, I go on holidays I never dreamt I would take, I live each day as it comes and I make the most of it. It is as though I was given a second chance on condition I made the most of it, so that's what I am doing."

Roy was understandably shattered by his daughter Janet's tragic accident. He has two other much-loved children, but felt particularly close to Janet because, as a child, she was the one who had inherited his asthma problem, and he sat up with her in the nights when she was struggling for breath.

"I am not a deeply religious man, but my own NDE made me very aware that there is a life after this one. When I saw Janet after her death, I could see from her face that she was at peace. I remembered the beautiful feeling I had when I was looking down on myself in the intensive care unit, and I know that's what she is experiencing. It certainly helps.

"I'm not afraid of death for myself when it comes. It is always sad for those who are left behind, but I believe that for the person who is dying it is not frightening or terrible. It is peaceful and wonderful."

It was a very rare illness that caused Maureen Daniels to be rushed into the hospital. Maureen, who was twenty-three at the time, was suffering from chronic paroxysmal hermicrania, a strange condition which sends signals to the brain that the body is in pain when there has been no injury or cause for pain. The result was that Maureen, a childcare worker from Idaho Falls, Iowa, was often crippled by acute pain, even though there was no physical cause.

In August 1983 she was rushed to the hospital doubled up in agony, and was given a morphine injection to help combat it. She collapsed. As doctors battled to save her, all her pain receded.

"There was a calming sound—it wasn't exactly music, it was more like the noise of waves lapping on the seashore. And there was a feeling of brightness and being surrounded by love. Approaching me from the front were my grandparents. My grandfather had died in 1968, and my grandmother had died three months before I was rushed to the hospital. My granddad was wearing his straight-legged trousers with cuffs, and my grandmother was in a housecoat type of dress. I knew it was them, although they did not look as old as they had when they died. They walked very upright, with no arthritis or wrinkles. They didn't embrace me, but I felt embraced by them.

"My granddad was telling my grandmother that I couldn't stay in their world. Although she was very excited to see me, my grandmother finally said, 'He's right, it's not your time, but we will see you again.' "

The next thing she knew, Maureen, who is married with one child, was back in the hospital being given mouth-to-mouth resuscitation. Medical experts have since suggested that her NDE was a hallucination triggered by the large amount of morphine she received, but she rejects this idea: "What happened was real, more real than this life. There is no question for me: it took place, it happened. I can't say I'm looking forward to death, because I have plenty to live for, but I know that when I do go, my grandparents will be there waiting for me."

Chapter 12

THE LIGHT SHINES
FOR CHILDREN

Children are the best witnesses of NDEs. Their minds are uncluttered: they don't know that what is happening to them is something that other people will regard as odd. They have never heard or read about other people's NDEs. They don't try to explain them away as hallucinations, or the result of any drugs they are being given: their clear, unprejudiced minds accept them for what they are, and the memory of them remains for the rest of their lives.

American pediatrician Dr. Melvin Morse, who has studied NDEs in children, found that they are more willing to believe their experiences than adults: "Children are filled with wonder without a lot of interpretation. I think we can get to the essence of the near-death experience through them."

The people whose stories are told in this chapter all had their NDEs when they were children, and for some of them that was many years ago. Yet all can recount them with great clarity, while they admit that other childhood memories have faded. For many of them, the effects of the experience are as enduring as the memory: they still feel their lives intangibly altered by their brush with death, and by their evidence of a life beyond this one.

Jonathan Saul astonished his mother Janet by announcing that he could remember his own birth. But from his description of the experience, Janet believes that what Jonathan actually remembers was not the start of his life, but an experience that very nearly marked the end of it.

Jonathan, who was born in 1980, made his startling announcement when he was twelve. His father, Ray, had been involved in a car accident and was in the hospital suffering from a concussion. Janet was at home with her two sons, Jonathan and his younger brother Matthew, who was ten. Friends had called at their home in Coventry to see if Janet was coping all right after the shock of hearing of Ray's accident, and the conversation led from concussion on to general functions of the brain, including memory. It was at this juncture that Jonathan said he could recall what he thought was his own birth.

He described traveling along a tunnel into a garden where there were lots of other children sitting around, drinking and playing. He said they glowed in the light, and described them as "a bit like fairies." He saw their faces very clearly, and although they were not the faces of any children he knew, he had a feeling of recognizing them. There was something familiar about them all. The whole scene was bathed in a bright light, the same light he had seen as he traveled down the tunnel. He talked for some time, describing the scene and particularly trying to get across to his mother the feeling he had about the faces of the children. He also said he felt relaxed and peaceful.

Janet was amazed and baffled by Jonathan's story, until she heard about NDEs and realized that he was describing a classic one. She immediately surmised that his memory was more likely rooted in the time when, at two and a half years old, he nearly died, rather than when he was born: he had had a perfectly normal birth.

Both Jonathan and Matthew suffer from asthma, and when he was little Jonathan had several severe attacks. His condition was well known to the medical staff at the local hospital, and Janet used to rush him there whenever she was unable to cope with his attack at home. "I'd become very efficient at treating him with Ventolin given through a nebulizer, but there were always times when the treatment just did not seem to work and he needed to go into hospital,'' she said.

On the day that Jonathan came close to death, his father Ray was away taking a class and Janet was at home with her small son. She could tell that the attack was a bad one, so she called the hospital to alert them to the fact that she was on her way with Jonathan. The call was usually a formality, but on this occasion an officious member of staff told Janet that her son could only be admitted at the request of a doctor. This was the correct procedure, but the hospital had always previously been prepared to bypass it.

It was a weekend, and it took a while for a doctor to appear at Janet's home. All the time Jonathan's condition worsened, so that by the time he was eventually taken to the hospital he was limp and unconscious. Janet was terrified that he was dying.

"He seemed to be completely gone. I just could not rouse him and nor could the hospital staff at first. It was a dreadful time, but I was always able to console myself that Jonathan had no memory of it. But I think now that he does, and the good thing is that it is a happy memory."

After a few minutes in the hospital Jonathan did regain consciousness and began to get better. Although he and his brother have both had bad attacks since, neither has ever been as ill as Jonathan was on that day.

Janet—now divorced from Ray, who survived his concussion with no lasting ill-effects—describes her son as a typical teenage boy: "He is into football, football, and more football. He loves all sports. He's bright and imaginative, but the story of going through the tunnel is not the sort of thing he would make up. He believes it happened—and so do I."

• • •

When Denise Kerry was seven years old she was rushed into Doncaster Gate Hospital for an emergency appendix operation. But although doctors removed her appendix, it was too late to prevent the onset of peritonitis, a serious condition which can be caused by the appendix rupturing. Poisons from the bowel leak into the stomach, and without emergency treatment can result in death within twenty-four hours. Denise was very ill, and was kept in the hospital, which in 1966 was a general hospital, for five months. After a second operation Denise was unconscious for weeks.

"I remember being taken down to the operating theater, and then the anesthetic worked and I was asleep. But suddenly I came back. I could see myself on the operating table with doctors and nurses rushing around me. I was up on the ceiling, looking down at my own body. I didn't appear to have a body up there, I was transparent, but it was definitely the real me and I was aware of having a shape. The body that was on the operating table was somehow connected to me, I knew it was me, but it was not the important 'me.' That was up on the ceiling.

"I could hear a nurse shouting my name, and she was holding something that looked like a rugby ball against my face—it was presumably a mask for me to breathe through. As I was watching them all panic I felt very calm and unworried. I looked sideways, towards a very bright light, and I could see an avenue of trees with green fields either side.

"I remember thinking that it looked like Paris, although I had never been there. I've been since, but never seen anything like this. It was like a long causeway lined with trees running through a park, and there were park benches at either side, although there were no people.

"The light was coming from the end of the avenue of

trees. It was very bright, but gentle, and I felt myself being drawn towards it. I started to move down the avenue of trees but I could hear the nurse shouting my name, and I suddenly felt frightened. Up to that moment I had felt wonderful, but the second the fear came I was back inside my own body, the vision had gone, and I don't remember anything else."

Denise's memories of her experience remain clear and sharp, even though she has forgotten a lot of other details about her long stay in the hospital. She was first taken in the week before Christmas, and on Christmas Day she was very sick, with tubes coming out of her nose. It was two days later that she had the second operation, and she was unconscious over the New Year holiday. "You would think a child would be more likely to remember a horrible Christmas like that than anything else. But the only part of it that remains as fresh as if it happened yesterday was the feeling of being on the ceiling and looking down the avenue."

Denise's mother was told that her daughter was lucky to have survived the operation. It wasn't until years later, when she was a teenager, that Denise shared her experience with her family: "I told some school friends and they laughed at me, and I realized it sounded stupid. So I shut up about it. But eventually I told my mum and dad, who were understanding about it."

Her husband David, an offshore oil-rig worker, remains skeptical. But Denise, who lives with David and their son Sean, who was born in 1984, says she believes "100 percent" in an afterlife. "I don't know that I would describe it as heaven, or what it is. But something happens after death, we don't just fade away. And I'm convinced that I had a glimpse of it, that if I had gone through that avenue of trees and into that light I would never have come back. It was not a frightening experience, although at the last minute I think I was frightened at the thought of going away from my family. But if the nurse hadn't brought all that back to me by shouting my name, I would have gone happily. It makes it easier to cope with death.''

Denise and her family had to cope with the death of her brother Steven, who drowned at the age of twenty while he was serving with the army in Germany. Denise was ten years old when the tragic accident happened.

"While my mother and father were away in Germany making the arrangements after his death, I slept in their bed. During the night, at about four A.M., Steven popped his head around the door and asked where our brother Stuart was. It all seemed so natural and real, he was wearing a T-shirt and jeans just like he did when he was home on leave. He said to me, 'Go back to sleep.' I thought nothing about it until the next day, but like the NDE it was so clear in my memory that I don't believe it was a dream.

"My mum and my brother Stuart also both saw Steven after his death. Stuart saw him the same night that I did, in the living room of our house in Maltby, near Rotherham, where there was a picture on the wall that my grandmother had painted. It was of a local park. Next to it was the budgie's cage, and the budgie suddenly started to make a lot of noise, then went completely quiet. Stuart looked across at its cage, and then saw the painting. Steven was walking up the lane in the picture, wearing his army uniform.

"Mum saw him the day after the funeral. It was one A.M., and she was in the kitchen washing her hair at the sink when he walked in, again wearing his uniform. She asked, 'What are you doing here?' and then he vanished.

"I don't think we are a particularly sensitive family, psychically. But Steven died very suddenly and unexpectedly, and I feel he needed to say good-bye to us all.''

For Denise, her own NDE helped her to come to terms

with the loss of her brother: "It has always been a comfort to me to know that death is a peaceful, happy experience, and that one day I will see Steven again."

In the famous "Narnia" chronicles by C. S. Lewis, the fantasy land for the children in the stories begins at the door of the wardrobe. For retired nurse Caroline Bloom, that is where her NDE started. And like the young fictional heroes and heroines who went through the wardrobe door, Caroline did not want to come back.

She was eleven when she became very ill with pleurisy and double pneumonia in 1930. In those days treatment for what was often a fatal condition was limited, and Caroline was being nursed by her mother in the family home at Streatham Hill in London. Although she was an active child normally, this was Caroline's third bout of pneumonia and her parents were very worried about her, as she was more ill than she had ever been. Every two hours the district nurse would call at the house to monitor her condition, and to help her mother apply poultices.

"I was in my parents' bed in their bedroom, and I felt myself get out of bed and cross the room to the wardrobe, which was a big, old-fashioned piece of furniture with huge heavy doors with mirrors, and when you opened the doors there was a chest of drawers inside. But on this occasion I was able to step straight inside, into a beautiful field where there were lots of other children making daisy chains. I was wearing a long white nightie, and so were they. There were lots of sheep and lambs in the field. I remember being shown how to thread a daisy chain by some of the children when one of them said, 'There's someone calling.' I said, 'Take no notice, it's my mother.' But the sound of her calling me persisted, and after a few moments I said to the other children, 'Oh, drat, I shall have to go.' I had a feeling that I needed to know what she wanted.

"The next thing that happened was that I opened my eyes and my mother was shaking me and calling me, over and over. She told me later that from the moment I opened my eyes she knew I was going to recover. But all I felt was terrible disappointment and I was very cross with her. I felt she had spoilt the super time I was having with the other children, and I was very resentful towards her for making me come back. It took a few years for me to realize how it was her wonderful nursing that saved my life."

Caroline then began a steady recovery. About a week later she was still being nursed in bed, but was well enough to climb out when her mother was out of the room busy with the housework.

"She had washed me and changed my sheets and she told me to lie down and rest. As soon as she was out of the room I got out of bed again and went across to the wardrobe. I wanted to go back to those children: it was all I had been able to think about since leaving them. Imagine my disappointment when it turned out to be just an ordinary wardrobe full of clothes and boxes. I could remember so vividly the smell of the meadow where I had played, yet all I could smell when I opened the door was the slightly musty odor of the clothes.

"I was so upset that I burst into tears, and I sobbed so loudly that my mother came dashing back into the room to see what was wrong. I told her what had happened, but she said it was just a dream. I know that it wasn't: it is the most vivid memory I have from my childhood."

The feeling that another world, a beautiful world, existed beyond the wardrobe persisted for Caroline. When she was twenty-three, she sat in the same room holding her mother's hand when her mother died, and she saw a happy smile spread over her mother's face in the minutes before her death. Once again, Caroline walked across the room and opened the wardrobe, half expecting to see again the meadow with sheep and smiling children.

"The logical part of me knew that it would not be there, but there was something about the way my mother smiled that made me believe that, like me, she was going somewhere lovely. I'm a very down-to-earth person, not someone who imagines things, and I've got a very practical outlook. But I'm convinced that what happened to me was real."

Caroline, who qualified as a registered nurse, was married to her husband John for fifty-two years until she was widowed in 1989. Although John and her daughter both accepted her account of her childhood experience, John believed it was better not to read too much into it. "But I have always found it a very comforting memory," says Caroline, who now lives in Arborfield, Berkshire. "I have complete faith that I will be united with him when I die, and that wherever we go after death is a happy place. There is nothing to fear."

For Joyce Wood, the lovely sights and feelings that she had during her NDE are as clear today as they were when she had it in 1941, when she was fourteen years old. Joyce was desperately ill with double pneumonia and pleurisy, and the family doctor had warned her mother that her condition was very grave. She was, he said, too ill to be moved, and, besides, the hospitals in Leeds, where she was living at the time, were overflowing with war casualties.

Instead of taking Joyce into the hospital, the doctor arranged for a specialist to visit her at home to perform an emergency operation to ease her breathing. The night before he was due to come, however, Leeds was blitzed. As the bombs were falling on the city, Joyce was facing a different kind of crisis: her life hung by a thread, and she traveled out of her own pain and suffering to a land of bright sunshine, flowers and trees and sweet music.

"I was alone in the bedroom when it began. I was lying in bed feeling very ill, and then suddenly it seemed like the most natural thing in the world for me to be traveling down a dark passageway towards a lovely bright light. There were bells ringing and sweet music playing, and as I came towards the end of the passageway I could see that beyond it there was a field full of trees and flowers, all bathed in a lovely sunny light.

"There were people walking around, wearing old-fashioned clothes. I saw my grandmother and grandfather, who I had lived with when I was small and who were both dead. They waved to me. I didn't recognize any of the other people, but I could see them all clearly. There was a very welcoming, peaceful look about the whole place.

"There was a golden gate across the end of the passageway, and I put my hand on to it, eager to open it and get through into the field. But I heard a voice telling me that it was not my time yet. Then the same voice, a man's voice, said I had to answer three questions, and that if I got them right I was going back. All my life since then I have tried to remember what the questions were, but I don't know. I did get them right though, and as I answered each one I went further back down the passageway, away from the light. The voice said, 'You have other things to do and your time is not now.' "

As she reached the dark end of the passage again, Joyce woke up and without warning was violently sick. The next morning, when the doctor came to perform the emergency operation, he decided he did not need to: Joyce had cleared the fluid and mucus from her lungs.

"He described it to my mother as a miracle, and told her

that the combination of double pneumonia and pleurisy usually ended in death.''

Joyce spent three months in bed altogether, but she made a complete recovery. Today Joyce, who has retired from her job as a quality controller with Grattons, the catalog firm, lives in Bradford, and has been married to her husband Robert, a war veteran, for over forty years. Robert, a retired television engineer, has always accepted her story of what happened to her as a child.

"I've been a Methodist for many years, so I've always believed that there was life after death. I feel privileged to have had the chance to see it, and I've never forgotten what that voice said about me having many things to do. I just hope I have done at least some of them, and done them well enough."

Later in the same year that she was so ill, Joyce sat by the bedside of her six-year-old brother when he died of diphtheria. "The look on his face as he got close to death, a kind of shining, bright look in his eyes and a relaxed expression, made me absolutely sure that he went through the gate into that beautiful field. It helped me cope with his death. Somehow, a year later, I had the strength and patience to nurse my mother and her newborn baby, another brother, when they were both desperately ill. I seemed to have the knowledge of what to do to help them, and I don't know where that came from, because I was very young. They both survived, my mum living until she was eighty-four. She, too, looked very happy and peaceful when she died.

"I know that we go through one door and into another when we die, and although I am obviously very upset and I grieve for those I love, I know that they are not suffering, they are happier than they have ever been. It is a great comfort and consolation.

"I don't want to leave my family, but I can still clearly

remember how much I wanted to go into that field, and how nice it was beyond that gate. It makes life all the more enjoyable, knowing that there is something so special to come afterwards.''

Chris Hughes was always a bit of a class clown at school. If there was a scrape to get into, he was first in line. He never did anything seriously wrong, but he was one of those schoolboys teachers despair of: always talking, never paying attention, showing off, leading others into trouble. But he was a likable lad, popular with the other kids and with the staff, despite his propensity for trouble. It was near the end of Chris's education at Gowerton Comprehensive School in Swansea that he got himself into a scrape that backfired—and could have had very serious consequences. As it was, Chris experienced an NDE which has stayed fresh in his memory since it happened in 1987.

''I was showing off, as usual, in front of a couple of girls. I was trying to impress them and amuse them, which was typical of me. It was in the afternoon and we were in an upstairs classroom which had big old windows with a swivel opening action. There was a rope to pull to open each window. I was messing about and put the rope around my neck and pretended I was hanging. It was such a stupid thing to do, when I look back, but at the time I would do anything for a laugh.''

Chris, who had been standing, suddenly slipped and fell, and what had been a bit of fun turned into a nightmare. He really was hanging from the rope, which only reached down to about two feet above the floor, and the cord had tightened around his neck.

''Instantly I was looking down at what was happening, from the ceiling. I could not see myself, but I saw lots of other kids crowded around, and a teacher I recognized, who

pulled me up off the floor to release the tension in the rope
and get it from round my neck. The scene was blurred, and
I could hear muffled voices far away, like listening to them
from underwater.

"The feeling was lovely. I was weightless and just floating above everything, quite content. Then I felt myself being yanked back into my body, as though I was being
sucked back violently through darkness. This part was
frightening, and I woke up on the floor, shouting and lash-
ing out. I passed out again for another few seconds, but
nothing happened this time."

Afterwards Chris was able to describe to his classmates
what he had seen from up above, correctly naming the
teacher who had removed the rope, even though by the time
he came around it was a different member of staff who was
with him. He was taken from school to his home in Pen-
clawdd, Swansea, where his mother, who was used to him
having accidents and being in trouble, told him off for being stupid enough to mess around with a rope around his
neck.

Chris, who is now a butcher, is still looking for adventure: he's tried parachute jumping and bungee jumping.
"I'm not afraid of anything, certainly not death. I know
that if I fell under a bus tomorrow I'd have a similar experience to the one I had at school, and it would be pleasant. I don't think life ends completely with death, although
I didn't have any vision of heaven with angels and harps
or anything. I just knew that it felt good to be out of my
own body, and I was aware that I wasn't in that body."

Chris has told a few people about his experience: "But
it's not the sort of thing you drop into conversation all the
time, because some people would think I was mad. Yet the
memory of it is still very clear to me. I'll never forget it."

• • •

Like Chris, Ian Thomson's NDE took him no farther than the ceiling of the room where the emergency happened, and like Chris he has perfect recall of what went on around his body—even though, in Ian's case, it happened in 1949.

Ian was twelve at the time, and in acute agony with appendicitis. His family was living in a farm cottage in Suffolk, and on the day of Ian's illness his dad was out working on the land and his brother was at school, leaving him at home with his mother. He was unable to get out of bed that morning because of the jabbing pains in his stomach and side, so she sent for the local doctor.

"The doctor felt my abdomen, and as he did that I seemed to leap from my body, and then I was up on the ceiling looking down. I was at the far end of the room above the wardrobe, floating with nothing to support me. There was no sense of fear or that it wasn't natural to be up there, although at the same time I remember wondering why I was there. I felt good, all the pain had gone away.

"I could look around the room and out of the door down the stairs to the stone-flagged kitchen. I couldn't see that from my bed. I watched the doctor on the right-hand side of the bed and my mother, who was holding my hand, on the left side. I could see my own shock of red hair on the pillow. I could see their mouths moving, but I could not hear what they were saying. I sensed that my life was ending, but I felt no sorrow or worry.

"Then the doctor scratched my stomach with a pin, and as he did that there was a flash of light and I popped back into my own body, and all the pain was back."

An ambulance was called, and on the way to Ipswich General Hospital Ian's appendix burst, and he was rushed into the operating theater to have his stomach drained. He spent the next four weeks in the hospital and a convalescent home. "I've never really been ill again in the rest of my life, so I've never had a repeat experience," said Ian, who is divorced and lives in Portsmouth.

"My mother remembers the day vividly, because the doctor told her that they nearly lost me. The funny thing is that I can remember that room in the house so clearly that I know where all the furniture was positioned, but I can't remember houses or rooms that I knew well later in my life.

"The experience did change my attitude to death. I feel no fear of it, because I know it's peaceful. I've told my story to other people, and they believe me even though they have never experienced anything like it. I hope it brings a little bit of comfort to anyone who is facing death: I know that when my time comes, I'll go quietly."

Norbert Atherton also experienced the first stages of an NDE, rising out of his own body and looking down on himself, when he was four years old and had diphtheria, a very dangerous and infectious disease which has nowadays been almost eliminated in Britain and the United States by immunization. The disease usually starts in the throat, causing a film to form over the back of it which can eventually block the airway completely.

Norbert, who lives in Wilmslow, Cheshire, remembers the experience with the same clarity that others report, even though his NDE happened in 1931: "I had caught diphtheria from turkey feathers, after my parents plucked their own turkey at home. I had to spend three months in hospital, mainly in isolation, because in those days diphtheria was a killer, and lots of children did not survive. My memories are very patchy: I don't remember going to hospital in an ambulance, I don't remember ever seeing a doctor, and my sister has told me about events like when she brought me a new toy, and I have no memory of them at all.

"Yet I clearly remember the incident where I went up to the ceiling. I've got no head for heights: I can't even climb a stepladder, yet I did not feel at all uncomfortable up there. It started with me being wheeled into a room, which I now believe was the operating theater. I remember seeing my father's worried expression peering at me from behind glass: I wasn't allowed any contact with my family because diphtheria is highly infectious. I was aware of cotton wool being put to my face, which was the way of administering anesthetic in those days. I was being given a tracheotomy operation to help my breathing, although I don't actually remember having breathing difficulties.

"The next thing I remember I was up on the ceiling, just floating there, looking down. I saw a little boy in a bed with a nurse sitting next to him. The covers were pulled tightly across so that only his little white face was showing, and he was very still. I could see him clearly although I was a few feet away: it was like looking across a road at someone on the other side.

"I don't think at four years old I had much idea of what I looked like, yet somehow I knew that the boy on the bed was me. It didn't matter that I was outside my body, it didn't feel odd. I had no idea about dying: nothing like that occurred to me. I just felt very comfortable up there."

As he looked down on himself, Norbert was aware of a very bright light, bathing the child on the bed. Looking back, he wonders if there was an electric light over the bed—electricity was a novelty to him then, because at his home the only form of lighting was gas. But he also thinks that it would have been very odd medical practice to have had a bright light over a child who was recovering from an operation, and who was dangerously ill. He has also, after thinking about NDEs in general, come to the conclusion that the light which is such a common feature of them is necessary because many people die in the dark, at night. He believes that being able to ''see'' is a vital ingredient of ''crossing'' into death.

The experience ended as suddenly as it started, and the rest of Norbert's memories of his time in the hospital are as hazy as those of any four-year-old child. It is only the NDE that he remembers clearly, although he has a few memories of being taught to walk again, and being taken out by the nurses, wrapped in one of their large capes.

He was in the hospital for a total of three months, and when he told his mother what he believed had happened she told him that he was rambling and delirious at the time, and the hospital had warned her that he might not live. She treated his memory as nothing more than a dream of his delirium, and her patronizing attitude made him hesitate to mention it again. On the few occasions that he did, he was met with disbelief and ridicule.

He recovered completely from the diphtheria, and although he is now a diabetic he has not had any other life-threatening episodes. But he believes the memory of his throat closing and the operation that was needed to save his breathing is still buried in his subconscious, because he occasionally wakes in the middle of the night with a terrible choking feeling in his throat. It clears as soon as he wakes up properly.

The memory of the NDE stayed with Norbert throughout his childhood and early life, returning to him at regular intervals entirely unprompted. When he was in his thirties, he read an account of someone else's NDE, and for the first time recognized his own experience. Ever since then the memory of the event has come less frequently, and only when actively recalled. Yet whenever he does think about it, he can once again feel the peace and calm that prevailed: "I don't suppose as a four-year-old I had many worries anyway: it's not as though you have to pay the gas or electricity bills at that age. But there was a definite feeling of well-being and peace about being up on the ceiling."

Norbert, a pensioner who is divorced, is still apprehensive about death, acknowledging that he has only experienced the onset of "the crossing": "But I am happy and confident in the fact that I know there is something after death, and I know that you go towards it without pain or fear."

Mary Newton is nearly fifty years older than Chris Hughes, but they have one remarkable thing in common: it was showing off to friends at school that led to their respective NDEs. Mary was eight years old, and not frightened by anything. To prove it, she climbed on to a wall that surrounded the playground of her school in Sheffield. The wall was two feet high on one side—with a thirty-foot drop on the other. Mary fell. She fractured her skull and a broken bottleneck lying on the ground where she landed was thrust into her forehead, just under her hairline.

Mary was conscious during the ambulance ride to Sheffield Children's Hospital, where she was operated on immediately. A steel plate was inserted to hold her skull together, and after the operation she was in a coma for two weeks. Her distraught parents sat by her bedside day and night, begging her to live. They were told that her life hung in the balance.

"While they were worrying and having a terrible time, I was enjoying myself. I did not see any bright lights or a tunnel, but I went into a lovely garden, with steps running down the center of it. There were cherry trees and roses, all in full bloom, everywhere. Coming down the steps towards me was a beautiful lady dressed in long black robes, with a black Chantilly lace shawl over her head, and a basket of flowers on her arm. She was very good-looking, in a dark, Spanish way, and she was holding out her hand and beckoning me to go to her. I tried to go towards her but I could not move.

"She came to me every day, and every day I struggled to get to her. I wanted to be with her. I felt happy and peaceful, except for my frustration at not being able to go to the lovely lady who was calling me. The garden was the most beautiful place I have ever seen, and I can recall it completely, even after all these years. And I have never seen anyone with a face to rival that of the lady: it was serene and gentle and loving.

"When I finally awoke from my coma I cried, because I was in a hospital bed and not in the beautiful garden. I could see the hospital windows and walls, but they were dull and blank and uninteresting compared to the place I had been. The ward sister was so excited to find me out of my coma, and she ran to fetch a doctor. They asked me why I was crying and I told them that it was because I would not see the garden or the lovely lady again. The sister hugged me and told me the lady had gone. She said 'Thank goodness.' At the time I did not understand that. As far as I was concerned, the only thing I wanted was to be back there.''

Mary, who still lives in Sheffield, has been a widow for more than twenty years, and has one grown-up daughter. In 1984 she had another brush with death, when members of her walking club had to pull her back from the brink of a sheer drop while she was out on a winter walk.

"It was a frightening experience, but more because of the shock of the accident than because I am scared of dying. Since my childhood experience I have always accepted that death when it comes will be rather nice, nothing to be afraid of. I shall, I hope, be in the same beautiful garden with the same lovely lady, and with the feeling of warmth and peace that I can still remember. I believe I had a glimpse of heaven.''

It was a trip to the hospital in 1954 which triggered Barbara Fuller's near-death experience, when she was nine years old. She was given gas before having a tooth out, and she fell into unconsciousness easily. The next thing she remembers is being whisked down a spiral tunnel at great speed. There was a bright but gentle light at the far end, and she was heading towards it when she heard voices calling her.

"Traveling down the tunnel felt very pleasant, very normal. I wanted to go on, but I could hear myself being called back. I had a very strong feeling that it was my choice whether I went on or not. I seemed to have the will to control the situation, to make the decision. I felt that both options were good: I wanted to go on but I also wanted to go back, although I was not clear at the time what either choice meant. I didn't consciously know that I was choosing whether to go back to my body or not. It was just something I had to make up my mind about.

"I obviously chose to go back, because I woke up to find several people around me calling my name. My mother, who had to wait in the room outside, told me afterwards that there was a great deal of commotion, with staff coming and going, because I did not come round from the anesthetic as quickly as I should have done.''

Barbara, a divorcee with two grown-up children, lives in Knowle, Bristol. She remembers the incident as though it happened yesterday: "That is one of the most striking things about it. It is etched in my memory. I can recall the feelings, and I can recall that deep sense of having a choice. I tell lots of people about it, because my friends all know that I am a very stable person who would not make things like this up, and that to remember it after all this time means it must have been important.

"I believe that I was actually close to death when it happened. Whether the choice to return was mine or not, I don't know. I felt it was, but I have no memory of making the choice. I can remember feeling that I didn't mind which way I went, because it was all very pleasant. I saw nothing inside the light at the end of the tunnel, but I sensed that it was a good place to be going."

Chapter 13

DYING TO BE SLIM

Its nickname may be the dieters' disease, but the psychological implications of anorexia nervosa are much more profound than simply wanting to be thin. Sufferers—the majority are girls and young women, though an increasing number of men are being diagnosed—start out wanting to be slimmer, usually for fashion reasons. Girls whose careers depend on how they look, such as models or ballet dancers, are particularly prone to it. But once the disease gets a grip, the dieting becomes compulsive, and is no longer anything to do with the pursuit of a sleek shape, even though the sufferers may still insist that it is. It is an obsession, as difficult to shake off as an addiction and much more dangerous, and as many as one in every 200 adolescent girls suffers from it. Their perception of themselves becomes so distorted that while to others they look like stick insects, and while they know they are seriously ill, they still look into a mirror and see fat.

Anorexia can kill. It can also take girls to the brink of death—so close that they have NDEs. For Sandra Mackay anorexia was a long, hard fight. A few bitchy comments from a couple of other girls took Sandra from being a pretty, bubbly model to the brink of death. Her nails turned black and fell out, her teeth chipped and rotted, her hair came out in handfuls, the hair on her body rubbed off, her periods stopped, her liver and kidneys were damaged, she lost control of her bladder and bowels, and she was too weak to stand. Her mom and dad were twice told that she had only days to live, and one night the hospital staff had to struggle to keep her awake to prevent her from slipping into a coma and dying. At the time, she wanted to be left alone: she was experiencing a lovely NDE, and she'd left behind all the pressures and worries that had driven her to within minutes of death.

Sandra had anorexia nervosa. She refused to eat, and in less than six months she slipped from being a healthy 133 lbs. to weighing 73 lbs. When she looks at pictures of herself taken when she weighed less than 84 lbs., she is appalled, but she knows that at the time she posed for them she still felt she was too fat.

"Anorexia robs you of your sanity," says Sandra, who lives in Belfast. "Even at just over seventy pounds, I felt my hips were too big. I felt I had rolls of fat round my tummy. I wanted to eat but I was terrified of eating. I would cut up some melon, some lettuce, and a quarter of tomato. I'd slice that tiny piece of tomato into ten thin slivers. Then I'd take a mouthful of melon and two slices of the tomato, and I'd push the plate away, disgusted with myself. I'd be thinking 'Calories, calories,' as I looked at it, even though the amount of calories I was eating was so tiny.

"One day I ate an ounce of chicken and some lettuce and in my diary I wrote, 'I have been a pig today. I have gorged myself. Tomorrow I will eat nothing.' If I got through a day without eating anything I felt great."

Sandra's anorexia started just after her twenty-second birthday in 1993. She has been working as a model since she was sixteen, and has an album full of lovely photographs of herself looking slim, happy, and healthy. She had a good appetite; she was energetic, talkative, the life and soul of any party. She kept her figure trim and firm by doing three aerobic classes a week.

"Then I began to do weight training, and decided to

enter a physique competition. Some of the other girls who were going in for it were bitchy: they said I was getting too fat round my waist. I looked in the mirror, and decided they were right. I set out to lose seven pounds, which I did through sensible dieting. Then I looked in the mirror and decided that the loss didn't show, I'd lose another seven.

"That's how it started, and it went on and on. I always believed I would look great if I could lose another seven pounds, and when I got there I was always convinced I was still fat."

Looking back, Sandra blames a destructive three-year relationship with a boyfriend for the start of her anorexia. "He was very possessive and he completely knocked my confidence. I split up with him and felt great: it felt as though I had got my own life back. But it was a month later that I started weight training, and I became obsessed with diet and exercise. It was as though I had to have something else controlling my life."

Sandra's diet was balanced for the first few weeks, but by the time she got down to 112 lbs. she was living on toast, fruit, and diet drinks. When her weight loss slowed down, she gave up eating altogether. As well as going to exercise classes, she was working out with a video several times a day, going out jogging, and walking her puppy Sasha for miles. If she sat down in front of the television, she felt guilty because she was not burning calories. She lives on her own, so it was easy at first to deceive her family and friends about how thin she was getting.

"I became such a liar. I went to my mum's house every day, but I always told her I had just eaten, or I was going home to cook for myself. I wore big baggy sweaters, so it was hard to see how thin I was getting.

"I was so cold, even in hot weather. I wore at least two

sweaters with a jacket on top, and I had the electric fire on all through the summer.''

Like all anorexics, Sandra was obsessed by food. She got a part-time job in a restaurant kitchen and loved cooking for others. ''I'd make food for my family, I was always cooking puddings. But I wouldn't eat them myself. I even used to spend ages cooking for my dog; I loved watching others eat, and felt good because I wasn't eating myself.

''I believed that if I started eating again, people would not like me, and my family would be disappointed. I felt they were proud of me being a model, and they wanted me to be thin.''

But that was far from the truth. Sandra's older sister Linda was worried within the first few weeks of Sandra starting to diet, and she warned their mother Joan that she would go too far with it.

As the pounds fell off, Sandra's personality changed: ''I shouted and screamed at anybody who dared to suggest I was too thin. My family just couldn't mention it to me. We joke about it now—my brother-in-law says I nearly threw Linda through a window when she tried to persuade me to get help.

''I lost my memory—I can still only remember odd details about that time, and I used to forget things so fast that I'd get halfway through a sentence and have to give up because I didn't know what I was saying. I also lost my hearing, but I've been lucky because it has come back. The doctors thought it might be permanently harmed.''

Sandra's health began to deteriorate. She had to give up work when she bent down to pick up some chips off the restaurant floor and found she was unable to get up again because she was too weak. Her mother and sister took her shopping one day, and it took her twenty minutes to walk along one aisle of the department store. One of her brothers did not recognize her in the street until he looked twice, and her sister-in-law, who hadn't seen her for a couple of months, walked past on the other side of the road without knowing her.

After four months, she could no longer work as a model. "I went on a shoot with one photographer who had taken other pictures of me and he could not believe it. He told me he could not use me any more unless I put some weight back on. But I still felt I was too fat."

Sandra's sister and her parents contacted a woman whose own daughter had died as a result of anorexia, and they were given advice about how to help her. "They were told that it was no good lecturing me, and that I wouldn't get better until I wanted to myself, and that they should keep letting me know how much they loved me. I think it was the best advice."

Sandra believes it was the warmth and love of her family and her new boyfriend, Greg, that saved her life. She'd known Greg since they were both thirteen, but they only started going out together when she was ill.

"I don't think anyone who had not known me before would have been seen with me, I looked so awful. But Greg knew me and he was always sure I would get well again. He was very patient: I wasn't much of a girlfriend. I was so skinny that a cuddle hurt. People used to ask him why he was going out with someone who looked like me."

Sandra's periods stopped three months after she started losing weight, and even after she recovered doctors have told her that it would take a year or more for her to get back to normal fertility.

She was admitted to a hospital when she finally confessed to her sister that she needed help. "I had little flashes of sanity. Almost all the time I still thought I was fat, but every so often, especially after I had eaten something, however small, I'd have a few seconds of seeing clearly. It was as though when I had a certain amount of vitamins and protein in my body my mind started to function again, even if it was only for a flash.

"Once I looked down and realized with horror that the fattest part of my whole leg was my knee, because of the bone in it. But a minute later when I looked at it, all I saw was fat. One day at Linda's house I caught a glimpse of myself in a glass door, and saw myself as I really was. I broke down and asked for help."

By this time, Sandra was unable to control her bladder and her bowels. Her body hurt so much that she could not lie down on her bed to sleep, but had to sit on a soft chair wrapped in a soft blanket. She had to crawl on all fours to get upstairs. She also had an urge to harm herself. She'd asked her family to bring her some special rocks to make a rock garden in her yard: "But I had some strange plan that I could hurt myself with them, maybe even kill myself. I was so depressed."

Sandra's family was told there was a six-week waiting list for her to get help, but when they insisted that she would be dead by then, she was taken into the hospital the following day.

At first she cheated the staff and flushed her food down the lavatory, and after a few days she had lost even more weight. She scalded her leg badly, trying to carry a small pot of hot water to make herbal tea. She was suffering from jaundice, but tricked the nurses over the pills she was supposed to take.

"I put them in my mouth and spat them out later, because they contained calories. I thought all the hospital staff were against me, that they just wanted me to get fat and then nobody would like me. I was in tears all the time."

One evening after hospital visiting time, Sandra felt a

strange tingling all over her body. She dozed off to sleep, and woke up to feel her face and pillow damp—she was having a massive nosebleed. At the same time she lost control of her bowels.

When the hospital staff had cleaned her up she dozed again. This time, for the first time in weeks, she felt no pain. She felt as though her whole body was floating in the air, and she could see a long dark tunnel with a bright warm light at the end of it.

"For the first time in months, I felt very, very happy. I felt relaxed, my whole body was free of pain, which was something I had not felt for ages. I felt myself float up and hover just above the bed. I could see myself, but I hardly recognized myself. I felt peaceful and content. The doctor woke me up and when I told her about it, she told the nurses not to let me fall asleep again, as I would probably lapse into a coma and die. I just wanted to sleep, to get rid of my pain."

Sandra drifted in and out of this beautiful world for a while, constantly dragged away from it by the nurses who came in to wake her by calling her name. "I hated them for it. I wanted to stay there. I didn't want to come back to my body and all my problems. I felt a powerful urge to go towards the light."

The doctor was so concerned that she told a nurse to ring for Sandra's mother to come immediately, because her daughter was dying. "Hearing that my mum was being sent for triggered something in me. I thought about all the love she had given me, and how she'd make herself ill worrying about me.

"When she arrived she had cards from all my family, including ones that Linda's two little girls, my nieces Zoe and Zara, had drawn for me. Dad came, and he brought me presents from the people at his work.

"I thought, 'I'm going to fight it. I'm going to eat.' I ate a whole saucer of melon, and drank a black coffee. Then I felt guilty and tried to vomit, but nothing would come.

"That night I wanted to kill myself. There was a rope hanging from a scaffolding outside the hospital window, and I tried to lean out and grab it, to hang myself. But I couldn't get it.

"The next day I walked to the toilet on the ward—I was not supposed to get out of bed—and I caught sight of myself in a full-length mirror. I really saw what I looked like. I couldn't even remember having my hair permed, I didn't know myself. That's when I really started to eat.

"Every day my family and Greg would sit by my bed and tell me they loved me, and although it was hard, I forced myself to eat for their sake. I wrote a page in red ink in my diary, and every time I felt panicky I got it out. It said: 'You are not fat. You must eat.' Looking back in my diary, all the time I was dieting I started each entry with 'DO NOT EAT.' So now I started writing 'EAT EVERYTHING.'

"I had an old picture of myself next to my bed and the hospital staff all said, 'Is that your sister? She's lovely.' I felt proud—but it also gave me an incentive to get back to looking like that."

Sandra spent five weeks in the hospital, and then went home to live with her mom and dad. "I was almost bald because my hair was falling out in clumps, but the doctors said it would grow again. All the hair on my body turned fluffy, like a baby's, and rubbed off, and my eyebrows disappeared. My skin peeled in great sheets. My toenails turned black and dropped off: one day four came off at once. Five of my teeth had to be filed, because they chipped and then cut into my tongue."

Sandra recovered quickly. She was ill for eight months altogether. She still has some liver and kidney damage, which the doctors believe will heal in time, but all her other problems have gone, and her hair has grown back. She weighs 124 lbs., she's eating, and her exercise is limited to her aerobics classes. She is going to college to learn beauty therapy and she is hoping to become an aerobics teacher. She's already been back on the catwalk modeling clothes at a fashion show.

"Eating will be a struggle every single day for the rest of my life. I know that. But it is a struggle worth winning. I want a normal life. One day I want to marry and have children. I also want to help other girls with anorexia.

"I went to hell and back because of something someone said about my weight. I'd like to see everybody more relaxed about weight. At one modeling agency recently, since my illness, I was told I should lose a few pounds, but I told them to forget it. I will never diet again. I would rather miss modeling work than start that again."

One unexpected bonus for Sandra is finding a wardrobe full of clothes that she bought while she was ill. "I have no memory of getting them. Because I wasn't spending money on food I had money for clothes, but I obviously didn't wear them, as lots of them still have their labels on. However thin I was I still bought my normal size, ten or twelve. So I can wear them now. But my feet went down one whole size, so all the shoes I bought are too small."

The other bonus has come from the NDE: "I wouldn't, of course, want to go through what I've been through just to have an NDE, but it certainly was one of the few beneficial things about it. I had no doubt before that there was a life after death, but I had no idea what it would feel like. Now I can recollect that lovely peace, and I know that when I do die I will have nothing to worry about.

"I value life very highly now, and I value my own peace of mind. I'm not so anxious to please other people. I'm more easygoing, more relaxed. When you've been that

close to death, it makes you sort out your priorities. I knew
I wanted to live, although that night I would have gladly
gone to that lovely warm light forever. Now I am content
with what I've got in life, happy to take each day as it
comes, in the knowledge that this life is only the beginning.''

Chapter 14

WITH MINE OWN HAND

"Today is a good day for dying," says Kiefer Sutherland's character in the opening shot of the movie *Flatliners*. The story is about a group of young medical students who decide to take up the ultimate challenge: to discover what comes after death. They have heard the NDE stories and they want to test them for proof, by taking it in turns to be deliberately "killed" and then, after the heart monitor has flatlined for a given number of seconds, being resuscitated. Of course, being a Hollywood movie, it has to be more than just a succession of glorious NDEs: the students all end up having, in different ways, unpleasant experiences.

It is also, thankfully, not an idea that the medical profession is ever likely to take up, for all sorts of very good reasons, not least the ethical ones. But there are people who do experience NDEs through their own making: people who attempt suicide or who overdose on hard drugs. The two whose stories are told in this chapter have, understandably, asked that their full names not be used.

Helen is one of the few people interviewed for this book who has had more than one NDE. Her story is particularly moving: both of her close encounters with death were self-inflicted. Over a period of five years, Helen made fourteen suicide attempts, and after two of them she found herself in a peaceful and welcoming world which was much happier than the one from which she was trying to escape.

Helen, who was born in 1966, has had a succession of problems to cope with. Her hyperactivity as a child was dealt with by a doctor prescribing Valium for her when she was only nine years old. The addictive qualities of tranquilizers were not widely reported in the seventies, and it was only sixteen years later that Helen learned the hard way that benzodiazepine dependence is one of the hardest addictions to kick. The drug promotes both a physical and psychological dependence, and doctors are now urged to avoid prescribing it for more than a couple of weeks.

By the time she was fourteen, Helen discovered another addiction: alcohol. She started experimental drinking in the same way that many teenagers do, but she can, with hindsight, recognize that she was immediately drinking compulsively. "It was never social drinking, it was always something much more than that for me. By the time I was seventeen, I was drinking heavily, and was in trouble with it," says Helen.

Even though she was regularly using both tranquilizers and alcohol, Helen managed to keep up with her school work and moved on to study for a degree at Manchester University. Over the following few years her problems escalated. As well as her addictions, she also had to confront her own homosexuality. Although today she is very comfortable with the fact that she is a lesbian, coping with it has not always been easy.

"I think the hidden pressure to conform, from society and also from my family—although they have always stood by me and been very good about it—made it hard for me to completely accept myself," she says.

"By the time I was in my twenties I hated myself. I wouldn't keep a mirror in the house: I hated the reflection from my own eyes. I did not want to be me, I did not accept myself, and drink was one of the ways of getting out of myself.''

After writing suicide notes and taking an overdose of pills and drink, Helen was rushed to a hospital in very serious condition. Her heart stopped four times, she learned later from the medical staff. "I remember clearly floating up above myself, and looking down on my body. It was connected to numerous machines. I could see the drip and the oxygen mask. I could see the doctors working to restart my heart with electronic pads. I could see that my parents were there. It felt very peaceful, much better than where I had been before. I was bathed in warmth and light, and the calm was almost tangible. I felt it was up to me to decide where I wanted to be, up there or back in my body, but the peace was so overwhelming that I knew I wanted to stay.

"And then I was in a small supermarket, floating between the aisles. It was like any ordinary supermarket, with shelves loaded with goods. My grandmother, who died when I was very young, was at the checkout, and so was my auntie. I knew without anyone telling me that it was my auntie, my mum's sister, although she had died of a brain hemorrhage before I was born. They were beckoning to me to go to them, but through the plate-glass window I could see my parents and my immediate family, also beckoning and urging me to hurry.''

The next thing Helen remembers is waking from her coma with the oxygen mask pressing on her face and causing some pain. She felt regret at having left the peace behind.

"I had been in a coma for a week, and when I woke I recalled this experience with lucidity. It still felt good, especially the thought of having seen my grandmother and my auntie. I believe I had met her before, once when I was very tiny. She was in the army, although she had left it before she died. I was lying in my cot one day, and my mother had left my covers off. When she came back into the room I was neatly tucked up, and I told her that the lady in uniform had done it. I described her, and my mother recognized her sister from the description: we believe she came to have a good look at me.

"But there was also a slightly panicky feeling about the memory of the NDE, because I knew I'd had to choose between going to my grandmother and my auntie or to my living relatives, and in a way I had wanted both."

Helen's second NDE came a couple of years after the first, after another suicide attempt. This time she took pills and tried to swallow bleach. Her partner found her and called an ambulance.

"I was drifting in and out of consciousness, more out than in, but I remember being wheeled from the flat on a stretcher. Again, I floated above and could look down and see two men carrying the stretcher, and I felt secure and safe in the knowledge that I was walking away from all the chaos of my life. Again, I felt it was my decision to walk away. Then I remember a very powerful force pulling me towards a serene, very beautiful realm, a higher plane. I traveled very slowly along a tunnel towards a bright light, and I could feel an overwhelming sense of warmth and peace and whiteness. I wanted to walk into the whiteness, which was so tranquil and happy. It was like stepping into a vacuum, there was nothing tangible, no scenery to look at, but a tremendous feeling of being somewhere, like nirvana. I felt okay, as though this was where I was meant to be, as if I had arrived home, and I was at ease with myself for the first time in a long time.

"I also felt at one with the forces of the universe, as though I was part of something much much bigger, and yet I was also the whole of it. It was a tremendously powerful feeling, and such a contrast to the despair and depression that had led me there.''

This second time Helen did not see any relatives, and although she experienced the same sense of there being an element of choice in whether or not she returned to life or continued in that lovely place, she did not feel any panic when she awoke in the hospital a few days later. ''I knew I had not wanted to relinquish the good feelings the place had given me, but at the same time I did not feel regret at returning. This time, the experience seemed to give me strength. I felt refreshed.'' She was told by hospital staff that she was lucky to have survived.

Helen's two NDEs have taken away any fear she may have had of death, and she now anticipates that when it comes she will once again experience those feelings of peace and tranquillity. She does not believe that her NDEs encouraged her to make more suicide attempts: suicide, she says, is born of despair with this world, not a hankering after the peace and serenity of the next.

But she did make another serious attempt on her own life in 1991, when she slashed her wrists and then took an overdose. ''At that time I cut myself regularly. I was so insane with the illness of alcoholism that I felt I was trying to cut out the bad part of me. I felt that I was evil, and that if I cut myself I would let the evil out. I was also violent towards others: I'd attacked one partner very seriously on one occasion. Just before my final suicide attempt, I attacked another partner, hitting her with a broken bottle. I was completely unaware of what I had done because I was blacked out on booze. It wasn't until she came home with bandages round her head that I knew what I had done.''

The realization made Helen confront her alcohol problem: ''I'd tried to give up drinking before, but I'd always denied to myself how really ill I was. I thought I could just cut down. This time I knew it was all or nothing: my life depended on it.''

Helen detoxified and suffered withdrawal symptoms on her own in a small apartment in Manchester, her adopted city—not surprisingly, after the violence, her relationship had broken up. She attended a day center for recovering alcoholics, but the first three weeks without alcohol were very hard. After that, however, she began to feel physically better and mentally stronger. Today, she has not had a drink since 1991. She is back with her partner, studying for a master's degree and doing volunteer work.

''I look back on eleven years of my life which were dominated by drinking, and I ask myself, 'Where was I?' My memories of those years are very poor, and that is why the NDEs stand out so clearly. Initially, I tried to dismiss them as nothing more than dreams, but they are so vivid and so evocative that I know they were real. The feelings were so powerful, and the aftereffects have lasted for so long.

''I feel enormously lucky to still be alive, and I know I have to live each day to its fullest. I have had a second chance at life. But at the same time I have no fear of dying. I know what it will be like, and it will feel good. Whenever I have to move on to that next stage, whether it is tomorrow or fifty years from now, I will be ready.''

Steven, like Helen, also had his NDE as a result of a drug overdose, but an accidental one. Because of the circumstances of his experience, and his attempts to get his life back in order, he has asked that his full name not be used. His story is interesting because it underlines the conviction shared by all NDEers that what happened was not a dream or a hallucination, but something far more real. It would be easy to dismiss Steven's NDE as a drug-induced hallucination: he used drugs habitually, taking large amounts of speed and ecstasy, both of which are hallucinogens. Certainly, the objectivity of his account is undermined by the fact that he was very high when it happened.

But Steven consistently maintains that he knows the difference between a drug trip and what happened to him one night when he was eighteen, tripping on a combination of speed and magic mushrooms. His case is far more extreme than most, but his conviction about it parallels the conviction of all other NDEers, whether they were under anesthetic at the time of their experience or whether they were completely free from all chemical intervention. There is something about an NDE that convinces the person who experiences it that it is not a dream, not a delusion, not a hallucination, not a by-product of anesthesia, and not the result of a drug trip.

Steven was dabbling with drugs before he left school at sixteen. His attendance record at school was very poor, and although he had no criminal convictions, he had been caught shoplifting a couple of times, but let off with a caution. He came from a broken home, living in a flat in Edinburgh with his mother and brothers. His days were spent on the street, running with a group of kids who had also dropped out. From time to time he worked, once in a shop and twice in factories, but the jobs did not last long because he had a poor attendance record, usually as a result of bingeing on drugs every weekend. His main source of income was benefit, and after giving his mum £10 towards his keep, he spent the rest on drugs. He preferred ecstasy and speed to alcohol, because the kick came sooner and higher, and was, by some tortured reckoning which excluded all cost to his health and mental well-being, cheaper. Anyway, it was what the other kids did, and Steven during his teenage years wanted nothing more than to fit into the crowd.

He had spent the week prior to his NDE taking ecstasy

and speed. On the night it happened he was at a friend's house with three buddies, and Steven was still high from the drugs he had taken the previous night. He took some very pure speed, and ate some magic mushrooms that one of his friends had.

"I can't remember why we had so much drugs that night, but I know it was all free—somebody had got hold of it in some way, and we were able to take as much as we wanted without it costing anything. We were all very high on the mushrooms when the speed was handed round, and I obviously took far too much.

"I'd been having hallucinations from the mushrooms. I'd seen wee dinosaurs running around all over the place in my head, and I knew that was the drugs. I was feeling good, enjoying the trip. Then, after taking the speed, my limbs went completely weak and I could not stand up. I felt very, very strange, very ill. My friends put me to bed and even though they were all spaced out they were very worried about me. They could see I was not right, but they were too scared to call a doctor because of the drugs.

"I remember lying on the bed with my eyes open, and one half of my body felt as if it was spinning around. I literally felt my heart stop. I could feel every beat of it pulsing through me, and then it stopped. Immediately I could see a big light up above me, like the sort of light you see over an operating table in films.

"Then I could feel myself float out of my own body, and I could look down and see myself on the bed. I knew that I was fighting for my life, and just as suddenly as it had stopped, my heart started to beat again and I was back in my body, feeling very, very ill. A few minutes later the same thing happened: my heart stopped and I saw the bright light. It was a warm and welcoming light, very bright, but not harsh or dazzling.

"This time I saw myself running along, wearing long

white robes. I tried to chase myself, grabbing at the robes. I managed to catch hold of my own arm and yanked myself back into myself. The me that was chasing the other me was wearing normal clothes. Once I had pulled him back into me, I went back into the body on the bed and once again I felt terrible. Even though I had felt a bit panicky during the chase, because somehow I knew I had to catch myself, there had been a wonderfully relaxed feeling about it all. It had felt good, and I had been bathed in the warmth and comfort of the bright light.''

Seconds later Steven came back to consciousness. He was crying, feeling very sick, and the friend who was sitting with him said he had been grabbing his arm and calling out that he was going away. Steven, who now felt completely sober and not at all high on drugs, told his friend that he believed he had died or come very close to death. His friend dismissed it as a bad trip, as did the others when he told them about it. But Steven has experienced bad trips, and although he knows that they do not necessarily follow one pattern, he feels very strongly that what happened to him was not caused by the drugs.

"The feeling from a bad trip is totally different. You see weird things on a bad trip, and you know they are weird and frightening. I've seen wee cartoon characters running round, I've seen a skull and snakes, that sort of thing. It's hard to explain, but at the time it is happening it is frighteningly real, yet you always know it is the drugs.

"With the NDE it was totally different. I was there. It was a complete feeling that took me over. I know that I died for a few seconds, and nothing anyone can say will ever persuade me that I didn't. When you have a bad trip you feel terrible afterwards, but I felt better quite quickly after the NDE. I had no bad effects from the drugs at all, and the whole of the next day I simply felt calm and quiet.''

The brush with death shook Steven, but it was not the salutary lesson that made him kick his addiction. In fact, after the death of a friend from an overdose, he became even more immersed in the drug scene, taking frightening combinations of ecstasy, speed, acid, and magic mushrooms. He experienced more bad trips, but never anything like the NDE.

His life turned around when he met a girl who does not take drugs, and together they have struggled to free him from his addiction. He suffered appalling withdrawal symptoms, and for a time he visited a psychiatrist to help him cope with the temper tantrums provoked by the chemical withdrawal. He suffered blackouts, sometimes as often as three times a day, and his family and girlfriend were worried that he would injure himself falling over when these occurred.

Steven finally got completely clear of drugs, both the addiction and its aftermath, in early 1994. He is working hard to build up a totally different kind of life for himself, but he is still coping with housing and work problems.

"I hadn't given religion a serious thought until my NDE. I suppose I vaguely believed there might be something after death. But now I know there is something, and I know that it has got to be better than this life. The feeling I had when I floated away from myself and into the light was marvelous. My worries disappeared. When I came round, although all my problems were still there, I felt better because I had been given hope. It may have taken me a while to get off drugs, but I think that experience started my recovery. I could see that there was hope, even if it is only hope for a better time than this in the next world.

"I also felt I'd been given a second go at this life, and although it's not easy, with all the worries and hassles you get, I now feel it is precious. I'm determined to make the most of it.

"Although it is three years ago that I had my NDE, the memory of it is crystal clear: and that's another reason that I do not believe it was a bad drug trip. I don't remember those clearly, even the day afterwards. But that experience is etched in my mind.

"I realize that I cannot produce scientific proof that it happened. But inside myself I know it did, I also know that I came very close to death that night. And I know that what comes after death is good. I'm not afraid of it."

Chapter 15

"I KNOW THE DIFFERENCE"

Lots of people who have never had an NDE, including experts, reckon that they are nothing more than hallucinations. It is the most common explanation put forward for them: they are imaginary visions caused by mental dysfunction at a time of crisis. But studies have shown that NDEs have little in common with the "normal" hallucinations that come with psychotic illness like schizophrenia.

NDEs have a recognizable pattern, within which there may be endless variations but which share certain core elements; they also have an almost universal uplifting effect on the subject. Psychotic hallucinations, on the other hand, are infinitely varied, with no reliable characteristics in common; and although they can occasionally have a life-enhancing effect, they are far more likely to give rise to despair, depression, and feelings of great hopelessness.

NDEs are also over very quickly: if they are caused by brain malfunction, it very rapidly corrects itself. Although one-time schizophrenic breakdowns are common in the population at large—about one person in one hundred has a single psychotic episode in their lives—and do not presage a lifetime of mental illness, nonetheless the breakdown lasts for considerably longer than the few seconds needed for an NDE.

Subjectively, people who have suffered both psychotic hallucinations and NDEs know the difference. Even though, at the time they experience them, their hallucinations are as real to them as an NDE is, the NDE stays with them afterwards in the same way that it does for everyone who has one. Psychotic hallucinations do not: psychiatric patients are often startled and alarmed to be told what they "believed" during a psychotic episode. They don't remember it, or remember it only hazily, and are aware in their nonpsychotic times that it was a bizarre hallucination.

Julie has been in and out of the psychiatric hospital since she was fifteen, and has had a life as filled with trauma as it is possible to imagine. She has had plenty of delusions and hallucinations. She has also had one near-death experience and one out-of-body experience which have stayed crystal sharp in her memory, and which she can invest with a "reality" which, in retrospect, none of her hallucinations possess.

Julie's history of mental illness makes her no less reliable a witness than any other NDEer. She is an intelligent and, between her episodes of illness, capable woman, now crippled with arthritis. Because she has had both experiences, and can distinguish so clearly between them, her story is powerful evidence for the NDE not being triggered by brain malfunction in any way related to that which causes psychotic illness.

Julie, from Kent, had her first full-scale breakdown in 1965, when she was fifteen. Despite a high IQ she was forced to leave school without finishing, and over the ensuing years she has spent a great deal of time in the hospital. Since 1988 she has been married to Graham, and the two of them live a very fulfilled and happy life together. Before her marriage, Julie's life was a tortured succession of bungled suicide attempts, self-mutilation, anorexia, obsessions, and psychotic breakdowns. At one point she was stable enough to embark on nursing studies: she was doing very well when she had another breakdown and was forced to give up her hopes of a career. Today, she is so badly crippled with arthritis in her limbs and spine that she can only walk short distances with the aid of a cane, and the rest of the time needs a wheelchair.

Julie's NDE happened after she had taken a massive drug overdose in an attempt to kill herself. She has made several serious suicide attempts, but this one came closest to succeeding: she was in a coma for three days. She has little memory of how she got to the hospital, but before sinking into the coma she remembers seeing nurses around her bed.

"The next thing I knew I left my body, and I could see a long dark shaft with a bright light at the end, and I knew I had to go along the shaft. But I could not get to it because I was being dragged back by women in uniform, nurses, who were trying to make me put my head in a box. The box had spikes passing through it from both sides, like the sort of boxes that magicians stick swords through, and the spikes were pulled back to make way for my head.

"I knew that when my head was inside they would be pushed in again, decapitating me. I struggled hard, especially because I could see the light at the end of the tunnel and I wanted to get to it. But the nurses overpowered me and clamped my head. Yet somehow I managed to withdraw it from the box and the spikes had not damaged me.

"I ran like mad for the shaft, and began to go up it. It was a lovely feeling: I had no pain, no worries, there was nothing wrong with the world, and I knew that if I could get to the top I would find real happiness. I had to make a real effort to get up the shaft, as though I was swimming against the tide. At the bottom of it I could see the nurses, clamoring for me to come down so that they could put my head in the box again. I was in one way frightened, but in another I was feeling so relaxed and at ease with the world that I didn't care.

"When I reached the top I knew that if I touched a blue ribbon, which was stretched across the shaft, I would be free of them forever. I touched it, and as I did so I came out of the top of the shaft into a big open space full of people who were all cheering me. I did not know why they were cheering, although I felt very good. One of them told me it was because I had just got my nursing qualifications, which in real life I had failed to get because of my illness. Somebody gave me a badge. I felt happier than I had ever been before.

"And then someone came up to me, a man, and told me that I had to go. He didn't say where, but I knew without being told that I had to go back into my body. He was a kind-looking man, but there was nothing special about him: he was just one of this big crowd of people.

"As soon as he had spoken to me, I woke up in the hospital. I was told I had been out for three days, and that my condition had been touch and go for the most of that time. I realized to my horror that the nurses I had dreamt about putting my head into the box were some of the staff who had been looking after me: apparently my eyes were open through the coma, so perhaps I had been able to see them. The box and spikes may have symbolized the mental illness I was trying to escape from.

"I know that what happened was not a dream or a hallucination, because it happened about ten years ago, yet I can recall it vividly. I don't remember hallucinations, and I know afterwards that they are not real. But this was and is very real: I feel as though it actually happened. I have questioned myself about it, but my memory of it never changes, so I am convinced it was no dream or hallucination. I have had them: I know the difference."

It was in a psychiatric hospital when she was twenty-five

that Julie had her other out-of-body experience, which did not occur when she was physically near death. Her life was in crisis, but it was not a physical one.

"I'd had a breakdown, and I was feeling very low about being back in hospital. I went into my own room and shut the door. I lay on the bed, with the light on, and closed my eyes, hoping to go to sleep. But suddenly I was wide awake. I felt myself float up above my body, higher and higher until I was up to the ceiling. It was a lovely feeling, all my cares and problems slipped away. But something inside me told me it was wrong, and I spoke to myself, telling myself that I'd better get back into my body before it was too late. I forced myself with all my strength to get back in to the body on the bed, and just as suddenly as I had left it I was back in it again.

"As I lay there, I turned my head and I could see a beautiful old mahogany chest of drawers, covered with an intricate lace cloth. There was a bowl of oranges on top of it, and they looked delicious: the colors were so clear and beautiful. It was like the sort of thing you imagine you would see in a palace. I had a strange feeling of well-being, not quite like when I had been floating above myself, but a very positive sense of health and happiness, and an appreciation of life.

"When I turned my head away and then looked back again, of course all I could see was the old hospital chest of drawers, which was certainly not a thing of beauty. Yet the good feeling remained with me for a few hours."

Julie is adamant that neither of these experiences was part of her mental illness: "After years in and out of hospital I know the difference. I can look back at the times of my life when I was ill, and I can recognize my own obsessions and delusions. These two happenings were different, they were special, and they helped me with all the problems of life."

Julie and Graham are born-again Christians, and Julie believes in life after death: "I may have already had a glimpse of it: I don't know. All I know is that I felt completely free from all my usual problems, and it was lovely. I shall be happy to die if that peace is what is in store for me. Life has not been easy, and I would like peace more than anything. I think God gave me a glimpse of it to help me keep going."

Chapter 16

THE UNLUCKY ONES

Although the vast majority of NDEs are happy experiences, a minority are the opposite: the peace and relaxation that is such a familiar characteristic is replaced by fear and anxiety; the longing to go further into the experience is substituted by dread and terror; the welcoming beings who some NDEers meet are replaced by hellish characters who seem bent on destruction. The victim does not feel the typical rush of disappointment and regret at returning to the everyday world, but an enormous sense of relief at not being left behind in a landscape of nightmares.

Some NDEs are a mixture of enjoyment and fear: Mrs. Nella Parminter, whose story is told in Chapter Eleven, experienced a very clear sense that to her right was something pleasant and enhancing, while at her left was a "court" of black-robed men who were there to judge her, a frightening scene that left her relieved to return, yet still able to recall the enjoyment of the feelings engendered by floating through the tunnel and seeing the welcoming light on the right.

Other experiences, however, have no such redeeming features. They are the antithesis of the classic NDE: stark and unpleasant from start to finish. Yet they are not just nightmares which have been misinterpreted as NDEs, because they share the same vivid "reality" and the ability to implant and sustain themselves in the victims' memories for many years. They are as valid as the pleasant NDEs. Should they be interpreted as proof of the existence of "hell" as an afterlife, as most NDEers take their pleasant experiences as proof of "heaven"? Perhaps. But it would be wrong to assume that the people who experience them are those selected to be sent to this nether region: they may simply be those who have been allowed a glimpse of it, just as those who have the heavenly afterlife NDE have been privileged, they believe, to see a glimpse of the future that awaits all of us, not just them as individuals, after death.

Why the imbalance in the numbers reported, with only 3 percent having nasty NDEs? It could simply be that people who have nasty NDEs work harder at forgetting them, burying them in their subconscious, uneasy about the consequences of facing them. Or perhaps they do remember them but are reluctant to come forward and report them. Both theories are plausible, although to test the memory, NDEers were interviewed immediately after their experiences, and still only a very tiny number of unpleasant stories surfaced. When an American psychiatrist experienced an NDE himself, and saw visions of both heaven and hell, he was well placed to monitor how his memory worked: he found that the meeting with Jesus in a heavenly city was far more long-lasting and vivid to him years later than the scenes of human misery he saw.

Nancy Evans Bush, an American who is very involved in the International Association for Near Death Studies, has categorized nasty NDEs into three groups. The first are those which resemble the positive ones, except that the people concerned interpret them in a different way and are often terrified at the idea of losing control and going with their feelings: "A person who approaches the light and is fearful may see it as a reflection of the fires at the gates of hell, instead of seeing it as a radiant light," Nancy says.

The second group are those who experience a sensation of being caught in a void, a nothingness. They feel abandoned, despairing. The third and smallest group are those who see unpleasant things, and who believe they have been shown a vision of hell—some actually report seeing human souls being tortured, although such experiences are very rare.

Jim is thoroughly fed up with hearing about wonderful NDEs. His experience was anything but wonderful, and has certainly not given him any reason to look forward to life after death.

Jim was serving with an intelligence unit in Italy during the Second World War. He was traveling in a truck which went out of control and crashed. Jim lost consciousness, and was taken to a military hospital in Rome, suffering from a concussion and minor injuries. But he developed blood poisoning from one of his cuts, and over the next few days became very seriously ill, needing large injections of penicillin to bring him through. At the time he did not realize how ill he was, but he was told afterwards by medical staff that he came close to death.

One night during his illness he was lying in his bed in the darkened ward, surrounded by other injured servicemen. As he lay there he felt himself float away from his body, hovering about six feet above it as it lay on the bed. He was able to look down and see himself quite clearly. But Jim's experience was not the usual happy feeling of floating away from pain and trouble: he could feel himself being drawn out of his body, and stretched as though he were a piece of elastic.

"It was a terrifying experience, and somehow I knew that it was two other people who were pulling me away from my body. I also knew that they were trying to take me somewhere that I would not like, somewhere that was not very nice, although I had no idea where that might be. I tried to will myself back into my body, which I could see asleep below me, but all my efforts were countered by this strong force that was pulling me out.

"I tried to call for help, but no sound came out. The battle went on for some time, me pitting all my strength against these two characters who were pulling me. I could not see them, but I knew they were two other people who were dying, and I could sense that one of them was old and the other was a young chap about the same age as me—I was twenty-five in 1943, when this happened. I knew that if I relaxed my fight for one moment they would take me with them, and I knew that I desperately did not want to go.

"Suddenly the force that was dragging at me was released, and I was back in my bed, in my body. I let out a great shout for help, and the night nurse came running. She looked really alarmed: my shriek had been one of sheer terror. She asked if I was all right and I knew that she would never believe what had happened, so I fobbed her off by saying I had had a nightmare.

"As she walked away from me and out of the ward she paused by a bed opposite mine, and after examining the man in the bed she pulled the sheet up over his face. He was obviously dead. I thought, 'Well, there goes one of them.' I knew that this man had been the younger of the two who had been pulling me."

Jim, who lives in Surrey, was unable to sleep, and after a while he saw the medical orderlies bring a trolley and take the body away. Later in the night, as he was dozing, he was roused by the sound of the trolley being brought back into the ward. It was taken to a bed at the end, which had always been screened, so that none of the other patients on the ward had ever seen the occupant. After the body was loaded on to the trolley it was wheeled away, past Jim's bed.

"The face was not covered and I was surprised to see that it was an old man, which was strange because we were in a military hospital and everybody else in there was a

soldier. He looked ancient. 'There goes the other one,' I
thought.

"I never found out why the old man was there, and in
retrospect I cannot work out how I knew so conclusively
that where they were going was a terrible place. But I did
know it, with utter conviction. The whole affair was a very
nasty frightening experience, not at all in line with all the
stories that are reported of lovely near-death experiences.
It seemed to give me, on that night, the ability to predict
the deaths of two of my fellow patients, although they may
have already been dead at the time it happened. It also
makes me concerned that there may be a darker side to the
afterlife.

"I know that I was not dreaming. All these years later I
can recall the whole experience as if it was yesterday, and
I can see that old man's face as vividly as I saw it that
night, as it was wheeled past me."

Audrey had a premonition that something terrible was going to happen when she went into the hospital for a routine
test for blocked arteries in June 1988, when she was forty-
nine. Audrey, who lives in Essex, was suffering from high
blood pressure, and was taken into a London hospital for
an angiogram, a test involving a wire being inserted in the
groin and a dye traveling through an artery to the heart,
revealing any blockages. Only a local anesthetic is needed,
and patients can watch the whole procedure on the screen
that is being monitored by the doctor.

Audrey was terrified that something would go wrong,
despite all the reassurances of the medical staff. On the
morning of the test she was shaking when the doctor visited
her on the ward, and when he asked her what was wrong
she told him that she had a terrible fear that she was going
to die during the angiogram. He tried to relax her by mak-

ing a joke of her fears: "I haven't lost anybody yet—well, not this morning," he said.

Audrey was asked if she wanted to watch the dye moving up inside her body on a television monitor, but said she would prefer not to. The doctor talked to her as he carried out the test, telling her that he had inserted the wires in her groin.

"I heard him say, 'We're coming up on the right-hand side . . .' and at that moment I felt the most powerful surge in my neck, and I was no longer there in that room. Where I was I don't know, but in front of me was an oval ring with all my five children and my grandchildren—I had fifteen at that time—in it. My daughter Janet and her daughter Lucy, who was eight at the time, stood out in front. They all looked very distressed and they were shouting, but I could hear nothing. I could see their mouths moving, like a film with the sound turned down. I looked at them for a few seconds, feeling helpless, and then just as suddenly as I had gone I was back in the room at the hospital."

Audrey found herself the center of a great deal of activity. She had reacted to the dye, her heart had stopped, and she had been revived by electric resuscitation equipment. "My body felt like a rag doll. I had no control over it and I felt as though I had been thrown across the room. I had the marks of the resuscitation equipment on my chest for a long time afterwards."

Audrey was so terrified of what had happened that the next day she walked out of the coronary care unit and went home. She was still not well, and the following day her husband Bob took her into another hospital, where she was kept overnight and allowed to go home the following day.

"The whole experience was the worst of my life. I'll never forget the look on my children's and grandchildren's faces as they called to me. I am more afraid of death now than ever. Now I have a nightmare that I could be put into a coffin and still be alive, and I can't stand the thought of leaving my family. I didn't have any feeling of peace or relaxation, just terror.''

Audrey's husband, Bob, has had the same test that she did, an angiogram, and triple heart bypass surgery. ''When he had his angiogram, they asked him why he was afraid, and he told them what had happened to me. The doctor said that was a one-in-a-million chance, and fortunately everything went smoothly for Bob.

''I can't explain why I had such a strong feeling that mine would not work. I don't like hospitals and operations, but I'm not normally that scared. I just knew without any shadow of a doubt in my mind that something was going to go wrong. If that is what dying is like, I don't want it. There was nothing nice about it at all.''

Chapter Seventeen

SPIRIT IN THE SKY

You don't have to be near death to go out of your body. In fact, the sensation of leaving the body and looking down on it, or moving around in the air without it, is far more likely to happen to people who are not ill or in a life-threatening accident. Only about 10 percent of all people who report having experienced the feeling of leaving their body are near death at the time.

Out-of-body experiences (OBEs) are very common. Surveys show that around one in six of the population have had them, rising to as many as one in four students, possibly because students are more likely to have used marijuana, which is known to promote OBEs. For most the experience is short-lived, and involves nothing more than a feeling of floating upwards, and perhaps moving around very familiar surroundings, such as the room or even other rooms in the same house. But for a few, it is much more exciting and extensive: they travel long distances, go to totally new places, or "visit" friends and relatives in different buildings.

Most OBEs are very like the early stages of NDEs, and in fact it is often very difficult to see any difference, especially in comparison with an NDE that does not go beyond the primary stage of leaving the body and looking down on it from above. There is one major difference, though, even at this level: a high proportion (78 percent) of all OBEs occur when the person is very relaxed, physically more relaxed than usual. NDEs, on the other hand,

253

happen when the body is in crisis, and very far from being relaxed.

OBEs do not usually proceed along the same lines as NDEs. A person undergoing an NDE is more likely to be able to hear noises during the early stages (they can often hear doctors and nurses discussing their condition, and comments from passersby and relatives); they are more likely to travel through a tunnel and more likely to be able to look down on their own body (most OBEers float away from their bodies and do not see them again until they reenter them). The person having the NDE is far more likely to be aware of other beings—relatives, friends, strangers—and also far more likely to feel attracted to a strong and glowing light. NDEers are also more affected by their experience: they are more inclined to feel there was a purpose to their journey, and far more of them are changed by it, in terms of how they lead their lives and how it influences their spiritual or religious beliefs.

Another difference between the OBE and the NDE is the feelings they give rise to at the time it is happening. Almost all the OBEers interviewed for this book reported some element of fear or anxiety during their OBE. This is completely at variance with the NDEers, who almost unanimously talk of all their worries disappearing and being replaced by calm and tranquillity.

Not all surveys have found OBEs to be frightening, however: one major American study found that the most common emotion during an OBE was the same relaxed serenity that characterizes NDEs. Perhaps it is fairer to say that OBEers seem to be more aware of a range of emotions, not necessarily all pleasant, than NDEers are. Although the underlying tranquillity is there, they are also able to react more rationally than NDEers and register surprise, fear, anger, and so on.

Three American psychiatrists who carried out a detailed

comparison of OBEs and NDEs at Kansas University found that every aspect of the classic NDE—the feeling of tranquillity, the rising out of the body and looking down on it, the journey through a tunnel, the meeting with deceased relatives and friends, the encounter with ''a being of light,'' the sense of a past life being judged and evaluated, the reluctance to return to the body, and the feeling of life being changed afterwards because of the experience—has been reported during some OBEs when death has not been threatened or imminent, so the NDE has no completely exclusive features. But they came to the conclusion that, because of the infrequency of some of these features being reported from OBEs, it is right to treat the two experiences as different phenomena.

In other words, although a few people who have OBEs have some or all of the experiences of an NDE, the majority only have one, the floating away from the body: ''The results of our study suggest that the NDE cannot be written off as simply a typical OBE, bearing no relationship to survival threat. The proximity to death seems to provide it with certain characteristic features which differentiate it from other similar experiences,'' the report said in conclusion.

What, then, is an OBE, if it is not the same thing as an NDE? Most OBEs happen spontaneously and unexpectedly, usually when the person is lying or sitting in a very relaxed state, not particularly concentrating on anything. Nearly one in ten, though, happen in an active situation—one girl reported sitting on the roof of her own car watching herself taking her driving test; other people have had the experience during lovemaking.

Usually the person having the OBE floats out of their physical body and has no sense of having another body: they feel their essential ''self'' or soul leaving its physical shell. They are, they report, just a viewpoint outside the body, or in some cases they feel they are a source of light, or an ever-changing shape. Many of them say that they never looked to see whether they had another body or not, they were too intent on the experience. A few see themselves in another body, usually identical to the one they've left behind, although not necessarily wearing the same clothes. In rare cases the OBEer does not "float" away from the body but actually walks, in exactly the same way that they walk normally.

Almost all OBEers, in common with NDEers, report that their vision is better than normal: they can see things with amazing clarity. They talk of a soft, diffused light, which enables them to see clearly, even though they frequently have the experiences at night, in the dark.

Unlike NDEers, the vast majority of OBEers stay in the world they know: they don't travel down tunnels to strange and beautiful lands, they simply wander about their own earthly territory. So they are better able than NDEers to test the situation against "normal" rules of existence, to measure the capabilities of their out-of-body self. For instance, OBEers have attempted—and failed—to pick up objects, to write messages, to make others in the room aware of their disembodied presence. Even reading is much harder out of body than in body, apparently.

People who have OBEs come from all ages and classes: men, women, young, old, rich, poor, well-educated, uneducated. As with NDEers, religious belief has nothing to do with them. One of the few things that does induce them is drug use, particularly that of marijuana.

The history of OBEs goes back as far as the history of civilization. They have been reported in some form or another since records began. In many primitive cultures the shaman or medicine man would be required, as part of his job description, to have OBEs at will. By traveling out of his body, he would be able to raise the alarm when enemies were approaching, spy on the activities of other tribes, find out where to hunt for game. The Biblical prophet Elisha was reported to be able to spy for the Israelites by traveling out of his body to the bedchamber of the King of Syria, where war plans were being prepared.

Of course, shamans and spies like Elisha must have been able to have OBEs whenever they chose to, and although OBEs themselves are not rare, very few people can elect to leave their bodies at will. The vast majority of people who have OBEs, have only one or two in a lifetime, and each time they come unexpectedly and without preparation. Some people who feel they could have regular OBEs if they wanted to choose not to, and positively fight the feeling when it starts to happen. Although they admit that the sensation of floating away is pleasant, there is an underlying anxiety that they may never make it back to their body. Unlike NDEers, who go to a more attractive world, OBEers who are simply wandering out of body around their own homes or their own neighborhood do not want to stay in that state. When they get back into their bodies they experience a feeling of relief, not the one of regret and disappointment that NDEers have.

Because they travel around outside their bodies yet in the real world, it should in theory be possible to test OBEers scientifically. If they could "see" things while out of their body that they could not possibly know about if they remained in their physical body, it would be proof that they really did have an OBE. Early research into OBEs was prompted by the huge question of whether or not human beings have "souls" which are independent of their bodies. And, if it can be proved that they do by verifying OBEs, is that in turn proof that there is life after death, that the individual human spirit survives when the earthly shell ceases to function? Almost all religions provide some version of a life after death, and for that to be possible there must be a "self" which can be separated from the body. Belief is one thing and proof is another: to OBEers and NDEers alike, the experience was "real" and indisputable, but that doesn't hold up scientifically. So there have been many attempts to "prove" the veracity of OBEs.

Although it ought to be easier, it is in fact almost as difficult testing OBEs as testing NDEs. Even if the person being observed does report something he or she could not otherwise have known, it will not have been under scientifically acceptable circumstances and with witnesses on hand to verify that the physical body never moved.

Nonetheless, even though it may not satisfy the academics, there is much very convincing anecdotal evidence of OBEers seeing events and people while floating disembodied above. Children have reported what their parents were watching on television by traveling down from their bedrooms, and have described other activities. In one case a child was able to describe a visitor, a salesman who had been at the house, in accurate detail, including an unusual strawberry nevus birthmark on the man's bald head, which the child had seen from above. Neither parent had been aware of the mark, but when the man made a second visit to the house they make a point of surreptitiously checking, and found that the child was right. One OBEer reported seeing his neighbor digging a new vegetable garden behind a shed: the area was not visible from a window or from the fence around the neighbors's land. There are many more examples.

Serious research, of course, needs to be done with those few people who can trigger OBEs more or less at will, and are willing to try to do so under controlled conditions. California parapsychologist Charles Tart tested one young woman by asking her, while she was out of her body, to remember a number that was written on a piece of cardboard on top of a cupboard and which could not be seen normally without climbing up to it. The woman slept in the laboratory for four nights. On the first she had no OBE; on the second she was not able to get high enough to see the cardboard; on the third she traveled away from the laboratory and did not attempt to see it; and on the fourth she looked at it and remembered it perfectly. Unfortunately, but understandably, she could not continue to sleep in a laboratory for more testing to be carried out. Although her ability to record the number appears to be proof of her OBE, it could also be argued that she might know the number through ESP—extrasensory perception—meaning that she could have read it telepathically from Charles Tart's mind. Other, similar experiments carried out in the United States have failed to rule out clairvoyance as a possible explanation.

One side result of the laboratory research is that scientists know that OBEs are not dreams: they do not happen when the subject is dreaming. It is possible to know when someone is dreaming by recording their different types of sleep. Rapid-eye-movement sleep is the dream state, easily identified because the eyeballs move rapidly beneath the closed eyelids, which occurs about every ninety minutes during a normal night's sleep. The OBEs were reported after nondreaming sleep.

One interesting experiment with OBEs was carried out at Duke University in North Carolina, when a gifted psychic called Keith "Blue" Harary was asked to travel out of his body to a room where a kitten was. He knew and was very fond of the kitten. Eight times Harary "visited" the kitten, and researchers, who did not know when he was coming, recorded the kitten's activity throughout the time of the trial. When Harary was not "there," the kitten meowed and wandered around its enclosure; when he was "there," it did not meow once and appeared far more settled.

The stories in this chapter are as "unproven" as any of

the NDE stories, but that does not make them any less true. To the people concerned, they really happened. One enormous common denominator between those who have OBEs and those who have NDEs is this sense of the experience being real. Both groups remember the event vividly, often after many years, in a way they would not remember a dream or a hallucination. And in both cases their reports of their experiences do not grow or change as time goes by.

Pat Maddalena remembers her out-of-body experience better than she remembers events that happened yesterday, even though it happened in 1969. Pat was twenty-five at the time, married with two little boys. She'd had her usual busy day, running her hairdressing salon and then chasing around the family home in Bristol looking after two active children, and she remembers feeling quite tired.

"It was nothing exceptional—there was nothing special about that day at all, until after I went to bed. I was young and fit and healthy, with no particular worries. I went to bed at about nine-thirty P.M., because I knew I had a busy day the next day, but before I could go to sleep—I know I was not asleep—I was suddenly looking down at myself from the corner of the bedroom ceiling.

"I looked down on myself and I looked terrible, because my mouth was hanging wide open. I knew it was me down there in the bed, but I felt very removed from myself, as if I was just looking down at an old coat. The body meant no more to me than that: it seemed about as important as something you wear. The real me was up there on the ceiling.

"It was a strange mixture of feelings. I was very frightened, but at the same time I felt very calm and reassured. I knew that I was not dead. I knew, but I can't tell how I knew, that I had to get back into that body—or any other body, it didn't seem to matter. That one was handy, but it was just a body, completely separate from me. I knew I had to get in through the open mouth, and I had to do it as quickly as possible. I looked around the room and it was all very familiar. I could see the dressing table and the other furniture. Then I concentrated on getting back. I didn't have any interest in exploring or traveling about up there.

"I don't know how I did it, whether I just willed myself back, but I did get in, and I was wide awake. I told my husband, but he thought I had simply been dreaming. But it was much more vivid than a dream. I'm terrified of it happening again, because I have a fear that I will not get back in time. I go to sleep with my arms crossed under my chin, to keep my mouth closed."

It has never happened again to Pat, who has since had another two children. Although she is relieved, she is also fascinated by her experience: "I don't want to repeat it, but in some ways it has helped me. I'm now very clear in my own mind that we are more than just bodies. I discussed my experience with a nun, who told me that she could do it whenever she wanted, and she used to travel around the hospital where she worked at night checking on the patients, which I found comforting. She can choose to go and come back, so if it ever happened to me again, I'd try to do a little bit more before coming back into my body.

"It has reassured me about life after death: I now know that the body can be discarded, just like an old coat, without it damaging the person inside."

It was a hot, sunny day in July 1987. Wendy Buckingham's two children, Shelley, aged eight, and Gemma, four, were both at school, the housework was done and Wendy, who was thirty-six at the time, decided she'd snatch a few minutes sunbathing in the garden of the family home in Oxford. She settled down comfortably in a deck chair, and immediately felt herself floating upwards, out of her own body: "I felt as light and gentle as a feather blowing in the wind. It was a lovely sensation. I was wide awake, I know I was not dreaming. I hadn't even had time to fall asleep: it happened as soon as I sat down.''

Wendy did not look down and see herself: instead she looked upwards at a radiant and welcoming light which seemed to hover in the sky. The light swelled and took over her whole field of vision, surrounding her and, she felt, holding her up there in the air.

''I felt warmth and love in that light far beyond anything possible on earth. It was so beautiful, the most wonderful feeling I have ever had. The light had a central core to it, brighter than the rest, like the sun yet I was able to look straight at it without being blinded. But it wasn't as though I was looking out of my physical eyes, the ones I see with now, it was as though my vision was all of me. The light seemed to penetrate me, surround me, take me over, it was me and yet I was only part of it. It was an amazing sensation, and I think I could have stayed there forever if I hadn't started to think. As soon as I started to wonder about it, analyze, ask myself what I was doing there and try to see more, I felt myself being drawn back down into my own body. I was aware of slipping back in, an easy feeling.''

Wendy sat bolt upright in the garden chair, thinking ''Wow, what was that?'' The reality of the experience was something she never questioned, even though she could not explain it. The effect on her was long lasting and beneficial. ''Immediately afterward I was on a tremendous high, and the feeling of being uplifted lasted for about two years. My life turned from negative to positive. I could not see any problems, I saw no bad in anyone, I looked on the bright side of everything. I wanted to love everyone to bits.

''My mother had died ten years before and I was still mourning her, still depressed about not having her around. It was as though I could not move on from my grief: instantly, after my out-of-body experience, I did. Maybe it was the comfort of knowing that she in death must have had a similar experience, and gone into that warmth and love. Maybe I needed that experience of it to allow me to move on. But after that, although I still think about her and miss her, my grief for her is positive and joyful, not depressing and miserable. When I was up there in the light I felt it was a healing warmth, and perhaps I needed healing.''

Wendy had suffered from premenstrual tension for years, and this also cleared up instantly after her OBE: ''It has gradually come back again, but for a year or two I was completely free of it, and it is not now as bad as it was. I have returned to reality, which was probably necessary, because the high I was on meant that nothing seemed to matter very deeply, which may not always have been good. But everybody around me noticed how much happier and more fun I was: my joyous disposition was the talk of my friends and family. I was very content: everything I had in life seemed perfect.''

Because she was buzzing with what had happened to her, Wendy told everybody: ''Some people, including my husband Michael, looked at me as though I was a bit cracked. I was so enthusiastic about it that I couldn't stop talking about it. But even if he did not understand it, he could tell that something real had happened by the effect on my personality. A dream would not have given me a sense of euphoria which lasted for two years.''

Today Wendy has no fear of death, nor of having another OBE: ''I would love it to happen again. I don't want to leave my family yet, but another little trip like that one would be wonderful.''

Joan, who has asked for her full name not to be used, had one of the rarer OBEs that follow the pattern of an NDE, including traveling along a tunnel and seeing people at the end of it. Like Wendy, she feels that there was a purpose to her experience, which was to help her come to terms with her father's death a few months earlier. Joan was not ill when she had her experience, nor was she particularly under stress, although she was upset about losing her father. She had helped nurse him through a long and difficult illness, and when he finally died friends and family tried to comfort her by saying that he was better off, that he had been ready and wanting to die, and that he was now out of all pain.

To Joan, these sounded like platitudes. She understood them and paid lip service to them, but deep down she was still very worried about her father. The OBE put her mind at rest.

It happened one night after she had gone to bed and was drifting off towards sleep. She saw, in her mind, a vivid picture of her father's face, so clear that she woke up with a start. When she closed her eyes again, fully awake, the picture had gone, and she straightaway felt herself being lifted out of her own body and steered towards a dark tunnel. It was not, for Joan, a pleasant feeling: she was frightened, and tried hard to stop herself going into the tunnel.

"I struggled to focus my eyes on the blind at the window, thinking that if I could concentrate on ordinary things I would be able to stop. I remember thinking, 'I am not asleep, I am awake, I don't want to go.' But I closed my eyes again, almost against my will, and I was taken into the tunnel. I had a feeling of being 'taken,' as though someone or something was transporting me, but I did not see anyone else. As I went down the tunnel the most brilliant light appeared, so bright that I had to shield my eyes from it. I passed out from the end of the tunnel into the light, and found myself on a country path winding its way between trees and hedges. The colors were all autumnal:

the leaves were lovely golden and russet-brown and yellow. I was gently pushed towards a field, and I can clearly remember thinking that I could not go in there. There was a fence separating me from the field, and as I looked over it I could see in the distance a man in an old-fashioned smock lifting hay on to a cart. He turned and looked towards me and waved, and in that instant everything vanished. I opened my eyes and I was back in my bedroom.''

Interestingly, Joan did not feel that the man in the field was her father, yet somehow she knew from the whole experience that her father is happy and at peace. ''Perhaps I simply saw that there are other lovely worlds that can be reached. Although I had no direct contact with my dad, I knew the whole happening was connected to him. I lay in bed when it was over feeling happier than I had since his death. I could believe for the first time all the things people had been telling me. I knew he was better off than when he had been alive and in pain. Autumn was always his favorite time of year, and he loved the countryside.

''The whole thing was totally amazing. I did not dream it: it definitely happened. It was thirteen years ago now, but it is clear as crystal in my mind.''

Ann Neaum does not like heights, so she was terrified to find herself up on the ceiling of her sitting room, looking down on the top of her husband Geoff's head. Ann, who runs a guesthouse in Swavesey, Cambridgeshire, had her OBE while sitting peacefully in an armchair, with Geoff on the sofa next to her. Without any warning she found herself floating upwards.

''I screamed Geoff's name, but no noise came. I was petrified, and I was hoping he would see me and pull me down. I tried shouting even harder, but still nothing happened.''

Ann, who was forty-five when she had the experience,

in 1984, was aware that there was someone else in the room below her, in the chair where she had been sitting: "In retrospect I know it was me, but I wasn't conscious of that at the time. I was concentrating on trying to get Geoff's attention. But then I noticed that I was moving very slowly towards the wall. I braced myself to collide with it. I stretched my arm out, but to my astonishment there was no arm there. Before I had time to worry about that, I passed effortlessly through the wall. As I went through for a fraction of a second I got an impression of the side section of the wall: it was an outside wall, and I saw brick and wood and plaster. For a brief moment I was on the outside of the house, but almost at once I found myself back in my body.

"I don't remember any sensation of getting back into myself. But I remember that as soon as I was back I was overwhelmed by the realization that consciousness and the physical body are not the same thing, they can be separated, and that the consciousness will survive bodily death. I said 'Oh, yeah' to myself, as though I had just become aware of something obvious. It seemed as though something amazing had happened to me, but at the same time something quite natural."

At the time of her OBE Ann was near the end of a course of radiotherapy treatment for breast cancer. Her marriage was also in trouble: she and Geoff have since split up, although they remain good friends. "It was a stressful time in my life, although on that particular evening I was not under any more pressure than usual. I was physically very relaxed, although it was a worrying time.

"The experience helped me cope with the breast-cancer treatment. It made me very aware of the fact that there is life after death, and I knew that even if the worst had happened I would have survived, if not in body."

Ann, who has three grown-up children and three grandchildren, made a successful recovery: "Perhaps my more relaxed attitude helped: they do say that worry and stress contribute to cancer."

Repeated and frightening OBEs dogged the childhood of Steven, who prefers not to have his full name used. They started when he was about four or five. He would go to bed and fall into a deep sleep, only to be roused by a feeling of levitating or being lifted above the bed, and then floating around the house, usually downstairs to the living room.

"It felt as though I was then lifted and carried back into my bed, and then my chest would be tickled, my body shaken violently, and I would hear a strange cackling laugh. It was a female voice, like the witch in *The Wizard of Oz*. As soon as the laugh came I would sit up and everything would be back to normal, except that I would be shivering and sweating. I would lie back in my bed feeling scared, but after it had happened a couple of times I also knew that each time it was over I wouldn't have to endure it for a few months. So there was a feeling of relief, too."

Steven's experiences lasted for four or five years, happening to him in several different houses, as his father's job took the family around the country. It was only when he reached the age of nine or ten that he realized he could stop himself going on his OBE travel.

"If I could stop myself lifting off the bed, I could stop the whole event. I learned to recognize the feeling of it coming on, and I learned—I don't really know how—to break away from the feeling and stop it carrying on. Sometimes I had even begun to rise off the bed and I would force myself down again, and the whole trip would stop.

"I never enjoyed the floating travel, because I always knew it would end with the tickling and shaking and that horrible laughter. I remember that I floated through objects, like the door, to get downstairs, but I have no memory of what I saw on my journeys. I think I was too preoccupied with the horrible part that was still to come.''

Steven did not tell his parents until he had learned to control it. They had no explanation: they had never seen or sensed him coming into the living room during the evenings, when he should have been in bed. His mother believed him, but was unable to suggest any reason why his OBEs always ended in such an unpleasant way.

''To me, as a child, I was being taken by this witch creature, but there never seemed to be any reason why. Why did I float around before being shaken and tickled? It wasn't a recurrent nightmare, because I was very aware at the time that it was real. I've had nightmares, I know the difference.''

Steven, who was born in 1970, still occasionally feels the sensation of beginning to slip out of his body—and fights it, just as he did as a child. ''I have occasionally wondered if I should go with it, just to see if it is still the same experience. But even though I am now grown up, I can still feel the absolute terror it brought to me as a child. I have no wish to repeat that. There was certainly no peace or serenity attached to it, and I don't think I will ever be completely free of it, because I can remember it so clearly.''

Steven was not a sickly child: he was a typical sports-mad boy, with a strong constitution. Nor is he aware of having had any particular worries: he has always been a good mixer, never had any problems at school, got on well with his sisters and his parents: ''There was never then, nor is there now, any particular reason why the OBE feeling comes on some nights and not others. It was never when I was unwell, or under stress, or anything. It seems to come entirely at random.''

Chapter 18

THE VERDICT OF THE EXPERTS

So what do the scientists make of all this astonishing evidence? Many NDEers accept what happened to them without question as a profound spiritual phenomenon. Others are more curious: they want to know if the experts can shed any real light on why it happened and what it means.

The answer is essentially no. There are lots of different scientific theories, some with a certain amount of proof going for them. There are lots of possible interpretations of sections of the experience. But so far, nobody has come up with an overall explanation of what NDEs are and what they mean—apart from the obvious one that they are a foretaste of what death will eventually be like for all of us.

Much of the work being done by scientists in the study of NDEs is highly complex and difficult to reduce to simple terms, but this chapter is an attempt to do just that. There are, within it, some theories which may be difficult to understand; there are others which may not have been done justice because they are oversimplified. But altogether they give an idea of how far the experts have gone in their attempts to explain away the NDE.

One of the greatest strengths of the argument that NDEs are real is also one of its greatest weaknesses. The fact that all those who have NDEs follow the same path toward the light, going through similar stages on the way, makes a powerful case for the whole thing being a profound spiritual journey to an afterlife where everyone, from all ages and cultures, is welcome. But that same case, the "sameness" evidence, is also a fundamental part of the argument that the NDE is not a real experience, not a spiritual voyage, but a function of the dying brain. All brains, regardless of where in the world they come from, die in the same way, say the skeptics. And that is why all NDEs have essential core elements which are the same. It is not because the dying person is traveling towards a beautiful afterlife, but because the neurotransmitters in the brain are shutting down and creating the same lovely illusions for all who are near death.

But why? Why should the dying brain do this, if it is just a highly sophisticated lump of tissue? The question is one of the most fundamental and huge in the whole of human thinking. It boils down to asking, are we individuals with "personalities" and "souls" and "minds" that are exclusive to us? Or are we simply bodies controlled by very clever computers, or brains, each of which works a little differently from the rest, thus making each of us unique, just as an Apple computer is different from an Amstrad, although there are far more similarities between them than there are differences?

Scientists and researchers are divided. There are some who want to reduce the NDE to nothing more than a series of brain reactions. Others, who accept the realness and validity of the NDE experience, are nonetheless quite happy to see it put into a scientific context. In other words, they are not frightened of researching the experience rigorously, of finding out everything that we possibly can about it, perhaps even being able to explain aspects of it. But they can happily let that scientific aspect sit alongside the deeply personal, life-enhancing evidence of those who have actually been there.

There are very few people around, even among the skeptics, who would deny that people have NDEs, and that they are deeply affected by them: so many obviously sane and well-balanced people have now come forward and talked about what happened to them. What they do dispute is what causes an NDE and what it means. There are two main strands of research: one takes the psychological approach, which looks for reasons for human beings to behave the way they do, and to think and possibly to hallucinate the way they do. The other is the straightforward physiological approach, which is searching for that part of the brain which malfunctions and causes an NDE. Increasingly, as in all brain research, not just that connected with NDEs, the two approaches overlap.

The ruthless, depersonalized argument—that an NDE is just the result of the brain beginning to die—is not acceptable to the vast majority of people who have had NDEs. To reduce what was a profound and transforming experience to nothing more than a set of neurotransmitters going on the blink is a bit like seeing Michelangelo's statue of David as nothing more than several tons of marble.

If there is no afterlife, and the NDE is just the last throw of a fevered and dying brain, why does it bother? If everything, including the soul and personality, is going to dust and ashes, why does the brain lay on this last wonderful floor show for people near death or facing actual death, who relax into peacefulness and describe their wonderful visions?

One theory is that it is a deliberate ploy of the human race to help those behind adapt better to the inevitable ending of their lives. Darwin's simple theory of the survival of the fittest holds that every species is struggling to increase its hold on this planet and guarantee the survival of its descendants. That is our greatest primary urge. Other animals help their peers to survive: the dying elephant, for example, trails away into the bush so that he does not slow down the herd. Are the dying just "helping the herd" by putting out propaganda that death does not contain a sting? But this theory does not explain why NDEs are erratic, or why we shunted down an evolutionary sidetrack for years by making them something that people were reluctant to talk about. After all, in Darwinian terms, humans are the complete masters of the universe.

Some scientists from the camp that believes the NDE is one day going to be explained by brain functions have suggested that the dying secrete endorphins, hormones which act on the central nervous system to suppress pain and which are known to create the "runner's high," which happens when long-distance runners go through a pain barrier and find themselves running with ease and without tiredness, and with a feeling of elation. But endorphins are not hallucinogens and cannot re-create a state like an NDE, so although they may be involved in the process as a painkiller, they are not responsible for the whole experience.

Research on neurotransmitter receptors is highly complex and, in terms of our understanding of the functioning of the brain, in its infancy. It is known that a powerful anesthetic called ketamine can produce many of the features of an NDE, particularly the out-of-body element, and one theory is that a ketaminelike substance may be released by the body at the time of an NDE, and may attach itself to certain neurotransmitter receptors and be responsible for producing the whole NDE by blocking those receptors.

Some features of the NDE are known to occur in a type of epilepsy associated with damage to the temporal lobe of the brain, and researchers have found that by electrically stimulating this lobe they can mimic some elements of the NDE, such as leaving oneself behind, and the sense of life memories flashing past, although this is actually a relatively rare feature of NDEs. They believe that the stress of being near death, or thinking that you are near death, may in some way cause the stimulation of this lobe. There is some evidence to support this theory in the lower numbers of NDEs reported by people who suffer strokes which affect this part of the brain, or have tumors in this area. But there is also a case against: the characteristic emotions that result from temporal lobe stimulation are fear, sadness, and loneliness, not the calm and love of an NDE.

Other possible explanations are a lack of oxygen in the brain, or too much carbon dioxide. But these would not explain why some patients are able to give full and cogent reports of things that went on around them during their NDE. Cardiologist Michael Sabom has reported one patient who, while having an NDE, watched his doctor perform a blood test that revealed both high oxygen and low carbon dioxide. And comparisons of NDEs with the hallucinations produced by an oxygen-starved brain show that the latter are chaotic and much more similar to psychotic hallucinations. Confusion, disorientation, and fear are the typical characteristics, compared with the tranquillity, calm, and sense of order of an NDE. There are some features in common: a sense of well-being and power, and themes of death and dying. But people who have experienced both at different times say that there is an unmistakable difference.

Hallucinations, whether deliberately drug-induced, the result of medication, or caused by oxygen deprivation, almost always take place while the subject is awake and conscious, whereas NDEs happen during unconsciousness, sometimes when the subject is so close to death that no record of brain activity can be recorded on an electroencephalograph, the machine that monitors brain waves. Also, the medical conditions that take subjects to the brink of death, and to having NDEs, do not necessarily include oxygen-deprivation, or any medication. This is particularly true of accident victims. NDEs appear to occur at the moment when the threat of death occurs, not necessarily at the time, maybe hours later, when death is close enough to be starving the brain of oxygen.

The first modern attempt to explain NDEs in psychological terms was made in 1930 by a psychologist who argued that people faced with an unpleasant reality of death and illness attempt to replace it with pleasurable fantasies to protect themselves. They ''depersonalize,'' removing themselves from themselves—the floating away from their own bodies that NDEers have. It is a theory that is still sometimes put forward, but it can be countered by the fact that some typical features of an NDE just do not fit into the depersonalization model, such as the strong spiritual and mystical feelings, and the increased alertness and awareness.

Another popular theory is that the NDE is nothing to do with death at all, but a memory of birth. A baby being born leaves the womb to travel down a tunnel towards a light, and what waits for it in the light is, usually, a great deal of love and warmth. What happens at the point of death is only a stored memory of what happened when life began. Yet again there are a lot of points that don't match: a baby being born does not exactly float at speed down a tunnel, but is buffeted along with difficulty by its mother's contractions. And how does this model explain the meeting with friends and relatives who have died? The ''being of light'' is supposed to be the midwife or the doctor who rules the delivery room—but many babies are born without a midwife or doctor present, or perhaps with many people present. On a purely practical level, a baby's nervous system is not sufficiently developed to allow it to assimilate and store memories of the birth process.

Those who argue this theory say that the feelings of peace and bliss are a memory of the peace of the womb, when all physical needs were met by the mother and there were no stresses and strains. Why should this be any more likely than the feelings of peace and bliss are relief from the pain of illness and injury at the point of death?

James Alcock, a professor of psychology at Toronto's

York University, describes an NDE as "a distorted perception of reality." He says that even when unconscious or anesthetized, the brain can take in a certain amount of what is going on around it. "There may be some things from the world mixed with other material from memory. It doesn't take much exposure to religion to believe it's real," he says. Although research shows that the more religious a person is does not increase their chances of having an NDE, it is also true that no adult, however atheistic their own views, will be completely unaware of the teachings of religion. Children might, though, especially very young ones.

Another psychology professor who rejects the spiritual and mystical importance of NDEs is Ronald Siegel, from the University of California at Los Angeles. He argues that hallucinations can be triggered by fear, loneliness, or isolation. When a person is close to death, he says, the brain reacts to the threat to the body with fantasies and memories of childhood. Yet only a small proportion of NDEers have memories of their past life. He also suggests that those who have NDEs have a strong psychological need for the reassurance they bring: again, this runs counter to the evidence that those who have a strong need for religion in their normal lives are no more likely to have them than heretics and unbelievers.

Siegel claims to have reproduced NDEs in his laboratory by giving LSD to volunteers, but, as we have seen, other researchers say that although drug-induced hallucinations may have some resemblance to NDEs, they are not the same thing.

One of the most dedicated researchers into NDEs is Dr. Susan Blackmore, a senior lecturer in psychology at the University of the West of England. She believes that NDEs are caused by a combination of physiological and psychological reactions, triggered by disturbed brain function at the point of death or in great stress. She has impressive arguments for every stage of the NDE. The tunnel, she claims, is caused by oxygen starvation, which causes certain cells in the brain, inhibitory cells, to die first, the excitable ones taking longer.

"In the visual system many cells are packed into the center, and they thin out towards the edge. The excitable ones are all firing away like mad, in a hyperactive way, and because there are masses and masses at the center and fewer at the edges, it looks like a big, bright light. As the light gets bigger, you get the illusion of traveling down a tunnel."

In her book, *Dying to Live*, she lists four key arguments used as evidence that NDEs are the key to life after death—and then proceeds to demolish them all. The first is that NDEs are so consistently the same. She says, rightly, that this is no more proof that they foretell life after death than that all brains behave in a similar way when dying. But it is also no less proof.

The second is the deeply held conviction of NDEers that what happened to them was real. She does not argue with the fact that they actually had an experience, and that they are reporting it truthfully. What she maintains is that it is an illusion of reality, that we constantly construct models of reality to accommodate our lives and that there is no one constant model. This complicated idea, which Dr. Blackmore bases on cognitive psychology, also has a parallel in Buddhist teaching.

The third key argument is that, because most people cannot explain away NDEs, they turn them into evidence of an afterlife. Dr. Blackmore argues that people are looking for this kind of evidence to bolster their beliefs, to reinforce the reality they have created. To accept NDEs as paranormal experiences, glimpses into another world, a lot of physics, biology, and psychology would have to be overthrown, she says. Yet, as we've seen, NDEs happen to people who don't appear to have any need to believe in an afterlife: they are as common among atheists as they are among the devout.

And the fourth and final argument in favor of NDEs being real, spiritual experiences is that people are transformed by them. She counters this by saying that the very experience of being near death, with or without an NDE, is enough to make people less selfish and more concerned for others. This was not, however, borne out by a study done by Dr. Bruce Greyson of the University of Connecticut of three groups of people, some who had not been near death, some who had been near death without an NDE, and some who had had an NDE. He found the NDEers had changed more profoundly than, and in a different way from, those who had no NDEs but were close to death. Dr. Blackmore also says that the activity of the dying brain can provoke real insights—into the theory, for example, that all "reality" is a mental construction—and that this will take away fear of death and lead to a greater acceptance of life.

Yet there is no recorded case of an NDEer being able to articulate this kind of astonishing revelation, or even appearing to make any attempt to describe it, however inadequate. NDEers who return and are full of the wise teachings that they have absorbed may not always recall what those teachings were. It is just possible that this might be because those teachings are as abstruse and difficult as Dr. Blackmore's theory about reality being a series of different models. Perhaps that is a little beyond most NDEers. But surely some of them would have had a shot at explaining it? And if they have translated it into another model— an angel, a being of light, a dead grandmother telling them things—why have they done that if they have finally been given this key to understanding the nature of "their" world?

Dr. Blackmore says, "All things considered, I can see

no reason to adopt the afterlife hypothesis. I am sure I shall remain in a minority for a long time to come, especially among NDEers, but for me the evidence and the arguments are overwhelming. . . . We are biological organisms, evolved in fascinating ways for no purpose at all and with no end in any mind. We are simply here and this is how it is. I have no self and 'I' own nothing. There is no one to die. There is just this moment, and now this, and now this.''

It is a very sophisticated and difficult concept and, yes, Dr. Blackmore is definitely in a minority. Dr. Bruce Greyson, who has done a great deal of work on studying NDEs, rejects all the scientific arguments advanced so far. That does not mean that he is burying his head in the sand: he's no scientific flat-earther. ''It doesn't mean that there isn't a physiological explanation,'' he says. ''Just that we haven't found one yet.''

Dr. Melvin Morse, who did all the ground-breaking research with young children, states unequivocally, ''There is no explanation for the light.''

Dr. Kenneth Ring, perhaps the most respected of all NDE researchers, and the one who did most to put the subject on the academic map, says: ''Any adequate neurological explanation would have to be capable of showing how the entire complex of phenomena associated with the core experience (that is, the out-of-body state, paranormal knowledge, the tunnel, the golden light, the voice or presence, the appearance of deceased relatives, beautiful vistas, and so forth) would be expected to occur in subjectively authentic fashion as a consequence of specific neurological events triggered by the approach of death. . . . I am tempted to argue that the burden of proof has now shifted to those who wish to explain near-death experiences in this way.''

These are a complicated couple of sentences, but what Dr. Ring is saying is that there are so many consistent features of NDEs that it is going to be very difficult to find a good explanation for them in terms of the physical workings of the brain. And that the evidence is so strong for them that sympathetic researchers should no longer feel that the burden is on proving that they happen, but rather, for the skeptics, on proving that they don't.

Perhaps the final word should go to Nancy Evans Bush, of the International Association for Near Death Studies, who said: "There is no human experience of any description that can't simply be reduced to a biological process, but that in no way offsets the meaning those experiences have for us—whether it's falling in love, or grieving, or having a baby."

Or coming close to death and having a transcendental experience.

DELL NONFICTION BESTSELLERS